The Antiquity of Nations

The Antiquity of Nations

Anthony D. Smith

Polity

First published in 2004 by Polity Press Ltd.

Polity Press
65 Bridge Street
Cambridge CB2 1UR, UK

Polity Press
350 Main Street
Malden, MA 02148, USA

ISBN: 0-7456 2745-5
ISBN: 0-7456 2746-3 (pb)

A catalogue record for this book is available from the British Library and has been applied for from the Library of Congress.

Typeset in 10.5 on 12 pt Palatino
by SNP Best-set Typesetter Ltd., Hong Kong
Printed and bound in Great Britain by MPG Books, Bodmin, Cornwall.

For further information on Polity, visit our website: www.polity.co.uk

Contents

Acknowledgements

The author and publisher gratefully acknowledge the permission granted to reproduce the copyright material in this book

Chapter 1, originally published as 'The Myth of the "Modern Nation" and the Myths of Nations', *Ethnic and Racial Studies*, 11/1 (1988): 1–26. Reproduced with the permission of the editors. (<http://www.tandf.co.uk/journals/routledge/01419870.html>)

Chapter 2, originally published as 'Memory and Modernity: Reflections on Ernest Gellner's Theory of Nationalism', *Nations and Nationalism*, 2/3 (1996): 371–88. Reproduced with the permission of the editors of *Nations and Nationalism*, Journal of the Association for the Study of Ethnicity and Nationalism (London School of Economics).

Chapter 3, originally published as 'The Nation: Invented, Imagined, Reconstructed?', *Millennium: Journal of International Studies*, 20/3 (1991): 353–68. Reproduced with the permission of the publisher.

Chapter 4, originally published as 'Nationalism and Classical Social Theory', *The British Journal of Sociology*, 34/1 (1983): 19–38. Reproduced with the permission of the editors of *The British Journal of Sociology*.

Chapter 6, originally published as 'War and Ethnicity: The Role of Warfare in the Formation, Self-images and Cohesion of Ethnic Communities', *Ethnic and Racial Studies*, 4/4 (1981): 375–97. Reproduced with the permission of the editors. (<http://www.tandf.co.uk/journals/routledge/01419870.html>)

Chapter 7, originally published as 'The Origins of Nations', *Ethnic and Racial Studies*, *12/3* (1989): 340–67. Reproduced with the permission of the editors. (<http://www.tandf.co.uk/journals/routledge/01419870.html>)

Chapter 8, originally published as 'The "Golden Age" and National Renewal', in Geoffrey Hosking and George Schöpflin (eds), *Myths and Nationhood* (London: Hurst and Co., 1997). Reproduced with the permission of the editors.

Introduction:
Paradigms of Nationalism

'When is the nation?' This question, posed by Walker Connor (1990) over a decade ago, has taken on new life and meaning. From being regarded as somewhat dated, the debate about the 'age' and provenance of nations has, once again, become a matter of serious scholarly concern.

This reappraisal stems, in part, from recent developments in our understanding of nations and nationalism. The belief that the age of nations is behind us and that the true unit of cultural identity is small, local and untainted by power, and/or vast and transnational, has not withstood the test of political reality. Stateless nations and subnational groups (regional, ethnic or religious) have certainly made their presence felt on the political stage, but they have not fragmented national states; instead, several stateless nations have since 1989 achieved independence and sovereignty, while resident *ethnies* (ethnic communities) have won greater autonomy within their national states. National states may have lost some of their powers, notably in the economic and military spheres. But, as the recent clash of great powers over the Middle East has shown, they have conceded none of their political will and national interests. The fact that we live in a more porous and interdependent world actually exacerbates the underlying national conflicts which have provided the fault-lines of politics since at least the eighteenth century. For, in many ways, the reach and penetration of the regulatory national state has intensified – in health and reproduction, mass education, culture and leisure, communications and the media, criminal justice, as well as in the more traditional roles of taxation and law and order enforcement.

The same is true of that other threat to the powers of the national state: wider transnational associations or cultural communities like 'civilizations'. The latter, in particular, have to date not been able to achieve the unity or wield the power attributed to them by some scholars (Huntington 1996). National states have been loath to surrender their powers and roles to external authorities, even when they have voluntarily entered into binding agreements to abide by certain rules and conventions. This is true even of the one part of the world where it might appear that the national state is being deliberately undermined: Europe. The deep divisions over visions of 'Europe'; the power play for hegemony within the European Union; the incessant bargaining over national interests; above all, relations with the USA and other national states: these developments have blocked any early movement in the direction of supersession of the national state as the ultimate repository of power, and the political goal of aspirant *ethnies*. Besides, compared to the vibrant linguistic cultures of its constituent national states, a 'European culture' remains nebulous and uncertain, a patchwork of national cultures included, but in no way transfigured, by the slogan of 'unity in diversity'. While national identities still evoke strong attachments and heroic conflicts, a European identity remains as yet as remote and idealized as the Arthurian Holy Grail, answering to few shared interests and needs.[1]

Outside 'old Europe', the strength of national passions continues to excite and alarm states and populations across the globe. The force of competing nationalisms has, if anything, intensified, despite the many efforts of supranational organizations and the great powers to contain it; and conflicts emanating from the grievances and claims of incorporated *ethnies*, from the Moro and Aceh to Kurdistan and southern Sudan, have not abated. In these circumstances, to posit a new world order in which nations and national states are necessarily obsolete is to overlook what Michael Billig (1995) has called the entrenched banality of nationalism in the West itself, and to close our eyes to the increasingly 'hot' nationalisms that erupt periodically in different parts of the wider world, threatening regional, and sometimes world, peace and order.

The Historicity of Nations

But there is also a more 'positive' reason for the renewed interest in the origins and development of nations. There are, in fact, solid historical and sociological grounds for the continuing devotion of individuals and peoples to 'their' nations and national states, and these have provided the staple of the main explanatory paradigms and debates in the field. It is surely no accident that the issue of the antiquity or modernity of nations and nationalism has been central to these debates. All the major works in the field, from Karl Deutsch's *Nationalism and Social Communication* (1953, 2nd edn 1966), Elie Kedourie's *Nationalism* (1960) and Ernest Gellner's *Thought and Change* (1964), through John Armstrong's *Nations before Nationalism* (1982), John Breuilly's *Nationalism and the State* (1982, 2nd edn 1993), Ernest Gellner's *Nations and Nationalism* (1983) and Benedict Anderson's *Imagined Communities* (1983, 2nd edn 1991), to Eric Hobsbawm's *Nations and Nationalism since 1780* (1990), Liah Greenfeld's *Nationalism: Five Roads to Modernity* (1992), Walker Connor's *Ethno-Nationalism* (1994) and Adrian Hastings's *The Construction of Nationhood* (1997), have taken the question of the nation's genealogy and historicity as their starting-point and axis of explanation, engaging, implicitly or explicitly, in a debate about 'when is the nation?'

There are a number of reasons for this. For many people, and not just nationalists, history and historicity are central to the very concept of the nation. Not only do historical claims figure prominently in most major nationalist conflicts, the very sense of belonging to a nation evokes in most people's minds the ideas of continuity, recurrence and persistence of a cultural community over a period of generations. Irrespective of the historical facts, many nations evoke a sense of immemorial belonging. For most people, the nation is an ascribed community, by self as well as by others, so that even when through immigration individuals may choose to belong to another national community, it is one that appears to members and outsiders as historically 'given', not made up each time anew. Moreover, even in the voluntaristic versions of nationalism, individuals must belong to *a* nation: that is, one of the given historic nations. To be nationless in today's world is to be like Peter Schlemiehl without his shadow, an object of suspicion and contempt. (See Smith 2001: ch. 1.)

As significant is the role of shared memory. Memory, which is so vital to the sense of identity, is also central to both the individuality and the unity of nations. That means that the members' sense of their own history, their 'ethno-history', the memories that they share and the myths that they narrate, are crucial to the particular fabric and profile of the nation. These myths and memories are, of course, highly selective. They are also subject to considerable dispute and change, with rival versions of communal ethno-history competing for popular allegiance; one thinks of Norman Trojan or 'Arthurian' and Anglo-Saxon myths of origins in early modern England, or Hellenic and Byzantine golden age memories in nineteenth-century Greece. In the process, the sense of national identity is reinterpreted and reconstructed at periodic intervals. Nevertheless, given the highly specific nature of shared memories and myths, the distinctive character of particular national identities is likely to persist, because their expressions remain within the orbit of the community's basic cultural heritage and values, allowing us immediately to recognize the profile and forms of particular nations.[2]

But perhaps the most important reason for the centrality of the debate about the antiquity of nations is the vital role that historical sequence and periodization play in explanations of the constituent processes of nation formation. Such explanatory frameworks require the insertion of nations and nationalism into wider historical and sociological narratives of social change, without which they would have little meaning, just as in the absence of nations and nationalism, the narratives themselves would lack key components of historical development.

This is well illustrated by the main paradigms of nations and nationalism. Thus, 'modernists', who regard nations and nationalism as relatively recent and novel, link their emergence causally to wider changes in the fabric of society and politics at specific junctures in time, notably the age of revolutions in the later eighteenth century. It is because certain novel processes and ideas appeared at specific historical moments and came together in a certain sequence in the West, that conditions became favourable for the rise of nationalisms, which in turn enabled elites to construct nations. These processes of 'modernization' can be charted and placed in an overarching chronological framework, to create a convincing account of the genesis of nationalisms and nations, first in the West and later in Eastern Europe, Latin America, Africa and Asia.[3]

In contrast, 'perennialists', who claim that nations are recurrent or continuous (or both) throughout recorded history, link the emergence of nations, if not of nationalism, to more general processes of human activity and politics which can already be discerned in the earliest civilizations. The chronological framework here is much enlarged. It takes in the ancient and medieval epochs of human history (or at least some part of each), and relates the appearance of nations to cultural community and state formation in all continents and in every period. Here nations are treated, not as constructs of modern nationalists, but as age-old communities which generate their specific national sentiments and nationalist ideologies.[4]

Primordialism

Now, in both of these paradigms, nations are placed in wider frameworks of social change and historical periodization, and tied to particular sequences of events. This is in marked contrast to the outlook of 'primordialists', for whom nations and nationality constitute not only basic forms of human association, but intrinsic features of human nature and the human condition. In this view, nations cannot be regarded as either 'ancient' or 'modern', for they stand outside historical time, being coeval with humanity. Primordialists are generally thought to regard nations as 'substantial' and 'natural', possessed of 'essences' and 'organic' qualities, terms with negative connotations of inherent biological constraint and ahistorical fixity 'outside time'. This is, of course, a rather crude and partial characterization. 'Primordialism' takes many forms, and to grasp the complex relations between 'history' and 'nature' in these approaches, we need to disentangle them.

Early beliefs in the primordial nature of nationality centred on their God-given status and role in the divine plan. For Herder, nations were natural in the sense that they constituted an essential part of God's plan for humanity, as they had for his Pietist predecessors. In the later secular version of this belief, nations came to be regarded by *some* nationalists as analogous to organisms in the natural world, and therefore subject to the same laws of growth and decay and rebirth. However, this kind of organic nationalism, in which individuals bore the indelible stamp of their birth community throughout life, remained a minority view until the late nineteenth century, being eclipsed by a much more voluntarist liberal-democratic nationalism of revolutionary fervour espoused by Mazzinian radicals who saw nations as the products of human endeavour as much as their sources and vehicles.[5]

The recent neo-Darwinian revival of sociobiology has encouraged a much more radical version of primordialism. Here, the nature and origins of nations are subsumed under larger issues of collective bonding. For Pierre van den Berghe (1978, 1995), nations, ethnic groups and races are types of large-scale kinship grouping distinguished by different cultural signs which help individuals to determine their inclusive fitness groups. For van den Berghe, the basic unit of explanation is the individual seeking to maximize his or her gene pool, and through such mechanisms as nepotism various extended kinship groupings like the ethnic community and nation help to achieve this end. The argument here is deliberately individualistic and reductionist; cultural phenomena are in the end explicable in individual biological terms, and sociocultural principles of reciprocity and altruism supplement individual genetic drives. The central difficulties of this argument are twofold. In the first place, there is the general problem of deriving large-scale groupings like ethnic groups and nations directly from small-scale kin groups without resorting to additional explanatory principles over and beyond gene maximization through nepotism. In this sense, to term ethnic groups and nations 'inclusive fitness groups' begs the question. Granted that kinship plays a significant part in the mass appeal of ethnicity and nationalism, and that myths of descent are vital for ethnic and nationalist claims and beliefs, the question of how far the latter accord with actual biological descent must remain at the very least open, and often improbable, given the presence of rival myths of origin. Similarly, the potent belief that 'we are of one blood' is frequently contradicted by historical research on the origins and ethnic composition of nations. (See Connor 1994: ch. 8.)

In the second place, the sociobiological argument is quite ahistorical. It fails to separate ethnic groups from nations, either sociologically or in historical terms. There is no sense or possibility of development from ethnic to national groupings, let alone any sequential framework of events or periodization in which either ethnic communities or nations may be said to emerge. They are already 'pre-given' in the mechanisms of inclusive fitness consequent on the overriding need to maximize gene potential for evolutionary advantage. This means that a separate theory of nations and nationalism is redundant, and the question of the 'antiquity' of nations is a matter of biology or 'nature' rather than one of society or 'history'.

A rather different version of primordialism comes from those who see certain cultural attachments as both prior to and overriding other civil and political ties. Already in 1957, Edward Shils distinguished various kinds of social ties – personal, sacred, primordial and civil. Whereas the last kind of tie was rational and calculative and underpinned the political order of society, primordial ties related to basic cultural elements of society like kinship, custom, religion and language. This distinction was taken up by Clifford Geertz in his essay 'The Integrative Revolution' (1963), and used to analyse the dangers facing the new societies of Africa and Asia then in the process of decolonization. Geertz argued that their attempts to build a polity and society based on rational, civil ties were threatened by primordial attachments to what he termed the assumed cultural 'givens' of society – namely, kinship, contiguity, custom, race, language, religion and the like – which were prior to other kinds of tie, and which were felt by the participants to be binding and overpowering. However, for Geertz, nationalism and nation building are part of the attempt to create a rational civil order and state. This means that the cultural givens and the primordial attachments that they generate fall under the heading of kinship and ethnicity, and stand opposed to the nation-building process. In this view, nations are relatively novel and 'artificial' constructs, threatened by the anterior forces of primordial attachments (Shils 1957; Geertz 1963).

Geertz's essay has provoked a lively debate among sociologists. Jack Eller and Reed Coughlan (1993), for example, challenge the utility of the very concept of primordialism, claiming that it mystifies the social order by placing such ties prior to and outside the usual networks of social interaction, and by giving priority to 'emotion' over rational calculation of means and ends. In part, this represents a misreading of Geertz's essay.

Geertz had been careful to qualify his use of the concept of 'primordial attachments' (he did not use the term 'primordialism') by making clear that any power and priority resided not in the tie itself, but in the significance attributed to it by the participants, and that these primordial 'givens' were culturally assumed to be such.

This was a point taken up and elaborated by Steven Grosby. Highlighting the importance of cognition and belief in the genesis of collective emotional ties, Grosby argued that people's sense of the prior, binding, overriding nature of the bonds that underpin societies stem from their beliefs about the life-enhancing qualities of these primordial ties. Territory and kinship, in particular, are seen as life-nurturing and life-sustaining, and in that sense prior and 'basic', in ways that the state and the civil order can never be. But, in an interesting twist to the argument, Grosby (1994, 1995) sees nationalities as self-defined, bounded but translocal territorial communities, also partaking of these same life-enhancing attributes. As a result, in a sociological sense, nations may also be viewed as 'ancient' and to some extent primordial collectivities.

In fact, this sense of 'antiquity' is not only sociological; it is also historical. Grosby's own work straddles the divide between 'primordialism' and 'perennialism' (and in doing so, reveals the necessarily schematic nature of these theoretical constructs). On the one hand, the nation is 'ancient' because it stems from the basic elements of territory and kinship and partakes of their life-sustaining qualities, in sharp contrast to the *Gesellschaft* attributes of modern society and the modern state. On the other hand, particular nations, or, as Grosby prefers to call them, 'nationalities', can be found in various periods of history, including antiquity: here Grosby names the ancient Egyptians, Armenians and Israelites as clear examples of ancient nationalities. Thus, both from the standpoint of 'nature' (human nature) and 'history', the antiquity of the category of the nation is confirmed (Grosby 1997, 2002).

The question that arises is whether, given the ubiquity of territory and kinship and the frequency of collective self-definition, Grosby's characterization of the concept of the nation (he does not supply a formal definition) in naturalizing, primordial terms does not direct, and even determine, his choice of historical examples. Might it not be the case here that 'nature' determines 'history', and that the discovery of plausible cases of nationhood in antiquity stems from the way in which primordial categories form the basic elements of Grosby's characterization of nationalities?

But this, I think, is only part of the story. Other factors enter into Grosby's choice of which groups can be categorized as nationalities in antiquity; these include language, the central cult and the state, as is made clear in his analyses of Aram, Armenia and ancient Israel. After all, Grosby claims that the ancient Greeks did not constitute a nationality, though they undoubtedly had a clear sense of kinship and of a translocal territory. But their multiple self-definitions (in the *polis*, in the ethno-linguistic group – e.g. Dorian, Ionian – and in the wider cultural community of Hellas) and the relative lack of a single god, cult or law of the land among the Greeks, impeded the rise of the sociological community of an ancient Greek nation. We see here that, for Grosby, 'history', in the sense of particular factors and sequences, takes precedence over 'nature', the widespread attachment to kinship and especially to 'primordial' territory, and this priority makes for a much more detailed, nuanced and interesting historical analysis of the sources and trajectories of nation formation.[6]

Perennialism

Undoubtedly, the main objection to any form of 'primordialism' is not its alleged rigidity and neglect of change, but its lack of explanatory power. Primordialists, as Donald Horowitz (2002) argues, have isolated a narrow, but vital set of problems, focusing on the issue of intensity of national passions and the self-sacrifice to which this can lead; but they have neglected many other aspects of ethnicity and nationalism. (See also Smith 1998: ch. 7.)

However, though the problem to which they direct our attention is crucial, they are unable to supply any causal analysis of the grounds for this intensity and sacrifice. The more they embrace a strict biological primordialism, the more they tend to ignore the 'superstructure' of history, and so fail to distinguish the specific problem of nations and nationalism from the wider issues of ethnic identity and ethnicity, both historically and sociologically. The categories they employ are general and all-encompassing, and while Geertz uses them to illuminate the problems of new states in the 1960s, even he does so in a schematic manner that severs nation building and nationalism from ethnicity, 'race', language, religion and even territory!

Is the question of the 'antiquity' of the nation, then, better served by the perennialists? Here, at least, we seem to be on firm historical ground, without recourse to a metaphysic of essential properties and primordial ties. In the perennialist view, nations form, change their character, and dissolve or are absorbed into other human communities, along with all other forms of human identity and community. For all that, nations, on this view, are not tied to a particular stage of history; they can appear in every period and continent, wherever the conditions are conducive. As a result, we find a propensity in earlier writings on the subject to see nations everywhere, from the ancient Egyptians and Chinese to the modern French and Russians.

But here, too, closer inspection reveals different kinds of 'perennialism'. One of these tends to see the nation as a recurrent, but not necessarily a continuous, phenomenon throughout history. This kind of *recurrent perennialism* underlies John Armstrong's seminal *Nations before Nationalism* (1982), which portrays the nation as a recurrent form of community, with particular nations emerging and disappearing in every period of history. While modern nations may differ to the extent that they can be, and in many cases are, inspired by nationa*lism*, which provides a blueprint for designing nations, there is really no fundamental difference between these modern nations and the nations that appeared in pre-modern epochs. For they all share the properties of 'ethnicity', the cluster of shared sentiments, attitudes and perceptions of ethnic groups, and the myths, symbols and codes that guard their borders (Armstrong 1982).

Taking from Fredrik Barth (1969: Introduction) the idea that the boundary between ethnic groups is more important than the content of their culture, and from the phenomenologists the notion of ethnicity as a shifting bundle of attitudes and perceptions, Armstrong (1982) constructs a history of the persistence of nations or ethnic communities in medieval Europe and the Middle East, which lays emphasis on their ubiquity, their recurrence and their ability to endure over *la longue durée*. I say 'nations or ethnic communities', because, on the one hand, Armstrong focuses on the emergence and dissolution of ethnic identities into religious or class allegiances in pre-modern epochs in Europe and the Middle East, while, on the other hand, he wants to show us how at least some of these groups persisted into the modern epoch, to emerge as fully-fledged modern nations, and for this purpose, in his concluding chapter, constructs a matrix of factors at different levels of generality involved in the emergence of presumably modern 'nations'.

This uncertainty over the terminological status of the groups that form the object of his analysis raises some problems. Throughout the body of his book, Armstrong speaks of ethnic identity and ethnic communities, whereas in his title, and in the first and last chapters, he appears to be thinking in terms of nations and nationhood (which may or may not be 'modern'). In a later essay (Armstrong 1995), he makes much more of the distinction between pre-modern 'nations' (which presumably are identical with 'ethnic groups') before the watershed of nationalism and those that emerged in its wake. But why is nationalism accorded such importance as the criterion of modern nations? Is this a concession to the modernist insistence on the creative role of nationalism? And does it undermine the antiquity of nations?

Not really. For the heart of Armstrong's thesis lies elsewhere, in the enduring role of myths and symbols (the 'myth–symbol complex') in the creation of group boundaries, which guard the community against outsiders and their cultures. These symbolic border guards, such as language and the communications codes and specialists who lend them power, can persist over many centuries, even though their meanings may change for later generations. It is this longevity of symbolism that creates a sense of the antiquity and immemoriality of ethnic communities and nations, not just among the members but also for outsiders. From this perspective, the distinction between ethnic groups and nations becomes secondary.

Now, there is no doubt that myths, symbols and communication constitute vital elements in any historically grounded account of nations and nationalism (and Armstrong's account is full of detailed macro-historical analysis and vivid examples). But such an account inevitably overemphasizes the links between nations and *ethnies* (where it does not make them identical), glossing over important differences between them, particularly in the absence of definitions of terms like 'ethnic identity' and 'nation' which, we are reminded, refer to potentially ephemeral clusters of attitudes and perceptions. Here again, there is ambiguity. On the one hand, we are told that symbolic borders endure. On the other hand, what they appear to guard is nothing more than shifting clusters of attitudes and perceptions. But what, we may ask, is the cultural stuff that the borders enclose, and why should they be so strenuously and ceaselessly guarded? Have these cultures not helped to differentiate ethnic clusters from each other, and are they not, in turn, composed of myths, memories, values and traditions which may persist over many generations, only gradually changing their forms and contents? (See Smith 1998: ch. 8.)

Questions like these also lie at the heart of another kind of perennialist approach, which we may term *continuous perennialism*. Here the emphasis falls on the continuity of *particular* modern nations with their medieval origins. This has led several medieval historians to argue for the existence of (some) 'nations' in the medieval epoch – an approach that tends to pit them against their modern counterparts (see Gillingham 1992; Scales 2000; but cf. Reynolds 1984: ch. 8). Once again, on this view the threads of national continuity are provided by the cultural factors of religion, language, myth, custom, art and historical memory, rather than political, social or economic factors. Given the massive disruptions caused by capitalist industrialization and the bureaucratic, professionalized state (the 'modern state'), it has been easy to point to the many discontinuities between medieval societies and modern nations, and to the novelty of the modern form of the 'mass nation' and the national territorial state (see Mann 1993). But, in the realm of culture and religion, the discontinuities are much less marked. Secularization has been accompanied by periodic religious revivals; secular systems of mass education have built on earlier religious and elite models; vernacular languages have evolved through different forms from their medieval counterparts; and earlier ethnic symbols, values and customs have persisted and adapted to changed conditions.

These observations provide some support for Adrian Hastings's recent thesis about the European and Christian origins of nations. For Hastings, the world is composed of fluid, and often ephemeral, oral ethnicities. The key transition to nationhood follows the introduction of written versions of the vernacular. Nations date only from the production of a vernacular literature, which 'fixes' a body of readers, who form the core of the emergent nation. At the heart of these European literatures stood the Bible and the Book of Common Prayer and, more particularly for the rise of nations, the Old Testament, which Christianity adopted while rejecting Judaism and the Jews, and whose translations into the vernacular Christianity sanctioned. Now, the Old Testament portrayed in the nation of Israel a model of a polity which the New Testament lacked, and that model was, according to Hastings, an almost monolithically national polity fusing people, language, land and kingdom. For Hastings, Islam and other religious traditions lacked this model, and failed to sanction translations of their scriptures; this is why nations and nationalism were an exclusively European development, imported only much later into the Middle East, Asia and Africa. Moreover, it was in the west of Europe that the nation form was pioneered. While there were, according to Hastings, earlier exemplars in Armenia and Ethiopia, it was only in England and her neighbours, Scotland, Wales and Ireland, and later in France, Spain and Sweden, that the national form became continuous with modern nations. England, therefore, stood at the head of the column of medieval, and later of modern, nations and of their nationalisms. In contrast to the modernists, for whom nationalism precedes the nation, Hastings argues that it is a defensive response of threatened nations, and, in any case, a theory or ideology of nationalism is really quite secondary. What matters is the national sentiment (which he calls 'nationalism') of the nation under threat, a sentiment that is found frequently in the medieval sources (Hastings 1997).

To the specifics of Hastings's thesis, there are several cogent objections. For one thing, it lays too great an emphasis on the creation of a vernacular literature as the main, if not the sole, criterion of nationhood. The concept of the nation is far too complex and elusive to be pinned down in this fashion. For another, it underplays the role of both New Testament Greek and Vulgate Latin as sacred languages in Orthodoxy and Catholicism, with a similar function to that of Qu'ranic Arabic, which for long precluded the development and wide dissemination of vernacular translations, something that really took off only after the Reformation. As for his portrayal of Islam, the concept of the *umma* which he emphasizes signally failed to prevent the early development of rival Islamic centres, schisms and kingdoms, each with their own histories and cultures, despite the dominance of classical Qu'ranic Arabic (see Suleiman 2002.) Hastings's thesis also claims an identity of meaning in terms like 'nation' between the fourteenth and nineteenth centuries – at least in the English language. But the meanings of key terms often change radically with historical context, especially over such long periods witnessing vast changes. On the other hand, Hastings would claim that theological and religious texts may 'fix' certain meanings for long periods, and that this is very much the case with such a key Old Testament and biblical concept as the 'nation'. (Besides, such changes in meanings should not preclude a search for general definitions that are not derived from specific historical contexts.)

Again, Hastings's dismissal of the possibility of pre-modern nations outside the Christian orbit is rather too sweeping. On his own criterion of production of a vernacular literature, something very like the nation can be found in the medieval Middle and Far East – in Egypt, Persia, China, Korea and Japan. If we add in factors (other than religion or language) like geography and statehood that Hastings thinks are particularly conducive to nationhood, then we could add to this list such medieval kingdoms as those of Burma, Sinhala and perhaps Siam – though not in the modern, Western sense of the term.[7]

Nevertheless, the main thrust of Hastings's thesis has much to commend it. The ideology of nationalism emerged in Western Europe, albeit a secularizing one, and was heavily influenced by Judeo-Christian beliefs and motifs. Even earlier, ideas of the nation and national character were elaborated in a Christian Europe and were justified by reference to the Bible, including its influential 'Mosaic' genealogical schema in chapter 10 of the Book of Genesis, and its ideas of chosenness and covenant in the Pentateuch. Clearly, the role of Christianity *has* been crucial, and even more so has been the example of ancient Israel. This latter aspect is, if anything, underplayed by Hastings. Old Testament influence and, as a result, the example of the nation of ancient Israel have been strikingly apparent in the rise of national identities out of medieval European *regna*, as well as for the much later genesis of nationalist ideologies.[8]

Indeed, Hastings could have gone further. He does not address the question of whether, apart from the Jews, we can speak of other nations in antiquity, like the ancient Egyptians, and perhaps the Persians, and as a result his account of the antiquity of nations is curtailed, being confined to the medieval world from about the tenth or eleventh century (in England and Ireland). This is not to sanction nationalist myths about the Celtic or Germanic origins of modern nations and the like, but to make us enquire how far back the *model* of the nation can be traced, or whether *per contra* we should really only be speaking of *ethnies* (ethnic communities) in pre-modern epochs. In fact, as I try to show in Chapter 5, a case can be made for both positions. (See Poliakov 1974.)

The Critique of Modernism

Perhaps one reason for Hastings's omission of antiquity was the desire to steer clear of those nationalist myths that located the origins of their nations in the mists of the so-called Dark Ages, the early medieval epoch, and to found his thesis of continuous perennialism on firmer, better attested ground after the Carolingian Empire. Their nationalist myths have been the object of a recent critique by Patrick Geary (2002), who attributes to their pernicious influence the creation of an intellectual 'toxic wasteland' with its fatal mixture of language and 'race' which served as the basis for the manifold horrors of the twentieth century. I think this rather overstates the case. Certainly a fanatical minority of nationalists embraced these origin myths whole-heartedly, but for most people they were secondary; a sense of national identity and antiquity does not, and never did, require belief in the veracity of shadowy Celtic or Germanic tribal myths. More-over, Geary's chosen period, one of immense flux and movement of many factions, groups and peoples from the decline of the Roman Empire to the Carolingian Empire, is not one in which most people, let alone historians, would confidently locate their national origins.

Geary's own account of the period is firmly modernist, and constructivist. It involves a critique of ancient classical authors who regrettably departed from Herodotus' alleged sense of the fluidity and subjectivity of ethnicity by imposing a rigid, stereotypical framework of objectively conceived and ranked ethnic groups on much more fluid processes, thereby providing the framework for much later nationalist objectifications of ethnicity. Geary himself favours an account which focuses on the shifting nature of 'ethnicity' in the 'Dark Ages' and which singles out political and military factors as the key formative processes of shifting ethnic identities.

This is an analysis very much in keeping with the spirit and method of 'modernism', the dominant explanatory paradigm in the field of ethnicity and nationalism, and I would like to consider briefly its assumptions and limitations.

As indicated earlier, by 'modernism' I refer to a historical and socio-logical paradigm which holds that nations as well as nationalism are entirely modern, in the specific sense that

1   Nations are recent and novel.
2   Nationalism is recent and novel.
3   Both nations and nationalism are the product of 'modernization' and the conditions of modernity.

It is the third of these propositions that is crucial. It makes for structural, or sociological, modernism, as opposed to the purely chronological mod-ernism of the first two propositions. Nations, like nationalism, are located in the last two centuries, beginning with the aftermath of the French and American revolutions and the Napoleonic wars. But they are also embed-ded in the unique conditions of modern industrial society, with its mobil-ity, equality, secularism and individualism. This view is predicated on a model of historical change that emphasizes the sharp discontinuity between 'traditional' and 'modern' societies, harking back to the familiar contrast between *Gemeinschaft* and *Gesellschaft* types of society, and positing an inevitable progression, more or less gradual or violent, from the first type of society to the second. (See Smith 1998: part I.)

These are the assumptions underlying the modernist theories and approaches which I address critically in the first part of this book. My general approach to the study of ethnicity and nationalism stems, in part, from a dissatisfaction with

their limited, ethnocentric characterization of the nation;
their tendency to separate off the study of nations and nationalism from that of ethnicity;
their often doctrinaire 'foreshortening' of ethnic history;
their overemphasis on elite action and manipulation;
their failure to consider the long-term ethnic and popular sources of national identity.

All these make it difficult to account for the passions ignited by national-ism and the mass self-sacrifice it can often elicit. Moreover, the notion of the 'modern nation' put forward by many modernists possesses something of that same 'mythical' quality which they rightly discern in the national-ist ideal and which they seek to deconstruct.[9]

My general criticisms of the modernist position are set out in the first three chapters of this book, so I shall not elaborate on them further here. Instead, I shall confine myself to the preliminary problem of definitions of the nation, and then to outlining an alternative 'ethno-symbolic' position that underlies both the theoretical criticisms of the first part of the book and the historical and sociological chapters in the second part.

Ideal-types of the 'Nation'

For modernists, the concept of the nation is not only 'modern' – that is, recent and novel – but also essentially political. The nation, in their eyes, is a form of human association that is

1 Territorial – it has a definite territory of its own with a centre of authority and fixed borders.
2 Legal-political – it forms a specific legal and political type of community, with common rights and duties for all members.
3 Participatory – all its members are citizens able to participate in its political and social affairs.
4 Culturally homogeneous – it possesses a distinctive, uniform, public culture disseminated through a mass education system.
5 Sovereign – it has complete autonomy and is the fount of authority, and possessed of a state of its own.
6 Inter-national – it is part of a wider inter-national system of 'nation-states', of which it is a sovereign member.
7 Nationalist – it is conceived and legitimated by the ideology of nationalism.

It is clear that such a conception of the nation could emerge only in the modern period, which it faithfully mirrors. But, perhaps more important, the modernist ideal-type of the nation has a quite specific provenance. It came into being in the late eighteenth and early nineteenth centuries in Western Europe, and it bears all the hallmarks of its time and place of birth. This conception of the nation is a product not just of the ideology of nationalism in general, but of a particular variant of nationalist ideology, the 'civic' and territorial version which was an offshoot of a particular milieu and its specific history. This means, in effect, that we are using a particular version, or part of a general term, to stand for the whole range covered by that term – one, moreover, that is the product of a specific period and culture of which it bears all the signs. Hence we are using a partial term for the whole, in the double sense that it covers only one kind of nationalism and only one particular type of nation.

As a result, a definition framed in and for modern Western Europe suffers from a double limitation: it becomes difficult, if not impossible, to apply it in areas outside the West; and it precludes any discussion of the possibility of pre-modern nations. I discuss this latter issue in some detail in Chapter 5 below. For the present, I want to focus on its limited relevance for non-Western cases of nationhood, and to outline an alternative ideal-type.

One has only to travel east of the Rhine to see the limited applicability of the Western ideal-type of the nation. In a dismembered nineteenth-century Poland, one could not begin to speak of a clearly bordered territory of 'Poland', or of a legal-political community, or of mass participation of citizens, let alone sovereignty or membership of an inter-national community, but only of an elite Polish nationalism and elements of a distinctive public culture. Was Poland, then, not a nation? Had it been a nation before 1772, ceased to be one thereafter, and become a nation once again in 1918? Is it only the state that makes a nation?[10]

Though nineteenth-century Poland was a particularly poignant example, these are questions that can be addressed to many other communities in Eastern Europe and Asia, incorporated as they were in various kinds of empire. Whether we speak of Czechs or Finns, Serbs or Bulgarians, Arabs or Armenians, Sikhs or Tamils, none boasted clear borders; none could be called legal-political communities or were mass participant communities; and few till the twentieth century were sovereign states (though some could claim that they derived from medieval kingdoms) or were part of an international system. But, unless we take the view that they can be called 'nations' only after they have gained independence and become sovereign 'nation-states', the modern Western ideal-type has little relevance for these cases. (But, in that case, it is difficult to see how such communities could be transformed overnight into nations simply by gaining, or being given, a state of their own.) And this is very much in line with the conclusion of Stein Tønnesson and Hans Antlöv, the editors of a collection entitled *Asian Forms of the Nation* (1996, Introduction), who found that modernist approaches to nations and national identity were only of limited value in the study of Asian nationalisms.

For this reason alone, there seem good grounds for seeking to revise the modernist definition of the nation, and if possible frame a broader ideal-type. This is exactly what I attempt to do in more detail in Chapter 5. Here I shall only outline the main processes involved in this ideal-type. For, in so far as the nation is a form that is never finally achieved, but is always being developed, its features are the outcome of incremental cultural, social and political processes. Typically, these processes involve the following.

1 Self-definition – the growth of a sense of 'we' as opposed to 'them', those around us versus outsiders.

2 Myth and memory cultivation – the growth and cultivation of a fund of shared myths, symbols, traditions and memories of one or more culture communities.

3 Development of a uniform public culture – that is, the spread of a distinctive public culture forged from this common heritage to all the members of the community.

4 Territorialization – the possession of particular historic lands, or ancestral homelands, within recognized borders, and the development of collective attachments to them.

5 Legal standardization – the spread of common customs and laws and their observance by all the members of the community. (See also Smith 2002.)

These appear to be the main processes at work in the creation of communities that would approximate to the ideal-type of the nation. When we can demonstrate that a particular community manifests these processes to a sufficient degree and in mutually reinforcing combination, then there is a *prima facie* case for designating it a 'nation'. On this account, we may define the nation as a named and self-defined human community whose members cultivate common myths, memories and symbols, possess a distinctive public culture, occupy a historic homeland, and observe common laws and shared customs.[11]

Within this general framework, there are more specific sets of resources underlying national identity. These resources are at once 'usable' and 'sacred': they can be, and are, used for strengthening the sense of national identity, and at the same time they are regarded by the members as fundamental and canonical, and are revered as such. These include myths of origin and election, the territorialization of memories to form sacred landscapes, the shared memories of communal 'golden ages', and the ideal of struggle and sacrifice to fulfil a national destiny. Some of these 'sacred foundations' and resources of national identity I discuss below and in later chapters.

An Ethno-Symbolist Approach

Underlying this alternative ideal-type and the selected processes is an approach that involves the development over long time-spans of symbolic elements associated with culture communities of imputed descent. Here I can only outline some of the key dimensions of this historical 'ethno-symbolic' perspective.

Ethnicity and nationhood

Unlike modernists whose approaches to nationalism have little to say about
ethnicity, and reject, if only implicitly, any theoretical connection between
ethnic identity and nationalism, an ethno-symbolic perspective places the
link between nations and core *ethnies* (or ethnic communities) at the centre
of its concerns. However, unlike perennialists and primordialists, ethno-
symbolists refuse to conflate ethnicity and nationhood. While recognizing
that there can never be a simple one-to-one correspondence between a prior
core *ethnie* and a subsequent nation, ethno-symbolists argue that the
concept of *ethnie* and the model of an ethnic core are crucial for the development of the idea of the nation, as well as for particular nations. Conceptually and historically, nationhood and nations are most fruitfully seen
as specialized developments of ethnicity and *ethnies*, ethnic networks and
ethnic categories. This means, of course, that there is some degree of conceptual overlap between the features of the ideal-types of *ethnie* and nation,
but at the same time there is also a clear difference. This can be seen by
a glance at their respective features.

Ethnie

    1   self-definition, including a collective proper name
    2   a shared myth of common origins and ancestry
    3   shared memories of past communal events, places and personages
    4   one or more elements of shared culture
    5   some sentiments of solidarity, at least among the elites

Nation

    1   self-definition, including a collective proper name
    2   shared myths and memories of origins, election, etc.
    3   a distinctive common public culture
    4   possession/occupation of a historic homeland
    5   common rights and duties for all members

Here we see much overlap in the first two features, but considerable diver-
gence thereafter. Thus, in the case of nation, we are speaking of a much
more developed public culture, not just some shared cultural characteristics. Similarly, the members of a nation possess and occupy a historic
homeland; they do not have only a symbolic tie or memory of a special
communal place of origin. In the case of the nation, too, there is more than
solidarity among the members; there are common laws and customs for

all the members, and hence common rights and duties. (See Smith 1991: ch. 4; 2001: ch. 1.)

Any theory of nations and nationalism must, therefore, confront the centrality of ethnicity in the origins and persistence of nations, and consider the links and differences between core *ethnies* and nations. This element is central to the question of the 'antiquity' of nations, as well as to their 'modernity'. On the one hand, nations develop the self-definitions and the myths, symbols, values and memories of their pre-existing ethnic cores; this is what evokes among successive generations of members the familiar sense of the nation's immemorial character, its sociological 'antiquity'. On the other hand, nations, by definition, move beyond the ethnic character of their dominant cores – in terms of their territorialization, dissemination of public culture and legal standardization and observance by all the members (some of whom may not claim to belong to the ethnic core). In this, they reflect new and changing conditions, and to this extent are regarded as recent and novel. (See Smith 1986: especially part II.)

Ethnic myths and symbols

A second concern of ethno-symbolists is with the myths, symbols, memories and values of ethnic communities and nations. These are the main elements of collective continuity and cultural distinctiveness. Ethnosymbolism recognizes the many ruptures and discontinuities in communal existence occasioned by economic change and political action. Conquest, colonization, epidemics, immigration, commercialization, as well as political and religious movements, all disrupt the existing pattern of life of communities. But, short of total destruction or absorption, we can often discern elements of continuity amid change, and these are generally to be found in the sphere of culture and religion. These are the domains that must be investigated to see how far nationalist claims of continuous nationhood can be validated or rejected, and to discover which elements within these domains provide traditions and resources on which nationalists (and others) can build.

Of particular importance in this connection are myths of origins, election and sacrifice, and memories of golden ages. These have often formed the 'sacred foundations' of ethnic cores. Myths of origin have been crucial in defining and sustaining *ethnies*. Indeed, it was the belief that 'we are of one blood', because of shared ancestry, that differentiated and often mobilized the members of ethnic groups. Even when they diverge from what we know of the actual historical origins of peoples, these myths are of fundamental importance in creating a sense of common ethnicity. Equally important have been myths of ethnic election. The sense of chosenness and mission entrusted to a community by the deity has been one of the most powerful cultural resources, often helping to ensure the persistence of core *ethnies* across the centuries. Finally, myths of war and sacrifice have helped to forge powerful emotional bonds between the dead, the living and the yet unborn, often through monuments and ceremonies for the fallen, creating a cult of the 'glorious dead'; I touch on this in Chapter 6, when I analyse the impact of war on ethnic cohesion. As for memories of golden ages, these have acted as guides and models for the nationalists' mission of national regeneration, ensuring a sense of continuity, authenticity, dignity and destiny. These myths and memories have been accompanied by long-standing symbols – flags, emblems, words, scripts, songs, poems and the like – which ensure the mutual recognition of the members, as well as guarding the symbolic boundary with outsiders. Given the multivalent meanings of symbols and their flexibility of interpretation in successive generations, such symbols have been among the most enduring elements of ethnic continuity. (See Connor 1994: ch. 8; Smith 1999: chs. 2, 4; Smith 2003.)

La longue durée

This is why ethno-symbolists believe that, to grasp the nature and forms of ethnicity and nationalism, we need to extend our analysis over long time-spans. This is one source of their differences with modernists. It is not so much a question of disagreement about the dating of nations *per se* as of the need to trace the background and origins of nations to ethnic categories, networks and communities, often in pre-modern epochs. In this respect, modernists foreshorten the necessary time-span of historical periodization, by omitting the ethnic bases of nationhood and of many specific nations; while perennialists (and primordialists), in failing to distinguish nations from ethnic communities, abolish the need for historical sequence and periodization altogether.

Under the heading of *la longue durée*, we may distinguish three kinds of relationship between the ethnic past or pasts and the present. The first is that of *recurrence*. Here, both ethnicity and nationhood are regarded as recurrent forms of collective cultural identity and communal organization. Particular *ethnies* and nations may emerge and dissolve or be absorbed by other identities and communities, but *ethnies* and nations constitute cultural and social resources in every period and continent and, as forms of human association and identification, are not confined to any particular epoch or milieu. This means that, in principle, nations like *ethnies* may be found as much in pre-modern epochs as in the modern world.

The second kind of temporal relationship is that of *continuity* between modern nations and pre-modern core *ethnies*, or indeed a continuous nationhood from medieval to modern times. Here, we are dealing with specific cases, such as those explored by Adrian Hastings in Western Europe. This is a particular focus for the debate about the origins of nations, and as such hinges on the definitions of the nation employed by different historians, as well as on the wider theories in which these definitions are embedded. From an ethno-symbolist standpoint, the continuity in question is less a simple one of nationhood across the epochs than of tracing the origins of particular nations in the pre-modern ethno-histories and cultures of particular populations occupying specific territories, despite the disruptions of political and economic change.

The third kind of temporal relationship is that of *rediscovery and appropriation*, notably of communal ethno-history and its golden ages. This is the goal of intellectuals and professionals who seek out, select and reinterpret strands from the cultural heritage of the local populations whom they designate as 'their nation', usually an ethnic core. Rather than simply inventing national traditions (though that occurs too), the nationalist intellectuals, inspired by Romantic ideals, turn to folk cultures and ethnic memories and symbols in their search for authentic 'roots' for themselves and their community. Unlike many modernists who see in this a form of elite manipulation or even self-deception, ethno-symbolists seek to understand the underlying impulse to moral regeneration and authentication that inspires their researches and activities, and to sift the novel national categories and interpretations from pre-existing traditions of ethnic myth, memory, symbol and value. (See Hutchinson 1987.)

nativist

From ethnie to nation

Against this historical background, ethno-symbolic approaches chart the development of nations from various kinds of ethnic community. Here we can distinguish three kinds of *ethnie* and three routes of nation formation.

Historically, if we leave aside the distinct possibility of nationhood among a few peoples in the ancient world, the first kind are the 'elite' nations that emerged in Western and Northern Europe from, roughly, the thirteenth and fourteenth centuries – in England, Scotland, Wales, Ireland, France, Spain, the Netherlands, Denmark, Sweden and later Poland and Russia. The process involved is one of *bureaucratic incorporation*. Here we are faced with 'lateral' or aristocratic *ethnies* in which ethnicity is closely linked to class status. In some of these lateral *ethnies*, the ruling elites are able to forge strong aristocratic states; and in a few of them, their elites, for various reasons, become intent on using their strong, centralized, increasingly bureaucratic states to spread their aristocratic ethnic culture to the members of middling strata and to incorporate outlying regions around their core *ethnie*. The resulting state, though in fact polyethnic, is dominated by a core *ethnie* and its upper-class culture. (See Smith 1991: chs 2–3.)

A second type which, like the first, I discuss in more detail in Chapter 7, involves the development of a 'vertical', demotic *ethnie* into a politicized ethnic nation through a process of *vernacular mobilization*, a trajectory common to many communities in Eastern Europe and parts of Asia. Here smaller, often subject *ethnies*, in which a single culture permeates all classes, have been incorporated into far-flung empires, and are now mobilized by an intelligentsia that seeks to return to its 'roots' by rediscovering its ethnic history and culture. By educating 'the people' of the designated nation in selected native myths, symbols, traditions and memories, and in their vernacular codes and customs, the returning intelligentsia mobilizes and politicizes all classes of the demotic *ethnie*, thereby developing it into an ethnic nation able to claim independence.

Finally, there are the various immigrant part-*ethnies*, which through *pioneering settlement* in overseas territories, have been able to fuse together migrant fragments of other ethnic communities within a single overarching political culture in a newly won and expanding territory. This is the culture of the pioneer, dominant *ethnie*, whose members established the original settlements (often at the cost of indigenous peoples) and who later came to form the ethnic core of such nations as the United States, Argentina, Australia and New Zealand, and English Canada. (See Smith 1995: ch. 4.)

The role of nationalism

It is against this long-term background that we can gauge the impact of nationalism, the modern ideological movement and 'political religion'. Far from inventing nations, nationalism emerged from the secularization of religious traditions of ethnic election and mission, sacred territory, sacrifice and destiny, and has intensified and politicized ethnic bonds, hastening the processes of nation formation outlined above. The nationalist's typical activity has been the selection of ethnic motifs (myths, values, traditions, symbols, rituals and memories) and their codification to create a uniform, flowing history out of the many strands that form the traditions of the community. By providing a set of goals and a global legitimation for collective political struggle, nationalism has greatly expanded the number and role of the world's nations.

Nationalism may be defined as an ideological movement that seeks to ✦
attain and maintain autonomy, unity and identity for a population some of
whose members believe it to constitute an actual or potential 'nation'. In
this sense, nationalism is more than a collective sentiment or a discourse.
It combines an ideology with a political movement with clear goals of
national autonomy, unity and identity. To this end, it posits a nation that is
continuous, developing over time, and rooted in a specific terrain. The self-
appointed task of the nationalist is to rediscover that past, and to sift and
reinterpret its traditions, so as to mobilize the people and regenerate the ✦
community. But to do this, he or she must dig down to the 'authentic past'
of the community, like some political archaeologist, so that the nation can
be built in its ancestral homeland on its true foundations. (See Smith 1999:
ch. 6.)

Autonomy, unity, national identity, authenticity, the ethnic past, the
ancestral homeland: these are the recurrent motifs of the cultural heritage
of distinct communities which the Romantics popularized and which
nationalists readily took up, and these are the themes which I explore in
Chapter 9, in the context of a wider critique of modernism. Nationalism's
importance lies in its ability to provide a blueprint of nationhood for aspiring *ethnies*, something that is altogether elided by perennialists and primordialists, but greatly exaggerated by modernists who tend to see in
nationalism, the ideology and the movement, the prime source (along with
the state) of modern nations.

Plan of the Book

These, then, are the main assumptions of the approach which guides my
concerns in this book. The confluence of an ethno-symbolic historical and
sociological analysis, on the one hand, with a theoretical critique of both
modernism and perennialism, on the other hand, accounts for its overall
the plan.

I start with a critique of the modernist approaches. Chapter 1, 'The Myth
of the "Modern Nation"', highlights the 'mythical' quality of the modernist accounts of the nation, mirroring the perennialist and nationalist
myths which modernists seek to deconstruct. On the other hand, myths (in
a value-neutral sense of the term) are vital to the formation of nations and
nationalism; for the myths of nations can, and have, moved people to large-
scale collective action.

Chapter 2, 'Memory and Modernity', examines the explicitly modernist
theory of Ernest Gellner, and in particular his last public pronounce-
ment (in a debate at Warwick University in 1995), in which he espoused

a 'creationist' view of nations. Such a view, I argue, fails to account for
the role of historical memory and the systematic 'return to the past' which
are such typical features of nationalisms, and which are vital to the construction of nations. As a result, popular events and personages prior to the
advent of nationalism, which are neglected by modernists, become essential elements in the nationalist accounts of the nation. (Gellner 1983.)[12]

The third chapter, entitled 'The Nation: Invented, Imagined, Reconstructed?', examines more closely the theoretical sources of the accounts
of some recent historians, notably the concept of 'invented traditions'
propounded by Eric Hobsbawm and Terence Ranger (1983), as well as
the notion of an 'imagined political community' of a print-reading
public explored by Benedict Anderson (1991). Both, I contend, are
valuable but inadequate characterizations, let alone explanations, of the
formation of nations. Rather than invention and imagination, we need to
focus on the ideas of the rediscovery, reinterpretation and reconstruction
of nations.

Modernism in all its varieties sprang ultimately from the formulations
of the classical sociological traditions. Though Marx, Weber and Durkheim
failed to address directly questions of nation formation and nationalism,
their concepts and approaches indirectly furnished the basic assumptions
of the modernist and perennialist paradigms. This is the subject of Chapter
4, 'Nationalism and Classical Social Theory', the final chapter of Part I.

If Part I concentrates on theory, Part II is more concerned with historical and sociological issues, and focuses on the links between nations,
nationalism and ethnicity.

Chapter 5, entitled 'Were there "Nations" in Antiquity?', is an extended
essay on the vexed question of pre-modern nationhood. Through an exploration of several cases in Antiquity, notably ancient Egypt, Armenia and
Israel, it challenges the view that we cannot speak of nations in the generic
sense before the modern epoch, and argues for the replacement of the specific Western and modern definition of the nation proposed by the modernists with a broader, more neutral ideal-type. Modernists may be correct
in their empirical claim that most modern nations are chronologically fairly
recent, but the fact that the idea and the model of the nation, as well as
several examples, can be found in earlier epochs undermines the theoretical basis of their accounts, and forces us to re-examine our categories in
this field.

Chapter 6, 'War and Ethnicity', does much the same for the concept of
ethnicity. It analyses the arguments linking ethnic community with
warfare, and examines the evidence of linkage between them in the ancient
world, in the early modern wars of nations and in the total national wars

of the twentieth century. The effects of protracted warfare and its myths and memories on ethnic consciousness, cohesion and self-images are explored across the ages along a number of different dimensions.

Chapter 7, 'The Origins of Nations', develops an ethno-symbolic account of the formation of nations. Distinguishing two kinds of pre-modern *ethnie*, lateral and vertical, which serve as points of departure, it traces two main routes of nation formation. The first is through the creation of a strong state by an aristocratic *ethnie* and its bureaucratic incorporation of outlying regions and middle and lower classes. The second proceeds through the vernacular mobilization of 'the people' by an indigenous 'returning' intelligentsia, which seeks to use the myths, memories, values and symbols of poetic landscapes and golden ages which can resonate with larger populations in order to politicize their culture and achieve political goals.

The theme of the 'golden age' is the focus of Chapter 8, entitled 'The "Golden Age" and National Renewal'. This takes up, once again, the question of the return to 'antiquity' found so often in nationalisms, and the particular salience of memories of golden ages in ethno-history. These golden ages come in various forms and serve a variety of social functions, such as continuity, authenticity, dignity and a sense of collective destiny. Typically, there are rival interpretations and competing versions of the golden age, which the quest for an authentic antiquity so often encourages.

Finally, Chapter 9, entitled 'Romanticism and Nationalism', returns us to the onset of the modern epoch, and the Romantic 'roots' of nationalist ideologies. It was the ethnic myths, memories and symbols that the Romantics uncovered and disseminated that were crucial for the nationalist and vernacular mobilization of 'the people', and that meant drawing on the ethno-symbolic heritage of the populations that the nationalists wished to liberate. The 'romantic' themes of nature and homeland, authenticity and self-expression, 'history', 'destiny', autonomy and self-sacrifice, disseminated through all the arts, have given palpable substance and meaning to the sense of national identity among peoples across the globe.

Throughout, the book seeks to reveal the limitations of modernism and perennialism, so as to establish the 'antiquity' of nations in both a historical and a sociological sense. Historically, it opens up the question of pre-modern nations – that is, the possibility of designating at least some communities in pre-modern epochs as 'nations' in a generic sense of the term. At the very least, this entails the need to scrutinize critically modernist assumptions about (Western) nationhood, and to seek broader ideal-types that are not embedded in particular cultural and historical milieux. This is partly a matter of the use of terms; but it is also a question of the interpretation of sources and the handling of historical data in the light of general frameworks and concepts.

Sociologically, I argue that the members of even the most chronologically modern nations seek to return to their 'roots' – that is, to an 'antiquity' that is created to serve vital social and cultural needs. This entails a search for 'authentic' myths and memories that will encapsulate the 'origins' and 'essence' of the national identity. In the many other cases of long-established communities, it is a question of 'rediscovering' an authentic past or pasts that can serve as the foundation of national identity and resonate with the designated population. In this sense, the nation is revealed as an amalgam of the modern – that is, the recent and the novel – and the ancient – that is, the rooted, original and persistent elements. And while it is usual for scholars to focus almost exclusively on the modern aspects and deride the others as 'backward-looking', of equal importance for creating and sustaining a sense of national identity in an often heterogeneous population are those elements that are felt to be authentic and rooted because of their antiquity.

Notes

1 On European integration and cultural identity, see Delanty 1995, and the critique in Smith 1999: ch. 9.
2 On social memory and national identity, see Gillis 1994. For war memories, see Winter 1995. For a major study of 'sites of memory' in France, see Nora 1997–8. On competing ethnic myths in England, see MacDougall 1982; on Greek 'golden ages', see Kitromilides 1989.
3 On the diffusion of nationalism outside Europe, see Kedourie 1971: Introduction. For a fuller analysis of modernist theories of nations and nationalism, see Smith 1998: pt I. See also Hutchinson 1994.
4 See the recent 'perennialist' approaches of Fishman 1980, Armstrong 1982 and Hastings 1997.
5 For the liberal view, see Renan 1882, in Bhabha 1990 (cf. the essay by Thom in this volume). This is echoed in part in the well-known dichotomy of Kohn 1967, analysed by Hutchinson 1987: ch. 1.
6 For the multiple identities of ancient Greeks, see Alty 1982; Finley 1986: ch. 7; Hall 1992.
7 Hastings's contribution is discussed in a symposium in *Nations and Nationalism* 9 (1), 2003: 7–28; see also his article on Holy Lands in the same issue (Hastings 2003).
8 This facet is more fully discussed in my *Chosen Peoples* (Oxford University Press 2003: chs. 3–5), as well as in the symposium on 'Chosen Peoples' (1999), in *Nations and Nationalism* 5 (3). For the Mosaic 'ethnic genealogy' in Genesis, see Kidd 1999.

9 I have in mind the theories of Kedourie 1960, Gellner 1983, Hobsbawm 1990 and Breuilly (1993). See Chapter 3 for a critique of the constructionist element, notably in the work of Hobsbawm, and Anderson 1991.

10 Hans Kohn's (1967) dichotomy of 'Western' and 'Eastern' nationalisms does not appear to question the existence of nations east of the Rhine, and neither does Hroch's (1985) analysis of smaller European nationalisms. That is why they had to be placed in a separate category, for which the Western conception of the nation was largely irrelevant.

11 This presents a revised definition of the nation in place of the rather more specific and modernist one which I employed earlier; on which, see Smith 1983: ch. 7. See also Uzelac 2002 and the other articles in this special issue of *Geopolitics*.

12 For this debate, see Mortimer and Fine 1999: pt II.

References

Alty, J. H. M. 1982: Dorians and Ionians. *Journal of Hellenic Studies* 102, 1–14.

Anderson, Benedict 1991: *Imagined Communities: Reflections on the Origin and Spread of Nationalism*, 2nd edn. London: Verso.

Armstrong, John 1982: *Nations before Nationalism*. Chapel Hill: University of North Carolina Press.

Armstrong, John 1995: Towards a theory of nationalism: consensus and dissensus. In Sukumar Periwal (ed.), *Notions of Nationalism*, Budapest: Central European University Press, 34–43.

Barth, Fredrik (ed.) 1969: *Ethnic Groups and Boundaries*. Boston: Little, Brown & Co.

Bhabha, Homi (ed.) 1990: *Nation and Narration*. London and Boston: Routledge.

Billig, Michael 1995: *Banal Nationalism*. London: Sage.

Breuilly, John 1993: *Nationalism and the State*, 2nd edn. Manchester: Manchester University Press.

'Chosen Peoples' 1999: Symposium in *Nations and Nationalism* 5 (3).

Connor, Walker 1990: When is a nation?, *Ethnic and Racial Studies* 13 (1), 92–103.

Connor, Walker 1994: *Ethno-Nationalism: The Quest for Understanding*. Princeton: Princeton University Press.

Delanty, Gerard 1995: *Inventing Europe: Idea, Identity, Reality*. Basingstoke: Macmillan.

Deutsch, Karl 1966: *Nationalism and Social Communication*, 2nd edn. New York: MIT Press.

Eller, Jack and Coughlan, Reed, 1993: The poverty of primordialism: the demystification of ethnic attachments. *Ethnic and Racial Studies* 16 (2), 183–202.

Finley, Moses 1986: *The Use and Abuse of History*. London: Hogarth Press.

Fishman, Joshua 1980: Social theory and ethnography: neglected perspectives on language and ethnicity in Eastern Europe. In Peter Sugar (ed.), *Ethnic Diversity and Conflict in Eastern Europe*, Santa Barbara, CA: ABC-Clio, 69–99.

Geary, Patrick 2002: *The Myth of Nations: The Medieval Origins of Nations.* Princeton: Princeton University Press.

Geertz, Clifford 1963: The integrative revolution. In Clifford Geertz (ed.), *Old Societies and New States*, New York: Free Press.

Gellner, Ernest 1964: *Thought and Change.* London: Weidenfeld & Nicolson.

Gellner, Ernest 1983: *Nations and Nationalism.* Oxford: Blackwell.

Gillingham, John 1992: The beginnings of English imperialism. *Journal of Historical Sociology* 5, 392–409.

Gillis, John R. (ed.) 1994: *Commemoration: The Politics of National Identity.* Princeton: Princeton University Press.

Greenfeld, Liah 1992: *Nationalism: Five Roads to Modernity.* Cambridge, MA: Harvard University Press.

Grosby, Steven 1994: The verdict of history: the inexpungeable tie of primordiality – a reply to Eller and Coughlan. *Ethnic and Racial Studies* 17 (1), 164–71.

Grosby, Steven 1995: Territoriality: the transcendental, primordial feature of modern societies. *Nations and Nationalism* 1 (2), 143–62.

Grosby, Steven 1997: Borders, territoriality and nationality in the ancient Near East and Armenia. *Journal of the Economic and Social History of the Orient* 40 (1), 1–29.

Grosby, Steven 2002: *Biblical Ideas of Nationality: Ancient and Modern.* Winona Lake, IN: Eisenbrauns.

Hall, Edith 1992: *Inventing the Barbarian: Greek Self-definition through Tragedy.* Oxford: Clarendon Press.

Hastings, Adrian 1997: *The Construction of Nationhood: Ethnicity, Religion and Nationalism.* Cambridge: Cambridge University Press.

Hastings, Adrian 2003: Holy lands and their political consequences. *Nations and Nationalism* 9 (1), 29–54.

Hobsbawm, Eric 1990: *Nations and Nationalism since 1780.* Cambridge: Cambridge University Press.

Hobsbawm, Eric and Ranger, Terence (eds) 1983: *The Invention of Tradition.* Cambridge: Cambridge University Press.

Horowitz, Donald 2002: The primordialists. In Daniel Conversi (ed.), *Ethnonationalism in the Contemporary World: Walker Connor and the Study of Nationalism*, London and New York: Routledge, 72–82.

Hroch, Miroslav 1985: *Social Preconditions of National Revival in Europe.* Cambridge: Cambridge University Press.

Huntington, Samuel 1996: *The Clash of Civilisations and the Remaking of World Order.* New York: Simon & Schuster.

Hutchinson, John 1987: *The Dynamics of Cultural Nationalism: The Gaelic Revival and the Creation of the Irish Nation State.* London: Allen & Unwin.

Hutchinson, John 1994: *Modern Nationalism.* London: Fontana.

Kedourie, Elie 1960: *Nationalism.* London: Hutchinson.

Kedourie, Elie (ed.) 1971: *Nationalism in Asia and Africa*. London: Weidenfeld & Nicolson.

Kidd, Colin 1999: *British Identities before Nationalism: Ethnicity and Nationhood in the Atlantic World, 1600–1800*. Cambridge: Cambridge University Press.

Kitromilides, Paschalis 1989: 'Imagined communities' and the origin of the national question in the Balkans. *European History Quarterly* 19 (2), 149–92.

Kohn, Hans 1967 [1944]: *The Idea of Nationalism*, 2nd edn. New York: Collier–Macmillan.

MacDougall, Hugh 1982: *Racial Myth in English History: Trojans, Teutons and Anglo-Saxons*. Montreal: Harvest House; Hanover, NH: University Press of New England.

Mann, Michael 1993: *The Sources of Social Power*. vol. 2. Cambridge: Cambridge University Press.

Mortimer, Edward and Fine, Robert (eds) 1999: *People, Nation and State: The Meaning of Ethnicity and Nationalism*. London and New York: I. B. Tauris Publishers.

Nora, Pierre (ed.) 1997–8: *Realms of Memory: The Construction of the French Past*, English edn by Lawrence Kritzman, New York: Columbia University Press, 3 vols (orig. *Les Lieux de Mémoire*, Paris: Gallimard 1984–92, 7 vols).

Poliakov, Leon 1974: *The Aryan Myth*. New York: Basic Books.

Renan, Ernest 1882: *Qu'est-ce qu'une Nation?* Paris: Calmann-Levy (English trans. in Bhabha 1990).

Reynolds, Susan 1984: *Kingdoms and Communities in Western Europe, 900–1300*. Oxford: Clarendon Press.

Scales, Leonard 2000: Identifying 'France' and 'Germany': medieval nation-making in some recent publications. *Bulletin of International Medieval Research* 6, 23–46.

Shils, Edward 1957: Primordial, personal, sacred and civil ties. *British Journal of Sociology* 7, 13–45.

Smith, Anthony D. 1983: *Theories of Nationalism*, 2nd edn. London: Duckworth; New York: Holmes and Meier.

Smith, Anthony D. 1986: *The Ethnic Origins of Nations*. Oxford: Blackwell.

Smith, Anthony D. 1991: *National Identity*. Harmondsworth: Penguin.

Smith, Anthony D. 1995: *Nations and Nationalism in a Global Era*. Cambridge: Polity.

Smith, Anthony D. 1998: *Nationalism and Modernism: A Critical Survey of Recent Theories of Nations and Nationalism*. London and New York: Routledge.

Smith, Anthony D. 1999: *Myths and Memories of the Nation*. Oxford and New York: Oxford University Press.

Smith, Anthony D. 2001: *Nationalism: Theory, Ideology, History*. Cambridge: Polity.

Smith, Anthony D. 2002: When is a nation? *Geopolitics* 7 (2), 5–32.

Smith, Anthony D. 2003: *Chosen Peoples: Sacred Sources of National Identity*. Oxford: Oxford University Press.

Suleiman, Yasir 2002: *The Arabic Language and National Identity*. Edinburgh: Edinburgh University Press.

Tønnesson, Stein and Antlöv, Hans (eds) 1996: *Asian Forms of the Nation*. Richmond, Surrey: Curzon Press.

Uzelac, Gordana 2002: When is the nation? Constituent elements and processes. *Geopolitics* 7 (2), 33–52.

Van den Berghe, Pierre 1978: Race and ethnicity: a sociobiological perspective. *Ethnic and Racial Studies* 1 (4), 401–11.

Van den Berghe, Pierre 1995: Does race matter? *Nations and Nationalism* 1 (3), 357–68.

Winter, Jay 1995: *Sites of Memory, Sites of Mourning: The Great War in European Cultural History*. Cambridge: Cambridge University Press.

Part I
Theory

1

The Myth of the 'Modern Nation'

The nature and role of nations is undoubtedly one of the most significant and fateful subjects in human history, but it is also one of the most baffling and ambiguous, liable to mythical interpretation and political manipulation.

Nationalism itself can be regarded as one such political myth. It holds, after all, that mankind is naturally divided into distinct nations, each with its peculiar character, and that everyone must, again as a matter of nature, belong to a nation, which is the source of all power and every liberty. Nationalists further claim that nations have existed from time immemorial, but that, in the course of generations, the members of most nations forgot their identities and failed to recognize the ties that bound them; and it is only in recent times that nations have been reawakened, with the help of the nationalists and patriots, who have succeeded in re-minding members of their national bonds, so paving the way for a truly national regeneration.[1]

Now, however untenable and undemonstrable some of these proposi-tions are, nationalist claims cannot be dismissed as wholly illusory or totally without foundation. There are clearly factual elements here: most of humanity *is* now divided into national communities which often possess distinct cultural attributes, and nationalism is quite plainly reviving a sense of cultural identity among some populations which appeared to be without such an awareness. But there are also components that go well beyond any

'The Myth of the "Modern Nation" and the Myths of Nations', *Ethnic and Racial Studies*, 11/1 (1988): 1–26. Reproduced with the permission of the editors. (<http://www.tandf.co.uk/journals/routledge/01419870.html>)

observations or inferences: the assumed existence of nations 'from time immemorial', the forgetting of national ties, the nation as the sole source of freedom, and so on. These are dramatized interpretations, and they are clearly designed to serve the special short and long term goals of nationalists. Some indeed would go so far as to explain the whole nationalist enterprise in terms of the interests or dispositions of nationalist elites and movements; but it is not necessary to assent to this claim, in order to see how drama has been mingled with empirical generalization in the ideology of nationalism.[2]

Now this mingling of empirical observations with dramatic narrative interpretation is typical of myth and mythical thinking. Myth is very far from being the kind of illusion that it is often conceived to be; nor would we be justified in regarding myths as wholly without factual foundation. The myth of the Norman Yoke did, after all, set out from the indubitable fact of the Norman Conquest. But myth exaggerates, dramatizes and reinterprets facts. It turns the latter into a narrative recounted in dramatic form, and this is part of its wide appeal. For myths *are* often widely believed, and though their components change, they generally exhibit certain basic forms. They generally relate present needs to future hopes through a reference, more or less elaborate, to the past. This is just as true of revolutionary as of restorative myths; even eschatological myths presume a generally corrupt tradition of thought or history of existence. The myths of the Second Coming or the October Revolution are only intelligible in the context of a particular interpretation of a (human or national) past order.[3]

From these examples, it must be clear that myths do not only serve to legitimate particular orders or regimes.[4] Some myths envisage or promote radical change. But they all refer back to a past state of affairs, often in the distant past, an age that is usually seen as pristine and golden, which the myth-makers or promoters may use as a model for the new dispensation they hope to inaugurate.

If, then, myths are neither illusions nor mere legitimations, they may perhaps be regarded as widely believed tales told in dramatic form, referring to past events but serving present purposes and/or future goals. In that sense, nationalism's peculiar myth of the nation may be seen as a particularly potent and appealing dramatic narrative, which links past, present and future through the character and role of the national community.[5]

The nationalist myth is also an example of what is often termed a 'primordialist' approach to community, an approach that takes as given certain fundamental cleavages and attributes of humanity, notably race, religion, language and territory. It is an approach that still boasts devotees, including the recent sociobiological variant, but it is not fashionable in the scholarly community, even though at the popular level it commands wide assent.[6]

Myths of the 'Modern Nation'

But there are other myths of the nation that have, since the Second World War especially, proved more attractive to scholars and students, notably in the social sciences. These new myths share an underlying 'instrumentalism', which regards cultural attributes and cleavages as infinitely malleable and subject to manipulation by elites and vested interests. Rightly pointing to the many changes that such attributes undergo over generations, adherents of this approach treat the cultural groups which human beings form as vessels and instruments of special economic and political interests, with no independent status. To the question why human beings should then resort to cultural groupings to further such calculative ends, they tend to invoke rather vague or schematic social psychological concepts like 'communication' and 'affect', which then turn out to play a more pivotal role than the general 'instrumentalist' approach envisaged.[7]

Nevertheless, it is a broadly 'instrumentalist' spirit that pervades the various modern accounts of the nation that scholars debate today. In one way or another, they are all variants of a single motif and assume a common background. I shall call this motif the 'myth of the modern nation', and the background 'the modernization paradigm'. The basic idea of this recent myth is simple. The nation, it holds, is neither natural nor immemorial, much less self-generative. On the contrary, it is a relatively modern phenomenon arising out of specific modern conditions and ideally suited to those conditions. It is also a construct. Human beings, specifically nationalists, invent nations, though they may not do so wholly of their own volition. So, nothing could be really more misleading than nationalism's own reading of the nation, because it reverses the real causal chain and makes false or undemonstrable assumptions.

I hope to show later why it is legitimate to call this recent general approach to the phenomena of the nation and nationalism, and its basic motif, a 'myth', or perhaps a 'counter-myth' to that of the nationalists. For the moment, I want to illustrate some variants of the modernization approach, to show how they fit with the basic motif. I shall not dwell on such obvious 'modernization' accounts as Smelser's, for whom nationalism at first promotes flexibility and rationalization of the social structure, and later impedes it after an initial stage of modernization – a perspective as instrumental as any Marxist account; nor on the methodologically more refined position of Karl Deutsch, for whom 'nation-building' was the result of the twin processes of 'communications' and 'social mobilization', but which he nevertheless firmly tied to the era and process of modernization. In both these approaches, as in that of Lerner, the nation is a purely modern phenomenon, for only in the modern era can there be any question of a large, participant culture.[8]

It is the more recent accounts, which attempt to distance themselves from an overt 'modernization' approach, that illustrate my point most interestingly. Despite his strong animus against nationalism, Kedourie subscribes to the general myth of the 'modern nation', seeing nations as the creations of a nationalist opiate that was first cultivated by German intellectuals around 1800 and then proceeded to infect the intelligentsias of so many other lands. The important point for my purposes in Kedourie's account is not his stress on the role of ideas in history, but his belief that the nation is a relatively recent construct of self-interested and misguided nationalist youth, which has undermined legitimate and traditional communities like the family and religious confession. Nationalism has introduced a new era, the age of principles, in place of earlier epochs which were governed by pragmatic interest in the field of politics; and for Kedourie, principle in politics is infinitely more dangerous than mere interest. As a result, the modern era is inherently unstable and conflict-ridden; whereas in traditional societies, wars never threatened to undermine the basis of society.[9]

The same dichotomy between tradition and modernity, but arising out of a sociological discourse and informed by a far more optimistic spirit, can be found in Gellner's theory of nationalism. Gellner makes an explicit and forceful contrast between a stable but traditional agrarian type of society, and a growth-oriented, mobile, industrial society. He boldly asserts that the cultural stratification of agrarian societies, which divided off literate urban elites from a host of illiterate food-producing communities, allowed no room for nations or nationalism; whereas modern societies, with their need for literacy and educated citizenries to man the industrial machine, positively require nations and nationalism. It is because of these industrializing and modernizing drives that intelligentsias emerge who demand the creation of mass co-cultural nations; it is nationalism that invents nations, both its general idea and particular examples of the nation. But such nationalism only emerges when societies start to modernize; and nations only make sense in modern conditions.[10]

The same strong emphasis on the modernity of nations can be found in more Marxian accounts. Tom Nairn, for example, concedes that ethnic groups and nationalities existed prior to 1800, but they were politically unimportant, and had no connection with the ideology or process of nationalism. It is capitalism, or rather its jagged and uneven progress across the globe as it moves out of its Anglo-French heartlands, that incites nationalism to emerge in peripheral and colonized areas. It is the imperialism of

Western bourgeoisies that summons into being the nationalist protests of elites in underdeveloped countries whose only resource is their manpower; hence their appeal to the masses in the countryside, and the populism of their ensuing nationalism.[11] In the same spirit, though with a subtler sense of cultural dimensions, Benedict Anderson understands the nationalist demand for a sovereign but limited political community, a uniquely imagined community, as springing out of peculiarly modern processes and developments, at least from the sixteenth century in Europe – notably the technology of printing and the capitalist production of books and journals on a mass scale for a mass, anonymous readership, and the administrative pilgrimages that colonial elites made under imperial domination, which led them to see themselves as embryonic communities different from the metropoles. The point is, if anything, underlined by its cultural setting: the dissolution of old faiths with their assurance of other-worldly immortality, with the onset of science and modernity. The nation replaces the faith, posterity immortality, in the modern epoch.[12]

Finally, two recent analyses by historians may be cited. For John Breuilly, nationalism is typically a political argument, a tool for seizing the state by mobilizing, co-ordinating and legitimating the movement of the masses. It emerges in early modern Europe, when the state is increasingly differentiated from society, and a sense of alienation from politics requires a new type of community to overcome it. The nationalist argument appears to promise that community, though Breuilly remains sceptical of its success. The important point, again, is that by treating nationalism as a form of politics rather than culture and identity, Breuilly is able to locate it securely in the modern era, and view it as a wholly modern phenomenon, the outcome of modern problems.[13] Similarly, Eric Hobsbawm and Terence Ranger, in their recent volume whose aim is to illustrate the capacity and need for modern societies to generate traditions, suggest the enormous utility for modern states and their elites, but also for other classes, of the ideals and symbolism of the nation in counteracting divisive tendencies and creating cohesion in disruptive eras. Again, nations and nationalism are seen as constructs and visions needed by all kinds of groups in a modern era of dislocating and exploitative capitalism. The 'invention' of mass-national traditions is an inevitable consequence of the divisions generated by modern capitalism.[14]

Functions of the 'Modern Nation' Myth

Given such a wide theoretical and ideological spectrum of scholarly opinion in support of the general 'modernization' approach to nationalism, is it legitimate to regard the basic motif of the modernity of the nation as in some sense mythical? What purpose does it serve to call it a myth?

It is important here to recall that myths mingle factual observations and generalizations with dramatic narrative interpretations, and that they relate past events to present and/or future purposes. Now, the motif of the modernity of the nation exactly mingles empirical generalizations and observations with such dramatic interrelations, albeit each of them different. The element of observation and generalization is clear. Nationalism, as a doctrine and ideological movement, *did* arise in the modern era, in the eighteenth century, to be more precise.[15] 'Nation-states' *are*, largely, modern phenomena, though in the strict sense of that term (where nation and state are coextensive) fairly rare.[16] Similarly, nations as territorially bounded, even impermeable, communities are recent developments, consequent on the increasingly effective operations of the modern 'rational' state.[17] Citizenship, too, though known in classical antiquity in rather different forms, is a recent phenomenon; to argue that it is an essential characteristic of the 'modern' conception and practice of the nation is question-begging, but I think there are good reasons for so regarding it, an issue to which I shall return.[18] Besides, the rise of new states attempting to build nations in Asia and Africa suggests that nations are neither organic nor immemorial, but really quite recent constructs.[19]

Yet, it is exactly here that unease creeps in. Is the evidence quite so unequivocal? Just how many new nations are being forged? We may be tempted to lean towards a favourable verdict in the case of, say, Tanzania, but what about Nigeria, India and Yugoslavia? Or even Belgium and Canada? Is it really quite so rational and technical a matter to build nations, given enough will, activism and self-sacrifice? The time-span under consideration is admittedly short; but the overall picture of nation-building and ethnic splintering is hardly encouraging. Even in long-established European states, the edifice shows ethnic cracks. It seems that this particular drama of 'nation-building' may depend less upon mass or elite activism than upon the historical and structural situation in which the nation-to-be finds itself.[20]

The element of activism in 'nation-building' is, of course, only one aspect of the overall myth of the 'modern nation'. But it is an important element, because it echoes the activism of Third World leaders bent on inventing nations where they do not exist, and engaged in the project of constructing the nation-to-be.[21] There is a second aspect, which much Third World experience appears to cast doubt upon: namely, the belief in the assimilative power of modernity, an assimilative capacity that enables large, culturally homogeneous nations to be formed. That is, after all, the promise, some would say the lesson, of the American experience. But, even here, perhaps especially here, the same facts breed different interpretations and opposed myths. The ideal of the 'melting-pot' is countered by the myth of 'unmeltable *ethnie*', which seem to present an insurmountable obstacle from the past to a mobile, culturally assimilative modernity creating nations in its own image.[22]

Activism and assimilation represent two aspects of the myth of the modern nation. But they also represent two functions of the myth for political elites, especially but not only in the Third World. Nation-building today demands activism and mobilization of the masses; in a polyethnic setting, it also requires policies of integration and assimilation. But the myth has other aspects and functions, closer to the situation of the myth-makers, and not always in harmony with the ideals of the political elites in the Third World.

There is, for example, a strong element of sociological iconoclasm in the myth. It sets out to debunk the claims of nationalism's own myth of the nation. It seeks to demythologize the nation, to view it through a neutral lens of sociological detachment. The ideological attitudes of proponents of the myth of the modern nation, especially to nationalism, may indeed vary from favour or condescension to outright hostility; but their theoretical position, the 'instrumentalism' through which they seek to explain nations and nationalism, is one of ironic scepticism and non-involvement.[23]

Such a stance fits well with the position of social scientists in society and in the academic community. Broadly speaking, the internationalization of social science from the 1950s onward went hand in hand with the aspirations for upward mobility of social scientists and the expansion of social science in tertiary education. The myth of the modernity of nations, in so far as it encourages people to believe that the nation represents a specific historical configuration and a particular stage in history, serves the professional and international aspirations of social science. It enables social theory to look back, as it were, on a dying age of nationalism, and forward to the demise of nations in an increasingly interdependent and cosmopolitan world. It is from the stance of a cosmopolitan culture and vision that the role of the nation in the modern world can be best grasped.

Of course, the functions of the myth of the modern nation are part and parcel of the wider functions of the belief in modernization itself. The dramatic element in the narrative of the myth focuses on the radical break between agrarian and industrial, traditional and modern, society, and it views human history as ultimately progressive, if discontinuous. The sharp dichotomy this creates between two periods, and levels, of history forms the essential locus for theories of the nation as a specifically modern phenomenon, marked by the basic features of whatever the theorist considers the hallmarks of 'modernity'.

What function, it may be asked, does this radical dichotomy serve in respect of the nation and nationalism? I think that its main purpose is to solve a difficult ethical dilemma, particularly for intelligentsia and the social scientists among them. This is that many professionals and intellectuals do still retain attachments, however attenuated, to particular nations or ethnic communities, through their families, recreations, friends, customs and so on. At the same time, in their public roles, they espouse a cosmopolitan culture and assimilationist ideal. How can their private and public roles be harmonized, and how can they reconcile particularistic attachments with universalist aspirations? The answer lies in regarding the nation as a modern, and therefore temporary, phenomenon, an attribute, more or less basic, of a particular industrial, capitalist or modern phase of history. In the future, when technological and economic conditions have matured, nations, and the private roles and attachments they engender, will wither away.[24]

Some Elements of the 'Nation'

Once we accept that the notion of a 'modern nation' is just as much a 'myth', in the sense outlined earlier, as the nationalist myth, and that it too serves present purposes and future goals, then we are in a better position to evaluate different elements of the myth and of the definition of the nation enshrined therein. As we saw, some of these elements have proved problematic. 'Nation-building' through planned activism has run into many problems. The American ideal of assimilation and integration, too, has encountered strong resistance, not least in America itself. Worse, despite growing world interdependence, the nation appears to be taking an unconscionably long time dying; in some areas like Western Europe, old communities have re-emerged to stake their entitlement to national status. Besides, the whole theoretical apparatus of 'modernization', along with its political ethic, has been under fire for some time; modernization itself is viewed by many as an ethnocentric, unilinear myth. It hardly helps to define the problematic notion of the nation as an essential aspect of a modernity that is itself so vague and ethnocentric.[25]

I do not wish, however, to suggest that there is nothing of value in the myth of the 'modern nation'. For one thing, that would be to misunderstand the nature of myth, and the way it informs, often through metaphor, much of our social thinking. For another, the idea that there have been important breaks in historical development, and that one of them can be located in early modern Europe, with the advent of the 'rational' state, capitalism and industrialism, has its uses in historical explanation. But if this particular myth deflects our attention from the role of cultural and historical communities and identities in *pre*-modern periods in various parts of the world, its insights may be bought at too high a cost.

It seems to me that here lies the principal objection to the myth of the 'modern nation'. It is less its 'instrumentalism' than its myopic, modern Western perspective on nations and nationalism that prevents a proper recognition of the fundamental significance of pre-modern ethnic communities in providing a model and basis for the subsequent development of nations and nationalism. This is not just a historical mistake of giant proportions; it flows from the logic of modernization discourse itself, which forces nations to be seen as wholly modern phenomena. To have something so important and ramified as the nation straddling both sides of the 'traditional'/'modern' divide would make a nonsense of the whole purpose of modernization theory. That it is this commitment to modernization which obscures the role of pre-modern ethnicity, rather than the 'instrumentalism' of so many of the theorists of the 'modern nation', is borne out by the work of John Armstrong, who adopts a broadly 'instrumentalist' position (though of a special Barthian variety), but recognizes the fundamental role of ethnic identity and community in medieval Christendom and Islam.[26]

Can we nevertheless salvage some of the insights of the 'modernist' position, while extending our concept of the nation and nationalism to accommodate the important role of pre-modern ethnicity? I think we can, and in what follows I attempt a sketch of the main elements of such an extended historical conception.

I start from the fact that in the modern world we find two overlapping concepts of the nation, civic or territorial, and ethnic or genealogical. The civic conception treats nations as units of population which inhabit a demarcated territory, possess a common economy with mobility in a single territory-wide occupational and production system, common laws with identical legal rights and duties for everyone, and a public, mass education system, with a single civic ideology. Territory, economy, law and education constitute the four spheres in and through which nations, in this view, are formed. It is very much a Western conception, and fits well with the myth of the 'modern nation', since these kinds of unity – territorial, economic, legal and educational – require a modern, industrial base.

But there is another conception of the nation which harmonizes less well with Western modernity. It sees nations as named human populations claiming a common ancestry, a demotic solidarity, common customs and vernaculars, and a common native history. Genealogy, demography, traditional culture and history furnish the main resources for an ethnic view of

the formation of nations. It is a conception of the nation that has found
favour mainly outside the West, and often opposes civic conceptions.[27]

Now ancestry, history, common culture and solidarity, along with a
common name, are precisely those features of community which define
'ethnicity' and 'ethnic' identity. An ethnic community, or *ethnie*, may, in
fact, be defined as a named human population possessing a myth of
common descent, common historical memories, elements of shared
culture, an association with a particular territory, and a sense of solidarity.
(I say 'association' with, rather than possession of, a given territory or
homeland, because some communities lose their homelands yet locate
themselves in the world by reference to it, as do many others.) I have
included a reference to 'solidarity' to distinguish an 'ethnic category'
which scholars and outside observers may deem to constitute an *ethnie*,
but where the members themselves appear to be largely unaware of their
ethnic ties, as among pre-twentieth-century Turks, or eighteenth-century
Slovaks. It is with communities that I am concerned, and here a sense of
solidarity among at least a significant proportion of the membership is
important.[28]

It seems to me that any useful definition of the nation must do justice
to both ethnic and territorial conceptions. In many ways, the nation is an
ideal of the nationalists which has come to be accepted by very many
people, and equally an abstraction and construct. But it cannot be defined
apart from the conceptions of the nation entertained by nationalist and
other participants, for these conceptions reflect the experiences and processes of the historical and present situations in which so many find themselves. That is why I have opted for a definition of the nation which, while
founded on ethnic elements, includes the civic components that emerge
in more recent periods of history. The nation then becomes a named human
population sharing a myth of common descent, historical memories and
a mass culture, and possessing a demarcated territory, common economy
and common legal rights and duties. In this way, the two overlapping
concepts of the nation are brought together, while allowing different
emphases, and ethnicity is closely linked to the nation and nationalism,
in a way that accords better with reality than the more common attempt
to oppose them.[29]

Ethnic Foundations of Nations

Of course, this is to state by way of definitions a more general perspective, perhaps an account, of nations and nationalism, one that is in some
respects sharply at odds with the 'modernist' view. But only in some

respects, because it accepts the fact that the nation is a modern construct, found only under modern conditions; but goes on to claim that it is not a *wholly* modern construct, it requires pre-modern ethnic elements, and is increasingly formed in the image of older *ethnies*.

Such a perspective provides, in my view, a more comprehensive and sharper understanding of the nature and formation of nations and the role of nationalism in this process. It does not entail acceptance of any 'primordialist' notions of nationality or ethnicity, nor of the nationalist myth itself. What it reintroduces is the much longer time-spans of pre-modern *ethnies*, and the survival of ethnic ties and ethnic mosaics from these periods into the modern world; and thereby makes it possible to explain the durability and widespread appeal of nations, and the intensity of ethnic aspirations today.[30]

Basic to this view is the contention that nations are formed out of 'civic' and 'ethnic' components. Perhaps the most important civic component is the extension of legal rights and duties to all strata, culminating in the ideal of citizenship for all classes. In the modern ideal of the nation, citizenship holds an honoured place. Nations are felt to be lacking in a vital respect, if citizenship is withheld from any region, class, race, sex or religious group of the adult population in the nation-state; or, in cases where the nation does not possess a state of its own, as in Catalonia, if equal legal rights and duties are withheld from any sub-category of the nation.[31] A second vital element on the 'civic' side is the acquisition of a 'homeland', a duly recognized historic territory for the nation. Lack of such a homeland, in the case of diaspora peoples like the Armenians and Jews, long prevented (and prevents) movement from the status of *ethnie* to that of nation with its concomitant development of a national economy and mass educational culture.[32]

Of the ethnic components, historical memories and myths of descent are particularly important. True, in the long-formed and well-established nations of the West, citizens tend to take their myths and memories for granted; only a minority speak of Saxon liberties or Gallic ancestry, let alone Varangian forbears. But even here the assumption of rootedness in a definite homeland with a particular life-style and historical culture is widespread, if less shrill than in smaller or more contested nations.[33] One of the major difficulties faced by the new states in Asia and Africa is precisely the lack of unifying memories and myths, symbols and values for the inhabitants of the territories created by the colonial empires, and conversely the frequent presence of a multiplicity of smaller nodes of 'myth–symbol' complexes among the several *ethnies* that generally make up these post-colonial states, nodes and *ethnies* that impede the chances of creating 'territorial' nations on the civic model. In other words, the civic concept of a modern nation with its common territory, economy, citizenship and mass educational culture often lacks or omits the solidarity and homogeneity stressed by an ethnic concept; the modern nation, to become truly a 'nation', requires the unifying myths, symbols and memories of pre-modern *ethnies*.[34]

What this suggests is that to create a modern nation, a unit of population requires not merely a territory, economy, education system and legal code to itself, but also needs an ethnic foundation in order to mobilize and integrate often diverse cultural and social elements. The first nation-states in the West were fortunate in this respect. Despite some internal divisions far back in the past, by the fifteenth century, one could speak with some justification of a French or English *ethnie* which formed the core of the French and English kingdoms, and which had begun to expand into outlying territories inhabited by other, smaller *ethnies*.[35] Russia similarly, once it had thrown off the yoke of the Golden Horde, was expanding in the sixteenth century outwards from the Russian *zemlya* around the earlier northeastern settlements into neighbouring territories inhabited by Tartars and others.[36] In Sweden and in the Iberian peninsula, a similar process of expansion through conquest, dynastic alliance and religious imposition took place, albeit in very different ways; and together, these European states became the models for others.[37]

Now the vital point that was, and is, sometimes missed is that such expansion took place from a culturally fairly secure base. The population at the centre was culturally relatively homogeneous; they were not riven by deep ethnic cleavages at the moment when expansion began to take place. In contrast, several African and Asian states which possess the 'civic' elements of nationhood far more effectively than did their late medieval European counterparts, are riven by ethnic cleavages at or very near the centre; typically, two or three main *ethnies* are engaged in a continuous competition for national power.[38] Their task is to create, out of the often sharply defined ethnic cultures of their component communities, a single overarching culture. But this is not something that can easily be manufactured in the classroom or even the peacetime barracks. Traditions may be 'invented', but they only last if they have resonance; and most of the resonance in Africa is ethnic and particularistic, not territory-wide. This means that creating 'ethnic nations' by endowing *ethnies* like the Ibo or Kikuyu with 'civic' components, including homelands of their own and ethnic citizenship, remains a tempting, if dangerous, option.[39]

One other general point about the perspective advanced here needs to be noted, and that is the increasing popularity of the 'ethnic model' of the nation. Not only are small nations far more numerous than large, secure ones, they are mostly defined by 'ethnic' features and their self-image is largely ethnic. A distinctive culture and history is, after all, the *raison d'être* for their separate existence. So, while the 'civic' elements of nation-hood are obviously required to maintain a nation in the modern world with its particular complex of economic and political conditions, ethnic profiles and identities are increasingly sought, if only to stem the tide of rational-ization and disenchantment. It is to their ethnic symbols, values, myths and memories that so many populations turn for inspiration and guidance, not in the everyday, practical business of running a state, but for that sense of fraternity and heroism which will enable them to conduct their affairs suc-cessfully. Ethnicity has, moreover, become an end in itself, if it ever was not. To belong to a 'community of history and destiny' has become for many people a surrogate for religious faith, over and above any individ-ual worldly ends that the collective action it inspires may serve.[40] One has only to consider the strong attachment that embattled communities like the Afrikaners, Basques or Sikhs have to their ethnic histories and cultures, to realize that, over and above the other goals they may serve, they have become end-values in themselves which in turn define the other goals that are worth fighting for. As wave after wave of people define themselves and their goals in ethnic terms, so the ethnic concept of the nation, and the ethnic model of national organization, becomes more and more widely diffused, forcing even groups which defined themselves in civic terms to regard themselves increasingly as ethnic nations, as happened in late nineteenth-century France.[41]

The Myths of Modern Nations

If we accept that the nation is a modern construct, built on pre-modern foundations and ethnic models, which are not obliterated, only modified, in the course of the formation of the nation, then we can see the continu-ing role of ethnicity today in many of the world's nations, and the special place of ethnic myths of descent. Of course, in saying that modern nations are built on ethnic foundations, we do not mean that each and every nation is built upon, and emerges from, a prior *ethnie* of its own. This is patently not the case. What is meant is that the first nations, which acted as models for many others, were built up by state elites on these ethnic foundations, that several other leading states were subsequently founded on core *ethnies* (in Russia, Japan, China, Burma, Egypt, Iran, Turkey, Ethiopia) and that, as we said, the ethnic model has become increasingly popular as the basis for nations among smaller populations. In addition, ethnic mosaics, that is interlocking networks of several *ethnies* in different class and political relationships in a given culture area like the Middle East or Eastern

Europe, have often furnished the bases of nationalism and nation formation.[42]

But to say that modern nations must have or create some elements of pre-modern *ethnies* if they are to endow their citizens with a sense of solidarity and destiny, does not mean that these ethnic elements remain in their pristine, pre-modern form and with their identical pre-modern meanings, when they are rediscovered and drawn upon by a returning intelligentsia intent on reconstructing a modern nation. This is where the nationalists with their peculiar myth of the nation generally make their most important contribution. For it is they who, in the first place, select the historical memories and elaborate the myths of descent of the relevant *ethnie*; just as they also deepen and extend cultural attributes like language or religion which appear to them most appropriate for unifying, and differentiating, the nation.[43]

Of course, nationalist intellectuals do not make their selections and elaborations in a purely arbitrary manner. Typically, they find already to hand various folk-tales, ballads, epics, customs and rituals, which they then seek to weave into a continuous, dramatic narrative of the 'rediscovered nation'. This means often choosing between alternative traditions of events, ironing out inconsistencies and contradictions, and elaborating from other strands of tradition those events, personages or periods that seem sketchy in the historical record. The aim throughout is to present a vivid, archaeologically faithful and comprehensive record of the nation from the dawn of its existence until the present in a convincing and dramatic narrative form, which will inspire the members of the *ethnie* to return to ancestral ways and ideals, and mobilize them to create on its basis a modern nation, or, in nationalist language, 'reawaken the nation'. That is what many painters and poets, musicians and novelists in late eighteenth-, nineteenth- and early twentieth-century Europe and America laboured to re-present in their tableaux of an imagined national past, on the basis of the historians', archaeologists' and philologists' researches.[44]

The premiss of their activities was a profound belief in the vitality and significance of the past. The past, in the eyes of these nationalist intellectuals and their followers, remained a living force. It represented a storehouse of collective memories, but it also embodied a communal standard and served as a model and inspiration. It was only the past that could define 'us', the collectivity which was the bearer of a future; and it was only messages from that past that the present community could transmit to its posterity. There lay the rub: in an era of increasing secularism, the gods were being replaced by societies of men and women, and the hope of immortality by the collective memory of posterity. What better hope for our immortality than a nation that could draw so freely on distant ethnic memories and entrust so much to the far-off generations of its offspring, always in the sure knowledge that 'we' and 'they' belonged together, in the self-same 'superfamily' of fictive descent?[45]

This is where the 'myths of nations' assume such significance, even today and even when they are implicit and taken for granted. Ultimately, it is the myth of origins and descent that links the modern nation to its ethnic basis, and defines it in relation to its destiny. Such myths are a defining characteristic of *ethnies*, and in more elaborate form and often with changed meanings and contents, they form one of the basic elements of nations. As we saw, there can be no real 'nation' without its tacit myth of origins and descent, which defines the fictive kinship basis of the nation and explains the network of affective ties and sentiments. Indeed, together with the historical memories of successive generations of members, myths of descent furnish the cognitive maps and mobilizing moralities of nations as they struggle to win and maintain recognition today.[46]

But there is more to national 'myths of descent'. Pre-modern *ethnies* boasted not only tales of origin and ancestry, but also narratives of descent from sages and heroes of a golden age in the early period of the community's history. The theme of a distant heroic age is often significant for later generations of *ethnies*, when the community is in decline and its members suffer oppression, division or exile. One has only to think of the role which the glories of the Byzantine Empire under a Justinian or Basil played in the minds and hearts of educated Orthodox Greeks in the Ottoman empire; or of the heroic Aksumite kingdom in the reinstated Solomonic dynasty which ruled Ethiopia in the fourteenth to sixteenth centuries.[47]

With the coming of nationalism, such myths take on a new life. Not only are they elaborated and fleshed out by historical and linguistic scholarship, they become standards and models for inspiring a national regeneration, and their very idealization allows for different messages of inspiration for the present. In this way, the Davidic kingdom in ancient Israel became a source of inspiration in the early *Haskalah* (Enlightenment) movement in early nineteenth-century German and Polish Jewry;[48] and the post-Vedic era of classical city-states on the Ganges similarly served to inspire a Hindu Indian national revival in the late nineteenth century.[49] Only now these visions of a heroic past are placed in the context of a wider myth of origins and descent, which becomes the nationalist charter myth of the nation, instead of being isolated traditions, or variants thereof, recorded in ancient epics, sagas and folk-tales.

Something of this elaborating and reshaping of traditional myths can be seen in the work of Irish cultural nationalists of the late eighteenth and nineteenth centuries. It is a three-stage process in which historians like O'Halloran in the eighteenth century, and artists like Barry, begin to recount episodes from early Irish history before the Norman invasions, often retailing exotic descent myths, like the one that traced Irish descent to Phoenician origins.[50] In this period, only some of the mythology of Ireland as an *insula sacra* of monastic culture is present. In the second period, this culture is vigorously recovered, especially through the labours of the archaeologist and artist, George Petrie, whose work on the 'map' of an early Irish Christian monastic civilization was to inspire many, including the members of Thomas Davis' *Young Ireland* movement in the 1840s.[51] But it was only in the third period, in the late nineteenth century, that the rediscovery of the Ulster Cycle of heroic sagas, which revealed a pagan warrior and bardic culture before St Patrick's conversions, allowed a new and earlier golden age of martial heroes to emerge and inspire a similar heroism in the Sinn Fein and Republican movements after 1900.[52]

This example also brings the multifaceted nature of myths of descent to our attention, and their varied uses in nationalist movements. Similar choices of 'golden ages' were to be found in a rediscovered Germanic culture. At first it was more a matter of emphasizing the linguistic unity of a culture area in opposition to Napoleonic France; hence the strongly linguistic basis of early German romantic nationalism from Herder to Fichte. But already with Müller and Jahn, there was a concomitant harking back to the glories of the Hohenstauffen and the early Holy Roman Empire, as German nationalists and bourgeoisie sought to define and enlarge the area of their jurisdiction and operations.[53] After the middle of the century, however, a new emphasis on the tribal primitivism of an Ur-Deutsch culture, with new heroes like Arminius, and Siegfried and Gunther, became apparent, and was popularized by Wagner's Bayreuth spectacles of old German sagas, and the racial theories of Lagarde and Langbehn, with their sharp contrasts between German and Slav, Latin and Semite.[54] In nineteenth-century France, too, while republican nationalists looked back to a free Gallic ancestry and Roman republican ideals, their conservative opponents lauded their aristocratic 'Frankish' origins and the noble chivalry of St Louis and Joan of Arc fighting for a Catholic kingdom.[55] And in late nineteenth-century Anatolia, the glories of the House of Osman and its Islamic pedigree were challenged by a secular and pagan picture of a purely Turkish history, locating the golden age of heroes in the tribal cradle of Central Asia in the early first millennium AD and the long wars and migrations which followed.[56]

In all these cases, there is not only a choice of golden ages for inspiration, but a historical succession of them in relation to the social and geopolitical situation of the *ethnie* and nation. But these descent myths also chart internal relations between social groups and classes, with one myth tending

(margin note: philology)

to find its locus in a particular class or institutional stratum, while another, perhaps opposed, myth is espoused by another class or group. The myth of a Byzantine restoration, for example, was obviously espoused by the Greek Orthodox clergy, but it also appealed to notables and peasants on the Greek mainland who tended to define themselves as Orthodox in opposition to the Muslim Ottoman officials. In contrast, merchant and professional-intellectual classes were increasingly drawn to the alternative myth of a Hellenic culture, locating its heroes in the golden age of classical Athens.[57] These two myths of descent and their associated golden ages struggled for supremacy in Greek education and politics throughout the nineteenth century, with disastrous consequences for Greeks in Ionia once Kemal had defeated the invading Greek army which had been sent into Anatolia after the First World War, under the direct influence of the Byzantine myth, the *Megale Idea*. No clearer illustration of the continuing power of self-definitions and self-renewals inspired by reshaped ethnic myths of descent and the golden age can be found.[58]

There are, of course, many other cases inspiring current ethnic separatisms or national irredentisms. The IRA in Ulster, the Gush Emunim in Israel, the Tamils in Sri Lanka and the Somali in the Ogaden are just a few of the many recent examples of ethnic conflict, which depend for their *raison d'être* on ethnic myths of descent and historical memories which bring them into direct conflict with ancient neighbours. Very often, the same events will be retailed quite differently by the two sides, not just because of vested interests or simple error, but because they are located quite differently in the old ethnic myth of descent which has been taken over and worked up into the new, more elaborate nationalist myth.[59] But even where there is no conflict of interests, even where, as in Western Europe today, independent nation-states are attempting to work out a more co-operative future together, nationalist myths of individual nations and of their role in a wider Europe persist to inspire different interpretations of catastrophic recent events, and thereby keep the nations apart. Such myths also imperceptibly feed very different perceptions of neighbouring nations, handed down as they are from generation to generation, and only gradually amended or eroded. And this is what we must expect, given the essential defining role of myths. If their mobilizing and directing role has diminished in a few parts of the globe, their defining role remains largely intact, and if anything enhanced by global economic interdependence. As long, therefore, as these collective self-definitions matter, and as long as collective immortality is felt to be best secured through group posterity, nations will continue to exist and influence social and political life, and national myths of the past will define and inspire groups.[60]

The Supersession of Nations?

The 'modernist' myth of the nation locates nationalism in the transition to industrial modernity, or pronounces it a feature of that modernity. The implication is that, once the peculiar aspects of modern industrialism have been replaced by new forms of society, nations and nationalism will necessarily decline. Nevertheless, in practice, modernists remain divided on this issue. The more usual course is to assert the decline of national*ism* as its goals are satisfied, and as mass education and industrial growth are fully implemented. In these conditions, there is no further need for a mobilizing nationalism. On the other hand, nations, seen as culturally homogeneous territorial units legitimating the political division of the world, are likely to continue in existence for the foreseeable future.[61] The less usual prediction claims that nations too will wither away with the coming of a post-industrial society based on mass communications networks; but this very decline of entrenched nations and nation-states may well allow a resurgence of smaller, communal ethnic nationalisms, so long as they do not challenge the basic ideologies of the two great power blocs, capitalism and communism. Here the argument focuses on the dominant role of the great multinational companies, and the enormous technological advances in systems of mass communications and education, which create a service society bound by new telecommunications and computerized information systems. In such an interdependent world, nations have little or no role, and their place will be taken either by international agencies and corporations or by local regional, religious, ethnic and other interpersonal social groupings.[62]

Once again, such predictions presuppose a fundamentally 'instrumentalist' view of ethnicity and nationalism, and one that roots ethnic ties in the exigencies of production, exchange and power. But, if nations and ethnic identities are rooted, not in any techno-economic order, nor in any form of domination and goal-attainment, but in modes of cultural communication and socialization, then changes in technology, economics and political formations, however radical, will not ensure the demise or supersession of nations and nationalism. If such modes of communication and socialization possess their own internal rhythms of change, which may well be 'out of step' with major alterations in the modes of production and domination, then again we cannot use the latter to explain changes in the former, much less predict the decline or transcendence of nations and nationalism.[63]

Of course, particular ethnic or national changes may be explained, at least in part, by alterations in the spheres of production, exchange and domination. The size and boundaries of given nations, for example, will obviously hinge on the results of warfare between competing states in the area, or the ecology and resources of particular ethnic habitats. Similarly, the chances of a particular *ethnie* obtaining a state of its own will depend on a variety of economic and geopolitical factors and circumstances. Even the long-term survival of specific ethnic identities will be bound up with broader political, and economic, developments. But none of this affects the basic division of mankind, in most times and places, into separate cultural communities of history and destiny, a division which, while its collective actors often change over the centuries, maintains itself throughout recorded history and furnishes the premiss of new and renewed nationalism everywhere. Thus we might well see the emergence of a new European identity and community, forging its own myths and symbols, and unifying itself around common values and memories, out of the many cognate traditions to hand. But, though it might spur other analogous large-scale communities of identity elsewhere, such a European identity would only transpose on to another level, the division of mankind into separate culture communities of history and destiny; and there is little guarantee that, in changed circumstances, it might not be subject to the same processes of fission that threaten some of the old-established European 'nation-states' today. Amalgamation and fission are characteristic of ethnic processes, as successive generations seek and find different *levels* of ancestry, history, culture and territory appropriate to changing circumstances and needs.[64]

Do we detect here an echo of the 'instrumentalism' that was previously rejected? Not exactly. Or rather, the 'instrumentalism' only extends to the scale and extent of the unit of identity and loyalty, which may well change (within highly circumscribed limits) over generations, to meet changing interests and needs. But note that, even here, the lower and higher (smaller and larger) units are historically determined: there must be *some* cultural-historical basis for the enlarged unit, to which it is desired to move, be it from Saxony to Germany, or Germany to Europe. It could not be an artificial construct, dreamt up in a bureaucratic office. That is exactly the trouble with several of the African 'state-nations'; their boundaries *were* artificial, in the sense that several of the enlarged units imposed by the colonial powers possessed no cultural or historical significance for the Africans incorporated in them, despite the efforts of some of the European powers to respect former divisions.[65]

It is the level, then, that may change in response to changing needs and circumstances, not the basic division of mankind into culture units and historical identities, nor the underlying processes of communication and socialization which give rise to 'superfamilies' of fictive ancestry and historical culture. This is not to say that the modes of even such basic processes as communication and socialization have not, and will not, undergo change; but it is unlikely, given the influence of former modes and identities on later ones, that such change will produce a unified, global mode of communications and socialization. Historical legacies are not so easily eroded in these spheres; and the identities and traditions they create are themselves powerful determinants of any new modes and units of association.

In conclusion, we find that the myth of the 'modern nation' greatly exaggerates the impact of modern conditions of industry, capitalism and bureaucracy on the nature and role of nations today. There is no doubt that modern conditions extend and exacerbate the need for communities of history and destiny today, while prescribing the new, civic forms in which those needs are best satisfied. But the 'modernist' myth mistakes form for content, and turns the nation into a one-dimensional unit, seeing in nationalism a resolution of the problem of boundaries and scale, and failing to grasp the nation as equally a temporal construct and a mode of education and culture.[66] The root of this neglect is its inability to locate the nation in a historical sequence of cultural forms of identity. This is largely due to its dramatization of the differences between the two 'poles' of tradition and modernity, and its insistence on placing the rise of the nation in the transition to modernity, without enquiring into the sociological and historical antecedents of the nation. Inevitably, this has meant minimizing the continuity of particular nations with the ethnic pasts which they must affirm or rewrite. More significantly, it may have given to much of their analysis a historically shallow quality, one that misses the often deep roots of nations and nationalisms in an ethnic 'substratum', and the models of inspiration and guidance afforded by ancient *ethnies* and their myths and memories. It is ironical that so iconoclastic and instrumentalist a perspective should end in producing an account that is almost as 'mythical', in the sense we have outlined, as the discredited nationalist myths that 'modernists' aimed to counteract. Until we find a way of taking the myths of nations seriously (though not at their face value) and treating the historical traditions of their ethnic pasts with respect (though agnostically), we shall simply debar ourselves from grasping the almost ubiquitous appeal of the nation and nationalism today.

Notes

1   For representative selections of nationalist writings, see Kedourie 1971; for the basic nationalist argument see Minogue 1967, and A. D. Smith 1971: ch. 1.

2 Such explanations figure largely in the work of Kautsky 1962 and Sathya-murthy 1983, as well as, from a different standpoint, Breuilly 1982 and Kedourie 1960.
3 For an enlightening discussion of political myths, see Tudor 1972.
4 This is the working definition of a recent analysis of political myths of apartheid in South Africa by Thompson 1985: ch. 1.
5 Tudor 1972: chs 1–2; cf. Kirk 1970: ch. 1.
6 For a sociobiological account, see van den Berghe 1979; other non-sociobiological, but predominantly 'primordialist', accounts may be found in Fishman 1980 and Isaacs 1975.
7 Examples of such approaches are Enloe 1973, Bell 1975 and Brass 1974, 1979.
8 Smelser 1968; Deutsch 1961, 1966; Lerner 1958. For a critique, see Connor 1972.
9 These points are forcibly argued in Kedourie 1960 in the concluding pages, and again at the end of his introduction to Kedourie 1971.
10 Gellner 1964: ch. 7 and, more fully, Gellner 1983.
11 Nairn 1977: esp. chs 2, 9.
12 B. Anderson 1983: esp. chs 1–2.
13 Breuilly 1982: esp. Introduction, ch. 16 and Conclusion.
14 Hobsbawm and Ranger 1983: esp. the essay by Hobsbawm: 'Mass-Producing Traditions: Europe, 1870–1914'.
15 On this dating, Kemilainen 1964 and Kohn 1967: esp. chs 5, 7–8; for an earlier dating, cf. Marcu 1976 and the critique in Breuilly 1982: Introduction.
16 The relative rarity of 'nation-states' in the strict sense is demonstrated by Connor 1972; on the modernity of such nation-states, see Tivey 1980.
17 For the operations of such 'rational' states, see the introduction and essays in Tilly 1975 and Wallerstein 1974.
18 On citizenship in ancient Greece, see Ehrenburg 1960 and Finley 1981; on modern citizenship in nations, see Bendix 1964.
19 For the 'nations of intent' created by nationalism in Africa, see Rotberg 1967; Martins 1967 similarly speaks of developmental nationalism in Brazil as a 'project' of national integration.
20 For fuller discussions of the difficulties of 'nation-building', especially in Africa, see Olorunsola 1972 and Markovitz 1977; cf. also A. D. Smith 1983.
21 Rotberg 1967 and Gellner 1964: ch. 7; cf. W. C. Smith 1965.
22 For the debate on the American experience, see Glazer and Moynihan 1975, Greeley 1974 and Gans 1979; on the particular case of Jewish assimilation, cf. Cohen 1983.
23 Demythologization is very much the concern of Breuilly 1982 and Hobsbawm and Ranger 1983 (especially Hobsbawm's essay), but it can also be found in Gellner 1983, who is otherwise more favourably disposed to the aspirations of nationalists. The Deutschian school, too, emphasized a more neutral, quantitative assessment of the 'nation', though not of national*ism*.

24 This, of course, is also the view of Marxist social scientists in the Soviet
    Union as well as the West; see Davis 1978 and G. E. Smith 1985.
25 For the attack on 'modernization theory', see Frank 1969 and Taylor 1979,
    among many; and for the critique of its neo-evolutionary underpinnings, see
    Nisbet 1969 and A. D. Smith 1973a.
26 Armstrong 1982. He combines it with a phenomenological approach to
    ethnicity that does not do full justice to the very elements of ethnic identity
    (myths, symbols, memories, communications codes) which he emphasizes in
    trying to account for the longevity of many ethnic communities in pre-modern
    eras; for a fuller discussion, see A. D. Smith 1984a.
27 B. Anderson 1983: ch. 5 elaborates this latter conception, as, in their dif-
    ferent ways, do Kohn 1967: chs 7–8 and Plamenatz 1976. For a more
    general discussion of the two concepts of the nation, cf. A. D. Smith 1986a:
    ch. 6.
28 On the growth of 'Turkish' self-definitions, see Lewis 1968: Introduction and
    ch. 10 and Kushner 1976; for the Slovaks, cf. Brock 1976. Connor 1978
    regards my 'ethnic category' as an 'ethnic group', i.e. an ancestry group which
    lacks self-awareness, and my 'ethnic community' as a self-aware 'nation'.
    For other definitions of ethnic groups that stress fictive ancestry, historical
    memories and extended family analogies, cf. Schermerhorn 1970: 12 and
    Horowitz 1985: ch. 2.
29 For fuller discussions of definitions of the 'nation', see Rustow 1967; A. D.
    Smith 1973b, 1986a: chs 6–7; Gellner 1983: ch. 5.
30 None of this implies that particular *ethnie* are necessarily durable, or that eth-
    nicity is a universal; it does seem to be a widespread 'resource', one of a few
    recurrent sociocultural patterns in human history since c. 3000 BC (see Kramer
    1963 and Moscati 1962 and the essays in Wiseman 1973 for the ancient Near
    East).
31 The growth of citizenship rights, through the inclusion of all strata in the
    political arena, is the subject of Bendix 1964; its application in nineteenth-
    century Europe is briefly charted by M. Anderson 1972; on the Catalan
    sense of 'Spanishness', alongside their Catalanism, see Payne 1971 and Read
    1978.
32 For diaspora nationalisms, see Armstrong 1976, 1982: ch. 7 on (esp.) what
    he calls 'archetypal' disasporas such as Armenians and Jews; and cf. Seton-
    Watson 1977: ch. 8 for other diaspora cases.
33 For 'political culture' in these 'old, continuous nations', see Seton-Watson
    1977: ch. 2 and Ranum 1975; for some of their myths of descent, cf.
    Poliakov 1974.
34 For fuller discussions of the difficulties of creating nations out of polyethnic
    territorial states in sub-Saharan Africa, see Olorunsola 1972, Young 1985 and
    Neuberger 1986, as well as A. D. Smith 1983: ch. 7, 1986b.
35 Of course, important ethnic divisions persisted (and persist), and even the
    'core' was beset by rival sets of ethnic myths and memories such as the Brutus
    legend and Norman Yoke myths in England, on which see MacDougall 1982,
    or the competing Gallic and Frankish ancestry of which Siéyès and others

made so much in France, on which see Poliakov 1974: ch. 2; more generally, cf. Seton-Watson 1977: ch. 2.

36 For the implications, see M. Cherniavsky, 'Russia', in Ranum 1975, and Pipes 1977: ch. 3; to this day, the Russian heritage forms the ethnic core of the federation of Soviet Republics, as it did of the Tsarist empire, despite recognition of cultural diversity.

37 On the Iberian case, see Atkinson 1960 and, for the early medieval period, the detailed study of Collins 1983; for Sweden, cf. Seton-Watson 1977: ch. 2 and Jones 1973 for the early history.

38 As Horowitz 1985 has shown, such competition is often intense, because the prize is now state power and hence the ability to control the destinies of rival *ethnie* through resource allocation, posts, education, etc.

39 Hence the relative frequency of secessionist bids, despite some protracted attempts (Shan, Moro, Karen, Achinese, Tamil, Sikh, Kurd, Eritrean, Oromo, Bakongo, Ewe, Lunda, Ngoni, Ibo) and their lack of success (except in Bangladesh and Singapore); the leadership of African and Asian states is well aware of the dangers, as are other *ethnie*, and make every effort to prevent secession; see Neuberger 1976 and Horowitz 1985: ch. 6.

40 For this religious 'surrogate' function of ethnic nationalism, see B. Anderson 1983 and A. D. Smith 1986a: ch. 8.

41 For the striking case of Afrikaner ethnic identification as an end-value, see Thompson 1985; its religious roots can be paralleled in many other instances, and suggests that the transformation of *ethnie* into nations is by no means that wholesale and dramatic development that 'modernists' propose; there is more continuity with the past than many care to admit (cf. A. D. Smith 1986a: ch. 9).

42 For some consideration of such 'ethnic mosaics', see the essays in Sugar 1980 and, for Europe generally, Krejci 1979; on the Middle East, see Cahnmann 1944.

43 This is the theme of some of the essays in Hobsbawm and Ranger 1983, notably by Morgan and Hobsbawm himself; it is an area that merits more scholarly attention, but see Brock 1976 for the Slovak and Hutchinson 1987 for the Irish 'reconstructions'; and in general, A. D. Smith 1986a.

44 On which, see B. Anderson 1983: ch. 5 and A. D. Smith 1986a: ch. 8; for the role of musicians and artists, see Rosenblum 1967 and Einstein 1947: esp. chs 6, 15–17.

45 For a recent penetrating study of the meanings of 'the past' in the Anglo-Saxon world, see Lowenthal 1985; for the past as museology, and the problems of preserving the 'past', see Horne 1984 and Chamberlin 1979. There is a deeper need-satisfaction here than re-presenting pasts for special-interest tourists; a national past confers collective dignity on present generations and reminds offspring of their social location and historical heritage. It also legitimates the loci of power-holding and the foci of social mobilization; bureaucracies and citizens alike require a common past.

46 This is elaborated in A. D. Smith 1984b and 1986a: ch. 8; the role of such myths in pre-modern times is a major theme of Armstrong's work (1982), but

only Connor 1978 and Horowitz 1985 have given them much attention in the modern world; cf. also Schermerhorn 1970.

47   On Byzantium, see Armstrong 1982: 178–81 and Baynes and Moss 1969; for Ethiopia in the Middle Ages, see Ullendorff 1973: ch. 4 and Levine 1965: ch. 2.

48   On the ideals of the Haskalah movement, see Eisenstein-Barzilay 1959 and Meyer 1967.

49   See the essays by Crane and Adenwalla in Sakai 1961, and cf. Heimsath 1964. For an analysis of some of these myths and their functions, see A. D. Smith 1984b.

50   For a detailed exposition, see Hutchinson 1987.

51   Hutchinson 1987; Sheehy 1980.

52   On which, see Lyons 1979 and Paor 1986: ch. 9.

53   For this period, see Kohn 1965; and even earlier, the basis of 'Germanism' in linguistic opposition to Welsche (originally Latin) culture is stressed by Poliakov 1974: ch. 5.

54   For a detailed account of German Volkisch ideologies, see Mosse 1964; and for Wagner and his contemporaries, see Poliakov 1974: ch. 11.

55   On this rivalry, see Weiss 1977 and Poliakov 1974: ch. 2.

56   The rise of 'Turkish' origins is traced in Kushner 1976; also Berkes 1964.

57   These myths and their social loci are clearly set out in Campbell and Sherrard 1968: ch. 1; for the Phanariots and their myths of Byzantine descent, see Mango 1973, and for the role of the Greek merchants, see Mouzelis 1978.

58   For the ill effects of classicism in law, education and vocational pursuits, see Pepelassis 1958; the political consequences of the *Megale Idea* are traced in Dakin 1972 and Campbell and Sherrard 1968: chs 4–5.

59   For a Sri Lankan case, see Horowitz 1985: ch. 4 and Roberts 1979.

60   It could, indeed, be argued that economic interdependence in Europe guarantees the survival of nationalism, albeit in less overtly aggressive forms, as was claimed by Benthem van den Berghe 1966 and Nairn 1977: ch. 9.

61   See Gellner 1964: ch. 7 and Seton-Watson 1977; this is also the standard Marxist position, and is applied within the Soviet Union, on which see G. E. Smith 1985.

62   Richmond 1984 is the most explicit formulation; cf. also Said and Simmons 1976. Curiously, the argument assumes today's *ethnie* cannot, or will not, become tomorrow's nations.

63   Again we are faced with a paradox: namely, that those who stress 'communications' as the very 'essence' of nationality are also those who forecast the imminent transcendence of nations and their nationalisms, cf. Deutsch 1969 and the critique in Connor 1972.

64   For such a thesis about pan-Europeanism, see Galtung 1973. At present, centrifugal pressures remain powerful enough to counteract any pan-European identity, except among elites. For the idea of ethnicity operating at different levels, and allowing 'concentric circles' of loyalty, see Coleman 1958: esp.

Appendix and Horowitz 1985: chs 2–3. Circumstances may help to determine the appropriate level, but the propensity for group-formation in fictive ancestry and culture units appears to be perennial.

65 For such 'state-nations', see Zartmann 1963 and Young 1985; and for African ethnic groups partitioned by colonial boundaries, see Asiwaju 1985.

66 Nationalism as a resolution of the question of 'boundaries' is the formula favoured by Dunn 1978.

References

Anderson, B. 1983: *Imagined Communities*. London: Verso Editions and New Left Books.

Anderson, M. 1972: *The Ascendancy of Europe, 1815–1914*. London: Longman.

Armstrong, J. 1976: Mobilized and proletarian diasporas. *American Political Science Review* 70, 393–408.

Armstrong, J. 1982: *Nations before Nationalism*. Chapel Hill: University of North Carolina Press.

Asiwaju, A. I. (ed.) 1985: *Partitioned Africans: Ethnic Relations across Africa's International Boundaries*. London: C. Hurst and Co. and University of Lagos Press.

Atkinson, W. C. 1960: *A History of Spain and Portugal*. Harmondsworth: Penguin.

Baynes, N. and Moss, H. (eds) 1969: *Byzantium: An Introduction to East Roman Civilisation*. Oxford, London and New York: Oxford University Press.

Bell, D. 1975: Ethnicity and Social Change. In Glazer and Moynihan 1975, 141–74.

Bendix, R. 1964: *Nation-Building and Citizenship*. New York: John Wiley.

Benthem van den Berghe, G. van 1966: Contemporary nationalism in the Western world. *Daedalus* 95, 828–61.

Berkes, N. 1964: *The Development of Secularism in Turkey*. Montreal: McGill University Press.

Brass, P. 1974: *Religion, Language and Politics in North India*. Cambridge: Cambridge University Press.

Brass, P. 1979: Elite groups, symbol manipulation and ethnic identity among the Muslims of South Asia. In D. Taylor and M. Yapp (eds), *Political Identity in South Asia*, London: SOAS, Curzon Press, 35–77.

Brass, P. (ed.) 1985: *Ethnic Groups and the State*. London: Croom Helm.

Breuilly, J. 1982: *Nationalism and the State*. Manchester: Manchester University Press.

Brock, P. 1976: *The Slovak National Awakening*. Eastern European Monographs. Toronto: University of Toronto Press.

Cahnmann, W. 1944: Religion and nationality. *American Journal of Sociology* 49, 524–9.

Campbell, J. and Sherrard, P. 1968: *Modern Greece*. London: Benn.

Chamberlin, E. R. 1979: *Preserving the Past*. London: J. M. Dent & Sons.

Cohen, S. M. 1983: *American Modernity and Jewish Identity*. London and New York: Tavistock Publications.

Coleman, J. S. 1958: *Nigeria: Background to Nationalism*. Berkeley and Los Angeles: University of California Press.

Collins, R. 1983: *Early Medieval Spain, Unity in Diversity, 400–1000*. London and Basingstoke: The Macmillan Press Ltd.

Connor, W. 1972: Nation-building or nation-destroying? *World Politics* 24, 319–55.

Connor, W. 1978: A nation is a nation, is a state, is an ethnic group, is a . . . . *Ethnic and Racial Studies* 1, 377–400.

Connor, W. 1984: Eco- or ethno-nationalism? *Ethnic and Racial Studies* 7, 342–59.

Dakin, D. 1972: *The Unification of Greece, 1770–1923*. London: Ernest Benn Ltd.

Davis, H. B. 1978: *Towards a Marxist Theory of Nationalism*. New York: Monthly Review Press.

Deutsch, K. 1961: Social mobilization and political development. *American Political Science Review* 55, 493–514.

Deutsch, K. 1966: *Nationalism and Social Communication*, 2nd edn. New York: MIT Press.

Deutsch, K. 1969: *Nationalism and its Alternatives*. New York: Knopf.

Dunn, J. 1978: *Western Political Theory in the Face of the Future*. Cambridge: Cambridge University Press.

Ehrenburg, V. 1960: *The Greek State*. Oxford: Blackwell.

Einstein, A. 1947: *Music in the Romantic Era*. London: J. M. Dent & Sons.

Eisenstein-Barzilay, I. 1959: National and anti-national trends in the Berlin Haskalah. *Jewish Social Studies* 21, 165–92.

Enloe, C. 1973: *Ethnic Conflict and Political Development*. Boston: Little, Brown & Co.

Finley, M. 1981: *Economy and Society in Ancient Greece*. London: Chatto & Windus.

Fishman, J. 1980: Social theory and ethnography: neglected perspectives on language and ethnicity in Eastern Europe. In Sugar 1980, 69–99.

Frank, A. G. 1969: *Latin America: Underdevelopment or Revolution?* New York: Monthly Review Press.

Galtung, J. 1973: *The European Community: A Superpower in the Making*. London: George Allen & Unwin.

Gans, J. 1979: Symbolic ethnicity. *Ethnic and Racial Studies* 2, 1–20.

Gellner, E. 1964: *Thought and Change*. London: Weidenfeld & Nicolson.

Gellner, E. 1983: *Nations and Nationalism*. Oxford: Blackwell.

Glazer, N. and Moynihan, D. (eds) 1975: *Ethnicity, Theory and Experience*. Cambridge, MA: Harvard University Press.

Greeley, A. 1974: *Ethnicity in the United States*. New York: John Wiley.

Hall, J. 1986: *Powers and Liberties: The Causes and Consequences of the Rise of the West*. Oxford: Blackwell.

Heimsath, C. 1964: *Indian Nationalism and Hindu Social Reform*. Princeton: Princeton University Press.

Hobsbawm, E. and Ranger, T. (eds) 1983: *The Invention of Tradition*. Cambridge: Cambridge University Press.

Horne, D. 1984: *The Great Museum*. London and Sydney: Pluto Press.

Horowitz, D. 1985: *Ethnic Groups in Conflict*. Berkeley, Los Angeles, London: University of California Press.

Hutchinson, J. 1987: *The Dynamics of Cultural Nationalism: The Gaelic Revival and the Creation of the Irish Nation State*. London: George Allen & Unwin.

Isaacs, H. 1975: *The Idols of the Tribe*. New York: Harper & Row.

Jones, G. 1973: *A History of the Vikings*. London: Oxford University Press.

Kautsky, J. (ed.) 1962: *Political Change in Underdeveloped Countries*. New York: John Wiley.

Kedourie, E. 1960: *Nationalism*. London: Hutchinson.

Kedourie, E. (ed.) 1971: *Nationalism in Asia and Africa*. London: Weidenfeld & Nicolson.

Kemilainen, A. 1964: *Nationalism, Problems Concerning the Word, Concept and Classification*. Yvaskyla: Kustantajat Publishers.

Kirk, G. S. 1970: *Myth, Its Meanings and Functions in Ancient and Other Cultures*. Cambridge: Cambridge University Press.

Kohn, H. 1965: *The Mind of Germany*. London: Macmillan.

Kohn, H. 1967: *The Idea of Nationalism*, 2nd edn. New York: Macmillan.

Kramer, S. 1963: *The Sumerians*. Chicago: University of Chicago Press.

Krejci, J. 1979: Ethnic problems in Europe. In S. Giner and M. Archer (eds), *Contemporary Europe: Social Structures and Cultural Patterns*, London: Routledge & Kegan Paul.

Kushner, D. 1976: *The Rise of Turkish Nationalism*. London: Frank Cass.

Lerner, D. 1958: *The Passing of Traditional Society*. New York: Free Press.

Levine, D. 1965: *Wax and Gold: Tradition and Innovation in Ethiopian Culture*. Chicago and London: University of Chicago Press.

Lewis, B. 1968: *The Emergence of Modern Turkey*. London: Oxford University Press.

Lowenthal, D. 1985: *The Past is a Foreign Country*. Cambridge: Cambridge University Press.

Lyons, F. S. 1979: *Culture and Anarchy in Ireland, 1890–1930*. London: Oxford University Press.

MacDougall, H. A. 1982: *Racial Myth in English History: Trojans, Teutons and Anglo-Saxons*. Montreal: Harvest House.

Mango, C. 1973: The Phanariots and Byzantine tradition. In R. Clogg (ed.), *The Struggle for Greek Independence*, London: Macmillan, 41–66.

Marcu, E. D. 1976: *Sixteenth-Century Nationalism*. New York: Abaris Books.

Markovitz, I. L. 1977: *Class and Power in Africa*. Englewood Cliffs, NJ: Prentice-Hall.

Martins, H. 1967: Ideology and development: 'development nationalism' in Brazil. *Sociological Review Monograph* no. 11, 153–72.

Meyer, M. A. 1967: *The Origins of the Modern Jew: Jewish Identity and European Culture in Germany, 1749–1824*. Detroit: Wayne State University Press.

Minogue, K. 1967: *Nationalism*. London: Batsford.

Moscati, S. 1962: *The Face of the Ancient Orient*. New York: Anchor Books.

Mosse, G. 1964: *The Crisis of German Ideology: Intellectual Origins of the Third Reich*. New York: Grosset and Dunlap.

Mouzelis, N. 1978: *Modern Greece: Facets of Underdevelopment*. London: Macmillan.

Nairn, T. 1977: *The Break-up of Britain*. London: New Left Books.

Neuberger, B. 1976: The African concept of Balkanization. *Journal of Modern African Studies*, 13, 523–9.

Neuberger, B. 1986: *National Self-Determination in Postcolonial Africa*. Boulder, CO: Lynne Rienner Publishers, Inc.

Nisbet, R. 1969: *Social Change and History*. Oxford, London and New York: Oxford University Press.

Olorunsola, V. (ed.) 1972: *The Politics of Cultural Subnationalism in Africa*. New York: Anchor Books.

Paor, L. de 1986: *The Peoples of Ireland*. London: Hutchinson.

Payne, S. 1971: Catalan and Basque nationalism. *Journal of Contemporary History* 6, 15–51.

Pepelassis, A. 1958: The image of the past and economic backwardness. *Human Organisation* 17, 19–27.

Pipes, R. 1977: *Russia under the Old Regime*. London: Peregrine Books.

Plamenatz, J. 1976: Two types of nationalism. In E. Kamenka (ed.), *Nationalism, the Nature and Evolution of an Idea*, London: Edward Arnold, 22–36.

Poliakov, L. 1974: *The Aryan Myth*. New York: Basic Books.

Ranum, O. (ed.) 1975: *National Consciousness: History and Political Culture in Early Modern Europe*. Baltimore: Johns Hopkins University Press.

Read, J. 1978: *The Catalans*. London: Faber.

Richmond, A. 1984: Ethnic nationalism and post-industrialism. *Ethnic and Racial Studies* 7, 4–18.

Roberts, M. (ed.) 1979: *Collective Identities, Nationalisms and Protest in Modern Sri Lanka*. Colombo: Marga Institute.

Rosenblum, R. 1967: *Transformations in Late Eighteenth Century Art*. Princeton: Princeton University Press.

Rotberg, R. 1967: African nationalism: concept or confusion? *Journal of Modern African Studies* 4, 33–46.

Rustow, D. 1967: *A World of Nations*. Washington, DC: Brookings Institution.

Said, A. and Simmons, L. (eds) 1976: *Ethnicity in an International Context*. New Brunswick, NJ: Transaction Books.

Sakai, R. (ed.) 1961: *Studies on Asia*. Lincoln: University of Nebraska Press.

Sathyamurthy, T. 1983: *Nationalism in the Contemporary World*. London: Frances Pinter.

Schermerhorn, R. 1970: *Comparative Ethnic Relations*. New York: Random House.

Seton-Watson, H. 1977: *Nations and States*. London: Methuen.

Sheehy, J. 1980: *The Rediscovery of Ireland's Past*. London: Thames & Hudson.

Smelser, N. J. 1968: *Essays in Sociological Explanation*. Englewood Cliffs, NJ: Prentice-Hall.

Smith, A. D. 1971–1983: *Theories of Nationalism*. London: Duckworth (1971); Harper and Row (1972); 2nd edn, Duckworth and Holmes and Meier (1983).

Smith, A. D. 1973a: *The Concept of Social Change*. London and Boston: Routledge & Kegan Paul.

Smith, A. D. 1973b: *Nationalism*, A Trend Report and Annotated Bibliography, *Current Sociology* 21. Paris and The Hague: Mouton.

Smith, A. D. 1983: *State and Nation in the Third World*. Brighton: Harvester Press.

Smith, A. D. 1984a: Ethnic persistence and national transformation. *British Journal of Sociology* 35, 452–61.

Smith, A. D. 1984b: National identity and myths of ethnic descent. *Research in Social Movements, Conflict and Change* 7, 95–130.

Smith, A. D. 1986a: *The Ethnic Origins of Nations*. Oxford: Blackwell.

Smith, A. D. 1986b: State-making and nation-building. In J. Hall (ed.), *States in History*, Oxford: Blackwell, 228–63.

Smith, G. E. 1985: Ethnic nationalism in the Soviet Union: territory, cleavage and control. *Environment and Planning C: Government and Policy* 3, 49–73.

Smith, W. C. 1965: *The Modernization of a Traditional Society*. London: Asia Publishing House.

Sugar, P. (ed.) 1980: *Ethnic Diversity and Conflict in Eastern Europe*. Santa Barbara, CA: ABC-Clio.

Taylor, J. 1979: *From Modernization to Modes of Production*. London: Macmillan.

Thompson, L. 1985: *The Political Mythology of Apartheid*. New Haven and London: Yale University Press.

Tilley, C. (ed.) 1975: *The Formation of National States in Western Europe*. Princeton: Princeton University Press.

Tivey, L. (ed.) 1980: *The Nation-State*. Oxford: Martin Robertson.

Tudor, H. 1972: *Political Myth*. London: Pall Mall Press Ltd.

Ullendorff, E. 1973: *The Ethiopians: An Introduction to Country and People*, 3rd edn. London: Oxford University Press.

Van den Berghe, P. 1979: *The Ethnic Phenomenon*. New York: Elsevier.

Wallerstein, I. 1974: *The Modern World System*. New York: Academic Press.

Weiss, J. 1977: *Conservatism in Europe, 1770–1945*. London: Thames & Hudson.

Wiseman, D. J. (ed.) 1973: *Peoples of Old Testament Times*. Oxford: Clarendon Press.

Young, C. 1985: Ethnicity and the colonial and post-colonial state in Africa. In Brass 1985, 57–93.

Zartmann, W. 1963: *Government and Politics in Northern Africa*. New York: Praeger.

2

Memory and Modernity

Perhaps the most original and wide-ranging of the modernist theories which I touched on in the last chapter was that advanced by Ernest Gellner, my former teacher. His theory formed the subject of my Ernest Gellner Nationalism Lecture given at the London School of Economics on 21 March 1996, under the auspices of *Nations and Nationalism*, to commemorate Ernest Gellner's untimely death a few months earlier.

Though I had read *Words and Things* at Oxford, my first real encounter with Gellner's thought was with his second book, *Thought and Change* (1964), especially the chapter on nationalism. This chapter has largely set the terms of subsequent debate in the field. From this encounter, and my subsequent work under Gellner's supervision, I took away four fundamental lessons in the study of nationalism.

The first was the centrality of nationalism for an understanding of the modern world. The fact that Gellner took up the issues of nationalism in the 1960s and that he kept returning to them, when most social scientists were interested in Marxism, functionalism, phenomenology, indeed everything but nationalism, and the fact that he established a Centre for the Study of Nationalism in Prague devoted to research and latterly teaching in this field, demonstrates how thoroughly he appreciated the power, ubiquity and durability of nationalism.

'Memory and Modernity: Reflections on Ernest Gellner's Theory of Nationalism', *Nations and Nationalism*, 2/3 (1996): 371–88. Reproduced with the permission of the editors of *Nations and Nationalism*, Journal of the Association for the Study of Ethnicity and Nationalism (London School of Economics).

The second lesson that I learnt from Ernest Gellner was the need to appreciate the sheer complexity, the protean elusiveness, of the phenomena that were gathered together under the rubric of 'nationalism'. This is why he insisted on comparative analysis, and on the need to formulate typologies that do justice to the complexities of nationalism.

A third lesson was the sociological reality of nations and nationalism. Unlike many latterday scholars for whom the nation is a cultural artefact and nationalism a discourse, Gellner insisted on the structural embeddedness of nations and nationalism. Hence, the need, as he saw it, to use sociological concepts and methods to provide an understanding of this most complex of phenomena. This meant of course jettisoning nationalism's own account of itself, as an awakening of the slumbering but primordial nation through the kiss of nationalist Prince Charmings; and, instead, grasping nationalism as the necessary outcome of a particular kind of social structure and culture.

The final lesson was the hardest, the one on which I have stumbled most. Nations as well as nationalisms, Gellner argued, are wholly modern. They are not only recent, dating from the period of the French Revolution or a bit earlier, they are also novel, the products of 'modernity' – that whole nexus of processes that went into the making of the West over the last four centuries, including capitalism, industrialism, urbanization, the bureaucratic state and secularization.

It was this final lesson that was at issue in our last encounter at Warwick when, at the invitation of Edward Mortimer and the university, Ernest Gellner and I debated the origins and functions of nationalism. That debate, just twelve days before his tragically early death, was entitled 'The nation: real or imagined?' But since we both agreed that nations, like buildings or works of art, are created – albeit over generations – and are therefore both real and imagined, the question became the different but perhaps more important one of the relationship between nations and their putative pasts. It is, after all, difficult to see how a purely cultural artefact could inspire the loyalty and self-sacrifice of countless people. On the other hand, the primordialist picture of natural nations, of nations inscribed in the natural order, was equally unacceptable. So the question then became: where do nations come from?

Do Nations Have Navels?

Or, in Gellner's words, 'Do nations have navels'? Speaking of the dividing line between modernists and primordialists, Gellner asked for the kind of evidence that would decide whether nations had pasts that matter, or whether the world and nations with them was created about the end of the eighteenth century, 'and nothing before that makes the slightest difference to the issues we face'. 'Was mankind', he asked, 'the creator of Adam and did it slowly evolve?' The evidence that was debated at the time this issue was alive revolved around the question:

> [D]id Adam have or did he not have a navel? Now, it's a very crucial question, you see. No, no you may fall about laughing, but obviously if Adam was created by God at a certain date, let's say 4,003 BC, obviously I mean it's a *prima facie* first reaction that he didn't have a navel, so to say, because Adam did not go through the process by which people acquire navels. Therefore we do know what will decide whether the world is very old and mankind evolved or whether the world was created about 6,000 years ago. Namely, all we need to know is whether Adam had a navel or not. The question I'm going to address myself to of course is do nations have navels or do they not?

> My main case for modernism that I'm trying to highlight in this debate, is that on the whole the ethnic, the cultural national community, which is such an important part of Anthony's case, is rather like the navel. Some nations have it and some don't, and in any case, it's inessential (Gellner 1995, 1–2). What in a way Anthony is saying is that he is anti-creationist and we have this plethora of navels and they are essential, as he said, and this I think is the crux of the case between him and me.

In my opening statement at Warwick, I had argued that the modernist standpoint which Gellner embraced – the idea that nations are products of modernization and could not have existed before the advent of modernity – told only half the story (Smith 1995b); to which he quipped:

> Well, if it tells half the story that is for me enough, because it means that the additional bits of the story in the other half are redundant. He may not have meant it this way, but if the modernist theory accounts for half or 60% or 40% or 30% of the nations, this is good for me. (Gellner 1995, 2)

I certainly didn't mean it that way. But, from his standpoint, it would actually suffice if there were just one case of a nation being accounted for by modernism, for modernism to be true. And he produced his case: the Estonians. This is what he had to say about them:

> At the beginning of the nineteenth century they didn't even have a name for themselves. They were just referred to as people who lived on the land, as opposed to German or Swedish burghers and aristocrats and Russian administrators. They had no ethnonym. They were just a category without any ethnic self-consciousness. Since then they've been brilliantly successful in creating a vibrant culture. (Ibid., 2)

And he went on to praise this 'very vital and vibrant culture', which is so vividly displayed in the Ethnographic Museum in Tartu with its 100,000 objects, one for every 10 Estonians, claiming that it was created by 'the kind of modernist process which I then generalize for nationalism and nations in general'. And Gellner returned to the Estonians, at the end of his opening statement, when he tried to list the factors that may help us to predict which potential nations or cultural categories will assert themselves, a question I had posed in my opening statement:

> Now obviously it does matter to predict which nations will assert themselves, which potential nations, which cultural categories will assert themselves and which will not. I would say it is inherent in the situation that you cannot tell. You can indicate certain factors. Size is an obvious one, very small cultural groups give up. Continuity is another one, but not an essential one. Some diasporic communities have very effectively asserted themselves. Size, continuity, existence of symbolism, are important, but again the Estonians created nationalism ex nihilo in the course of the nineteenth century. (Ibid., 3)

I could quibble here, and say that the issue was not whether the Estonians created nationalism ex nihilo in the nineteenth century, but whether the Estonian *nation* was created by the Estonian nationalists ex nihilo. And while we would both agree that Estonian nationalism, indeed any nationalism, was modern, where Gellner and I would differ is whether the nations that nationalism creates are wholly modern creations ex nihilo. Gellner returned to this question, when he disagreed with my reading of the classical legacy of modern Greece, but admitted that

> There is some continuity with Byzantium or at any rate with the clerical organisation left behind by Byzantium certainly, but sometimes there is and sometimes there isn't [continuity]. So I would say in general there is a certain amount of navel about, but not everywhere and on the whole it's not important. It's not like the cycles of respiration, blood circulation or food digestion which Adam would have to have in order to live at the moment of creation. (Ibid., 3)

Now here lies the rub. If we pursue the analogy, we recall that God created Adam, fashioning his body and then breathing life into it. Not even the most megalomaniac nationalist has claimed quite that power. They have, of course, seen themselves as awakeners; but the body of the nation merely slumbered, it was not without life. Should we confer on nationalists that divine power, to create ex nihilo?

Of course, Gellner wants to confer that power through nationalism ultimately on modernity, on the growth society, on industrialism and its cultural prerequisites. For Gellner, the genealogy of the nation is located in the requirements of modernity, not the heritage of pre-modern pasts. He is claiming that nations have no parents, no pedigree, except the needs of modern society. Those needs can only be met by a mass, public, literate, specialized and academy-supervised culture, a 'high culture', preferably in a specific language which allows context-free communication. A 'high culture' is the only cement for a modern, mobile, industrial society; and this is the only kind of society open to us today.

For Gellner, the world was irreversibly transformed by a cluster of economic and scientific changes since the seventeenth century. Traditional agro-literate societies were increasingly replaced by growth-oriented, mobile, industrial societies. The rise of high cultures and nations is a consequence of the mobility and anonymity of modern society and of the semantic, non-physical nature of modern work. Today what really matters is not kingship or land or faith, but education into and membership of a high culture community, that is, a nation (Gellner 1983: ch. 2).

So, just as Pallas Athene sprang fully armed from the head of Zeus, without parents, so nations emerged fully-fledged from the requirements of modernity. If nations did have navels, they were purely ornamental.

But, can we derive nations *tout court* from the needs of modernity? To be fair, it isn't modernity that directly creates nations. To quote Gellner's original formulation: '[Nationalism] invents nations where they do not exist, – but it does need some pre-existing differentiating marks to work on, even if . . . these are purely negative' (Gellner 1964: 168). The same sequence is restated in his later book:

> It is nationalism which engenders nations, and not the other way round. Admittedly, nationalism uses the pre-existing, historically inherited proliferation of cultures or cultural wealth, though it uses them very selectively and it most often transforms them radically. Dead languages can be revived, traditions invented, quite fictitious pristine purities restored. But this culturally creative, fanciful, positively inventive aspect of nationalist ardour ought not to allow anyone to conclude, erroneously, that nationalism is a contingent, artificial, ideological invention . . . (Gellner 1983: 55–56)

This is a crucial passage, but it is by no means an isolated one. Throughout his writings on nationalism, Gellner keeps returning to the idea that nationalisms frequently make use of the past, albeit very selectively. This reveals an ambivalence at the heart of his theory, one highlighted by the word 'Admittedly' in the passage I have just quoted. It is this ambivalence that I wish to explore, because here, I believe, lies the main limitation of all 'modernist' theories of nationalism, including Gellner's. I want to examine this ambivalence under three headings: the parentage or genealogy of nations, the question of cultural continuity and transformation, and the role of collective memory.

The Genealogy of Nations

As far as the genealogy of nations is concerned, Gellner is saying two things. Nations are navel-less, they don't have parents; and even if they did, it's irrelevant. Nations begin *de novo*, in a brave new industrial world.

One might start by asking which of these positions Gellner really claims. If some nations had navels, they had ancestors. We could then try to compare the navel-less, ancestor-less nations with the nations that had navels and ancestors, to see how each class of nations was faring. That is an interesting empirical question. But, if having ancestors is *a priori* irrelevant, then why should even some nationalisms make use of 'their' pasts? Note, it is not any past. For my nation, your past will not do. It has to be 'my' past, or pasts, or, more usually, some of my pasts. But why return to the past at all? If the past is irrelevant to the needs of a modern society, then why does any nationalism bother to return to some sort of 'past'? Is this just a delusion, a matter of false consciousness? That is a position Gellner would, I believe, strongly deny, but he does not really explore the issue.

The other answer often given to this question is that elites, or people in general, have to return to tradition and ancestry to legitimate the new type of industrial-capitalist society and control the changes it must undergo. But that only begs the question as to why elites or people in general feel the need to refer back to 'their' ancestral traditions, or 'invent' ones that are aligned with these older traditions. Can it be because they are still quite powerful, and many people still operate in terms of these traditions, however irrelevant they may seem to some elites and to the theorist of modernity? In other words, many people appear not only to believe they have navels; they believe in the reality of the situation which gave them navels, and which their navels symbolize. In short, they believe they have collective parents, and these parents are in important ways relevant to their present situation (Matossian 1962; Hobsbawm and Ranger 1983: Introduction and ch. 7).

This belief is not entirely unfounded. Historically, the members of a community can point to a considerable amount of evidence to support their belief in the genealogy of nations. They can refer to documents and artefacts which bear out their belief that many present-day industrial or industrializing societies from England and France to Russia and Poland, from Japan and Korea to America and Mexico, are closely related to, indeed grew out of, past communities with which they identify. Members can

point to the fact that, despite the many transformations they have undergone, their nations continue to share with past communities such features
as a proper name, a rough territory, a language, some artistic styles, sets
 of myths and symbols, traditions of heroes and heroines, memories of
golden ages, and the like. In other words, they conceive of their nation,
despite all these changes, as 'stemming from' older communities of historic culture with whom they share myths of descent and common memories, including links with a homeland (cf. Johnson 1992).

We do not have to accept the ideology of nationalism itself, with its
romantic belief in the awakening of the nation, its mission and destiny, to
realize that we cannot fully grasp the rise and character of so many modern
nations unless we explore their historical antecedents, and the continuing
influence of those antecedents in the modern epoch. Gellner's modernism
tells us how a modern nation operates, indeed must operate, in the modern,
industrial age. But it cannot tell us which nations will emerge where, and
why these nations rather than others.

To return to an example which Gellner used in the Warwick debate:
modern Israel, he argued, is furnished with all the cultural equipment
needed in the modern world: a literate, mass public education system, a
common modernized language, a modern system of communications and
legal system, in short, a 'high culture' of the kind required by the mobile,
anonymous society which industrialism creates. In a state like Israel, where
immigrants from over seventy lands and many cultures have been in-
gathered, this sort of standardized, public, unifying, 'high culture' is all the
more necessary. To cope with the challenges of modernity, which is what
any society must do if it is to survive today, you require a 'high culture'. In
the modern world, the culture and religion of the past is at best irrelevant,
at worst an impediment (cf. Friedmann 1967; Vital 1990: chs 5–6).

But equally, in my view, this example demonstrates that we cannot hope
to explain the rise and character of modern nations solely in terms of the
requirements of modernity. Even that arch-modernist Theodor Herzl conceived of Israel as a haven for an ancient diaspora people, a *Judenstaat*, a
state of and for unassimilable Jews, taking up where the last independent
Jewish state, the Hasmonean state, had left off, in Zion. It was this ultimately religious and political vision, rather than the needs of modernity,
that inspired and mobilized many diaspora Jews to become Zionists and
take the arduous road to Palestine; and it was a vision that assumed a
genealogy and an ancient pedigree and name for a nation-to-be, one that
addressed, as does every nationalism, a designated and particular 'people'.
To assert, with another modernist, Eric Hobsbawm, that there is simply no
connection between the age-old Jewish yearnings and pilgrimages to Zion
and the modern ingathering of Jewish exiles into Palestine, is to miss, not

only the element of ethnic ascription, but also the whole aspect of popular motivation and collective self-understanding which is essential to the success of any nationalism. This is what I meant when I argued that modernism can tell us only half the story. It tells us in general why there have to be nations and nationalism in the modern world; it does not tell us what those nations will be, or where they will emerge, or why so many people are prepared to die for them. Nor does it tell us much about the character of particular nationalisms, whom they address, and whether they are religious or secular, conservative or radical, civic or ethnic – issues that are vital both for the participants and their victims, and for a scholarly understanding of nations and nationalism (Hobsbawm 1990: ch. 1; Wistrich 1995).

I am suggesting, then, that to understand modern nations and nationalism, we have to explore not only the processes and requirements of modernity, but also the genealogies of nations. In fact, we have to explore the impact of the processes of modernization on those genealogies, and the way in which they give rise to selections and transformations by each generation of pre-existing ethnic ties and of the ethnic traditions they have inherited.

Now, we may admit that in the case of the nations I have cited, it makes sense to explore their genealogies. But, what of modern nations that have lost their parents or never had them, or are not quite sure who their parents were? This poses considerable problems for nationalists attempting to create nations. It is certainly one reason for the enormous popularity of the *Kalevala* with the Finns, and the *Kalevipoeg* with the Estonians. (Yes, the Estonians did have a navel, after all. As a leading historian of Estonia, Toivo Raun, writing of the Estonian national revival of the 1860s, put it: 'Among the Estonian population, the importance of *Kalevipoeg* was not so much literary – it took decades to reach a wide audience – as it was symbolic, affirming the historical existence of the Estonian nation' (Raun 1987: 56, 76; cf. Branch 1985: Introduction).)

Both epics traced the descent of the Finns and Estonians to Iron Age culture communities, and thereby provided these dispossessed and subject peoples with a sense of their dignity through native ancestry and an ancient and heroic ethnic past. In this way, they confirmed the worldwide belief in the virtues of national genealogies. To dismiss this by attributing it to the ubiquitous influence of nationalism again begs the question of why so many people have been mobilized on the basis of this particular belief in the genealogy of nations. Besides, nationalists have usually managed to find some historical antecedents for their nations-to-be, albeit often embellished and exaggerated, and this suggests that there are mechanisms at work which ensure some connection and even continuity between the modern nation and one or more pasts. To two of these mechanisms I now turn.

Cultural Change and Continuity

The first lies in the field of culture, and it provides us with a second focus for exploring the ambivalence in Gellner's and other versions of modernism.

For Gellner, modernity introduces a radical cultural break. This has two aspects. The first is underlined in the theorem which underpins his early formulation of modernism. That theorem states that in pre-modern societies, culture reinforces structure, whereas in modern societies, culture replaces structure. By this Gellner meant that kinship roles organized social life in simple, traditional societies, and symbols, myths, traditions and codes reinforced and expressed that kinship structure. Modern society, with the possible exception of bureaucracy, has no such structure. Instead, it has a common culture. In the polyglot, anonymous city, where most encounters are ephemeral, people can only relate to each other through context-free communication. This requires a common culture in preferably a common language. The pre-condition of membership in such a society and of citizenship in the state is literacy. Today, by necessity, 'we are all clerks' (Gellner 1964: ch. 7).

In a later article and in his *Nations and Nationalism*, Gellner focused more upon the changed nature of work and the generic training required for a mobile, industrial society. To train a mobile work-force and citizenry to master the techniques of semantic work, modern societies require a new kind of education system. For this, Gellner coined the term 'exo-socialization'. In the old, agro-literate society, rote learning at one's mother's knee or in the village school sufficed. In a modern, industrializing or industrial society, external, state-imposed, standardized, mass schooling was needed to create the literate and technically sophisticated work-force, necessary to man the industrial machine. And the teachers, too, had to be specialized educational personnel, able to service the new literate 'high culture' which characterizes and defines modern nations (Gellner 1973, 1982, 1983: ch. 3; cf. also 1994: ch. 3).

This concept of a 'high culture' became the key to Gellner's later theory of nationalism. In an interesting section of *Nations and Nationalism*, Gellner contrasts the 'high' culture of modern societies with the 'low' cultures of agro-literate societies. A 'high' culture, as we have seen, is a literate, sophisticated culture, serviced by specialized educational personnel and taught formally in mass, public, standardized and academy-supervised institutions of learning. It is a highly cultivated or 'garden' culture. A 'low' culture, by contrast, is wild, spontaneous, undirected and unsupervised. These are the cultures that readily spring up, unbidden, in societies where the great mass of the population are food-producers servicing the needs of tiny specialized elites – clerisies, aristocracies, merchants and the like – who are almost completely cut off socially and culturally from the peasant masses. In such a society, there is neither need nor room for nations and nationalisms, since the many 'low' cultures of the peasants are local and 'almost invisible'. Thus, in agro-literate societies, in Gellner's words: 'Culture tends to be branded either horizontally (by social caste), or vertically, to define very small local communities' (Gellner 1983: 16–17).

Now, for Gellner, all these 'low' cultures are doomed. They are cut off, like so many umbilical cords, because they are simply irrelevant in an impersonal, mobile modern society. If they are remembered at all, it is only through some symbols, in the same way that navels remind us of our origins. Nationalism, Gellner claims, is basically a product of modernity. It is, he says,

> essentially, the general imposition of a high culture on society, where previously low cultures had taken up the lives of the majority, and in some cases the totality, of the population . . . It is the establishment of an anonymous, impersonal society, with mutually substitutable atomized individuals, held together above all by a shared culture of this kind, in place of a previous complex structure of local groups, sustained by folk cultures reproduced locally and idiosyncratically by the micro-groups themselves. That is what really happens. (Gellner 1983: 57)

Nothing could be clearer. The many, old 'low' cultures vanish. They are replaced by a single, new 'high' culture, or 'nation'. This is the true meaning of nationalism.

But there are two problems here, of which Gellner was well aware. Some 'low' cultures are not severed. Instead, they become 'high' cultures. The Finns and the Estonians clearly fall into this category, as do many of the cultures of the other smaller, subject peoples of Eastern Europe and the former Soviet Union. The other problem is that certain old elite cultures become 'high' cultures. The literary cultures of the Jews, the Armenians and the Greeks clearly fall under this heading, as do several of the cultures of Western peoples like the Catalans, Scots and French. Awareness of the difficulties posed for modernism by both these problems is an important source of its ambivalence (Gellner 1994: 37–44).

How do 'low' cultures become 'high' cultures? Why does Estonian win out over German, Swedish and Russian cultures in Estonia, and Finnish over Swedish and Russian cultures in Finland? Both these cultures were local, popular, largely confined to the peasants, at least at first. Why do these 'Ruritanians' become conscious of their local folk cultures and seek to turn what were 'low' cultures into 'high' ones for the nation-to-be?

Or were they really such 'low' cultures? And is the contrast between 'low' and 'high' cultures as sharp as Gellner alleges? In the case of Estonia, we know of Estonian language religious texts during the Reformation; and certainly by the seventeenth century, with the establishment of the University of Tartu and later Forselius' school system, the basis of a literate Estonian culture emerged a century and a half before the arrival of the Romantic movement in the Baltic states in the mid-nineteenth century. True, Germans and Swedes made the running, but a native Estonian poem of 1708 lamenting the miseries of the Great Northern War between Peter the Great and the Swedes, fought over Estonian lands, reveals a growing Estonian consciousness. Moreover, written Estonian can even be found in the thirteenth-century Chronicle of Henry of Livonia recording the German conquest of Estonia in the face of much resistance. All this suggests that the transition to an Estonian 'high' culture was much more gradual and long-drawn-out than a modernist account would suggest (Raun 1987: 57, 76).

If this is the case with a so-called 'low' culture such as the Estonian, it is likely to prove even more true of old, literate, specialist-supported and therefore 'high' cultures like those of the French, the Arabs, the Jews and the Greeks. True, the languages and cultures of these peoples had to be 'modernized' to cope with modern conditions: they had to be simplified, standardized, secularized and expanded to cover all sorts of undreamt-of phenomena and novel concepts, and embrace all classes and regions of the nation-to-be. But the old 'high' caste literate cultures were not scrapped and replaced; they were adapted, purified, enlarged and diffused, often through self-conscious cultural reformist movements. Sometimes, as in modern Greece, this involved a measure of compromise with its pasts, between a popular Byzantine Orthodox heritage and a classicizing Athenian language and culture. In this case, the recovery of ancient Greek texts and sculptures did create considerable preoccupation with Periclean Athens among the Greek-speaking intelligentsia, but it had constantly to compete with the more popular memories of Byzantium carried by an Orthodox liturgy and congregation (Frazee 1969; but cf. Kitromilides 1989).

What I am arguing here is that most modern languages and cultures are not 'invented': they are connected to, and often continuous with, much older cultures which the modernizing nationalists adapt and standardize. By Gellner's criteria, many of these older languages and cultures were 'high' cultures. But, even where they were 'low' (or 'lower'), spontaneous, popular cultures, they could become the basis for a subsequent 'high culture'. Gellner hints at this when he speaks of Ruritanians in the metropolis of Megalomania who, faced with the problems of labour migration and bureaucracy, soon come to understand the difference between dealing with a co-national, 'one understanding and sympathising with their culture, and someone hostile to it. This very concrete experience taught them to be aware of their culture, and to love it (or, indeed, to wish to be rid of it).' In other words, it is the old 'low' culture to which they cling, or not, as the case may be. And it is the old 'low' culture which, far from being cut off and thrown away, will soon become the modern 'high', taught culture, albeit for several hundred thousands or millions of people (Gellner 1983: 61).

There are many examples of this cultural connectedness and continuity amid change, and we need to remind ourselves that cultural continuity is not the same as cultural fixity. Take the realm of language development. The English and French languages evolved over many centuries, with several admixtures of other languages, yet we can trace lines of development which reveal their underlying continuity. Alternatively, there is a conscious reform of language and culture, as occurred with the Turkic languages under the impulse of the *jadid* educational movement of Ismail Bey Gasprinski, or with Hebrew through the modernizing reforms of Eliezer Ben-Yehudah. In the latter case, the differences between biblical and modern Hebrew are considerable; yet modern Hebrew is clearly based upon, and developed from, biblical Hebrew (Zenkovsky 1960; Fishman et al. 1968; Rickard 1974; Edwards 1985).

In terms of names, territorial attachments and myths of origin, too, there are striking connections and continuities, despite changes of cultural contents over time. This is especially true of island cultures like Japan, with its relative continuity of territory, identity and origin myths. But it can also be found in mixed cultures like that of Mexico, whose modern cultural nationalists have sought to recover and reappropriate some aspects of the pre-Colombian, mainly Aztec, past. Of course, it can be argued that the very need to recover the past is evidence for discontinuity. There certainly had been discontinuity, especially after Hernan Cortes' invasion. But, among the many indigenous *ethnies* of Mexico, the old cultures still lived in varying degrees and guises, to be used as partial models and disseminated through the mass, public education system to the *mestizo* majority (Franco 1970; Lehmann 1982; Florescano 1993).

Collective Memory and Modern Nations

This leads us directly to the final focus of modernist ambivalence, namely, the part played by collective memory in the formation of nations.

Collective memories form another major link with an ethnic past or pasts. Gellner was very conscious of the role of memory in creating nations, if only because, like Renan, he emphasized the importance of national amnesia and getting one's history wrong for the maintenance of national solidarity. But there was no systematic attempt in his work to deal with the problems posed by shared memories of a collective past (Gellner 1982).

For Renan, memories were constitutive of the nation. The nation is built on shared memories of joy and suffering, and above all of collective sacrifices. Hence the importance of battles, defeats no less than victories, for mobilizing and unifying *ethnies* and nations – all too evident in such sensitive areas of national conflict as Bosnia and Palestine (Renan 1882).

Memory, of course, can be easily manipulated. Witness the sudden surge of feeling over the mosque built on the temple of Ram at Ayodhya in India, or the post-war Israeli cult of Masada, a formerly obscure episode and half-forgotten fortress on the Dead Sea. Besides, we need to distinguish between genuine folk memories and the more official, documented or excavated records of an often heroic past (Billig 1995: ch. 2).

Despite these caveats, shared historical memories play a vital role in modern nationalism. The question is: how far can the modernist theory of nationalism accommodate them? There are, I think, two problems here. The first is that the 'nation', which modernist theories of nationalism conceive as the object of explanation, is divested of 'identity'. It is either conflated with the state, to become the 'nation-state', or it is equated, as in Gellner's theory, with a modern 'high' culture, to become a more or less stable configuration of objective traits like language and customs in a large, anonymous, unmediated and co-cultural unit. Now the nation does, indeed, have some 'objective' attributes like a name, a demarcated territory and a common economy. But equally important are its more subjective properties such as a fund of distinctive myths and memories, as well as elements of a common mass culture. This means that we must take into account the perceptions, sentiments and activities of its members in the definition of national identity. The cultivation of shared memories constitutes a vital element of this nation-defining activity (Gellner 1964: ch. 7; cf. Grosby 1991).

The second reason why modernist theories give little space to the role of collective memories is their tendency to rely on purely structural explanations. With the exception of Benedict Anderson's analysis of the representation of national images, most modernists trace the origins, rise and course of nations and nationalism to the consequences of (uneven) capitalism, industrialism, militarism, the bureaucratic state, or class conflict, or combinations of these. Where the role of ideas is also admitted, the origins of nationalism are ascribed to the influence of secularism, the Enlightenment and sometimes Romanticism. Only in this last movement

is there any room for a consideration of the role of collective men
Romanticism is usually treated, if at all, as a secondary, even ~~...~~
explanatory factor (Nairn 1977: ch. 2; cf. Kedourie 1960).

I think that we can overcome these limitations and build into Gellner's
framework a fuller account of the role of shared memories, if we marry
his insistence that nationalisms create nations to the ethno-symbolic
resources that they must use if they are to succeed. Take the vistas opened
up by the emerging disciplines of archaeology and history. The excavations of Great Zimbabwe with its Elliptical Temple, of Teotihuacan on the
central Mexican plateau, and of the tomb of Tutankhamun in Egypt,
created no continuity between the modern nations of Zimbabwe, Mexico
and Egypt and 'their' presumed ancient or medieval ethnic pasts. What
they did was to suggest, in some cases establish, connections with distant
and glorious periods, or 'golden ages', of communal history, thereby
extending the collective self-imaginings and shared memories of their
members back in time through a reconstructed past, and conferring a sense
of dignity and authenticity on their citizens. It is modern citizens who need
and reconstruct a heroic ethnic past; but once reconstructed, that past exerts
its own power of definition through ancestry and shared, albeit taught,
memory (Chamberlin 1979; Ades 1989; Gershoni and Jankowski 1986;
Smith 1995a).

The 'territorialization of memory' provides another example of the
power of shared rememberings. By this I mean the ways in which shared
memories become attached to particular terrains, and over time forge
delimited 'homelands'. The term 'homeland' suggests an ancestral territory, one which has become communalized through shared memories of
collective experiences. The ancestral land is the place where, in the shared
memories of its inhabitants, the great events that formed the nation took
place; the place where the heroes, saints and sages of the community from
which the nation later developed lived and worked, and the place where
the forefathers and mothers are buried. This last element is particularly
important. It ties each family to the homeland through memories of the
last resting-places of their ancestors, and it sanctifies the homeland by
creating its sacred sites and popular pilgrimages (Smith 1986: ch. 8 and
1996).

Memory, then, is bound to place, a special place, a homeland. It is also
crucial to identity. In fact, one might almost say: no memory, no identity;
no identity, no nation. That is why nationalists must rediscover and appropriate shared memories of the past. Identification with a past is the key to
creating the nation, because only by 'remembering the past' can a collective identity come into being. The very act of remembering together, of
commemorating some event or hero, creates a bond between citizens

whose self-interest often brings them into conflict. Hence the constant need to reawaken public memories, to engage in commemorative rites and remembrance ceremonies, especially for those who gave their lives for the community; and to tie those memories to the homeland through daily routines and 'flagging' (Billig 1995: chs 3–4).

Collective memories, then, are active components in the creation and reproduction of nations. Whether they are familial and unmediated, as often occurs in sub-Saharan Africa, or mediated and public, a construct of elites enacted in rites and ceremonies, and recalled in epics and chronicles, flags and anthems, shared memories are necessary for the formation of nations. States may be established without recourse to memory and remembering. But nations require shared memories to give their often heterogenous citizenry a common habitat, a source of pride and dignity, and a common destiny. Indeed, if we define the nation as *a named human population sharing a historic territory, common myths and memories, a mass, public culture, a common economy and common legal rights and duties for all members*, shared memories are required by definition. Without them, the subjective element, the sense of being part of a nation, would be absent. There could be no passionate identification by individual citizens with a particular 'nation', only a generalized calculating loyalty to the state (Mazrui 1985; Smith 1991: ch. 1; cf. Viroli 1995).

We can go further. If the modern nation is, in large part, a creation of nationalism, as Gellner argued, then there are three vital elements of the nation which, in my view, depend on the role of collective memory. The first is the drive for regeneration which is based on memories of a golden age, or golden ages. This is the idealized former age of great splendour, power and glory, intellectual or artistic creativity, or religiosity and sanctity. It is the age of the community's exemplars – its saints and sages, poets and heroes, artists and explorers – the ideal against which to measure the present, usually lamentable, state of the nation, and the spur to emulation for successive generations. The memory of the golden age signifies the possibility and hope of national regeneration.

A second element is the sense of collective mission and national destiny. There is no nationalism, and few present-day nations, that do not proclaim some special mission and unique destiny. But a sense of collective mission presupposes shared memories of a past or pasts in which the nation was entrusted with that mission, and which shaped a unique community as the vehicle for the development and reproduction of 'irreplaceable culture values'. Similarly, a sense of national destiny presupposes a well remembered past, a history of a unique trajectory along which 'we' are destined to travel. Without such memories, without rituals of commemoration, the nation would have no distinctive task or future, and hence no *raison d'être* (see Weber 1947; Smith 1992).

The third vital component is a sense of national authenticity, and this too is closely bound up with shared memories. What is or is not mine, what is or is not distinctive, representative, or original, is closely tied to questions of remembering and forgetting. What is 'inauthentic' is, in part, what is alien to popular consciousness and folk memory. What is original and 'ours' is that which has been hallowed by the shared memories of 'the people'. The acceptance of the *Kalevala* as Finland's national epic owed much to the survival and resonance among the peasants of the Karelian folk ballads on which Elias Lonnrot based his modern compilation, even if the 'memories' contained in that epic were less than historical (Branch 1985: Introduction).

Together, these nationalist concepts of regeneration and the golden age, mission and destiny, authenticity and folk culture, all presuppose the influence of shared memories of a collective past, however distorted or dimly remembered. And, since it is nationalism that largely creates the modern nation, the modern nation must be built on shared memories of some past or pasts which can mobilize and unite its members.

Conclusion

Nihil ex nihilo. Nothing comes from nothing. Ernest Gellner called himself a 'creationist', but he attributed the sudden birth of nationalist humanity to a process, the process of modernization which, like the biblical creation process of 6,000 years ago, was sudden and discontinuous. And modernization keeps bringing nations into being, suddenly, explosively.

My view, on the contrary, Gellner termed 'evolutionist', indeed 'primordialist'. I hope I have made it clear that I, in no sense, subscribe to any of the forms of 'primordialism'. Nations are modern, as is nationalism, even when their members think they are very old and even when they are in part created out of pre-modern cultures and memories. They have not been there all the time. It is possible that something like modern nations emerged here and there in the ancient and medieval worlds. That is at least an open question, requiring more research. But, in general, nations are modern.

Can my position be called 'evolutionist' in opposition to Gellner's 'creationism'? Not in any strong sense of that term. There is too much discontinuity and change between pre-modern and modern communities to warrant the conclusion that modern nations are the ~~not~~ product of slow, gradual, incremental growth from rude beginnings. But, in a weaker sense, there is considerable evidence that modern nations are connected with earlier ethnic categories and communities and created out of pre-existing origin myths, ethnic cultures and shared memories; and that those nations with a vivid, widespread sense of an ethnic past, are likely to be more unified and distinctive than those which lack that sense (see Armstrong 1982; Smith 1986).

It is important to stress here that pre-modern *ethnies* are not nations, whether in Gellner's definition of the nation, or mine. They generally lack a clearly demarcated territory which their members occupy, equal legal rights and duties for all members, and a public, mass culture. What they do have, and what they bequeath, albeit selectively, to modern nations is a fund of myths, symbols, values and shared memories, some distinctive customs and traditions, a general location, and sometimes a proper name. Without these shared memories and traditions, myths and symbols, the basis for creating a nation is tenuous and the task Herculean.

Of course, there are exceptions to the rule. Some islands, like Trinidad or Mauritius, emptied of their original inhabitants, may gradually be forged, not without conflict, into unified and distinctive nations through the conscious creation or use of overarching myths and traditions, memories and symbols. The process of ethno-genesis, after all, goes on all the time, along with, and as part of, the creation of new nations. The same process may also be taking place in the former Italian province, and now independent state, of Eritrea with its two religions and nine language groups. Nevertheless, these exceptions only go to show that the widely accepted model of the unified and distinctive nation is derived from the many nations with a dominant ethnic past, and that, where such a past is lacking, the task of creating a modern nation – as opposed to a state – is very much harder (Cliffe 1989; Eriksen 1993).

This brings me to perhaps the most fundamental difference between my approach and that of Ernest Gellner. For Gellner it is possible and desirable to have a general theory of nationalism, one that derives from the postulates of modernity. For myself, no such general theory is possible. Though I prefer a certain kind of approach, which may be termed 'ethnosymbolist', I feel that the differences between nationalisms across periods and continents are too great to be embraced by a single Euclidean theory. For such a theory can never tell us, as Gellner admitted, which are the nations-to-be and why they have this or that distinctive character and trajectory.

At the same time, such is the force and sweep of Gellner's own theory that nobody can fail to be convinced of the centrality and ubiquity of nations and nationalism for the world we live in. Gellner has revealed the sociological foundations of our world of nations and shown us why nationalism must remain a vital and enduring force in the contemporary world. His originality consists in demonstrating why the link between culture and politics is so intrinsic to the modern world and why it must generate so much passion. As a result, Gellner was not among the many who foresaw an early supersession of nations and nationalism, although he was more optimistic about the diminution of its fires in affluent, democratic states. This is because he thought that the imperatives of industrialism and mass education would in the end override the power of shared memories of great events and ancient or recent antagonisms. Of this I am not so sure. The past cannot be swept away so easily.

So: to paraphrase Rousseau, a nation must have a navel, and if it has not got one, we must start by inventing one. And it is because nations have navels, and because those navels, and the memories and traditions, myths and symbols they represent, mean so much to the people that have them, that we are so unlikely to see the early transcendence of nations and nationalism.

References

Ades, Dawn (ed.) 1989: *Art in Latin America: The Modern Era, 1820–1980*. London: South Bank Centre, Hayward Gallery.

Armstrong, John 1982: *Nations before Nationalism*. Chapel Hill: University of North Carolina Press.

Billig, Michael 1995: *Banal Nationalism*. London: Sage Publications.

Branch, Michael (ed.) 1985: *Kalevala: The Land of Heroes*, trans. W. F. Kirby. London: Athlone Press.

Chamberlin, E. R. 1979: *Preserving the Past*. London: J. M. Dent and Sons.

Cliffe, Lionel 1989: Forging a nation: the Eritrean experience. *Third World Quarterly* 11 (4), 131–47.

Edwards, John 1985: *Language, Identity and Society*. Oxford: Blackwell.

Eriksen, Thomas 1993: *Ethnicity and Nationalism*. London: Pluto Press.

Fishman, Joshua et al. (eds) 1968: *Language Problems in Developing Countries*. New York: John Wiley.

Florescano, Enrique 1993: The creation of the Museo Nacional de Antropologia of Mexico and its scientific, educational and political purposes. In Elisabeth H. Boone (ed.), *Collecting the Pre-Colombian Past*, Washington, DC: Dumbarton Oaks Research Library and Collection, 81–103.

Franco, Jean 1970: *The Modern Culture of Latin America*. Harmondsworth: Penguin.

Frazee, C. A. 1969: *The Orthodox Church and Independent Greece, 1821–52*. Cambridge: Cambridge University Press.

Friedmann, Georges 1967: *The End of the Jewish People?* London: Hutchinson and Co.

Gellner, Ernest 1964: *Thought and Change*. London: Weidenfeld & Nicolson.

Gellner, Ernest 1973: Scale and nation. *Philosophy of the Social Sciences*, 3, 13–38.

Gellner, Ernest 1982: Nationalism and the two forms of cohesion in complex societies. *Proceedings of the British Academy* 68, 165–87.

Gellner, Ernest 1983: *Nations and Nationalism*. Oxford: Blackwell.

Gellner, Ernest 1994: *Encounters with Nationalism*. Oxford: Blackwell.

Gellner, Ernest 1995: Do nations have navels? Transcript of opening statement in a debate on nationalism with Anthony Smith at the University of Warwick, 24 October.

Gershoni, Israel and Jankowski, James 1986: *Egypt, Islam and the Arabs: The Search for Egyptian Nationhood, 1900–1930*. New York and Oxford: Oxford University Press.

Grosby, Steven 1991: Religion and nationality in the ancient world. *European Journal of Sociology* 31, 229–65.

Hobsbawm, Eric 1990: *Nations and Nationalism since 1780*. Cambridge: Cambridge University Press.

Hobsbawm, Eric and Ranger, Terence (eds) 1983: *The Invention of Tradition*. Cambridge: Cambridge University Press.

Johnson, Lesley 1992: Imagining communities. Paper for Conference on *Imagining Communities: Medieval and Modern*, University of Leeds, Centre for Medieval Studies.

Kedourie, Elie 1960: *Nationalism*. London: Hutchinson.

Kitromilides, Paschalis 1989: 'Imagined communities' and the origins of the national question in the Balkans. *European History Quarterly* 19 (2), 149–92.

Lehmann, Jean-Pierre 1982: *The Roots of Modern Japan*. London and Basingstoke: The Macmillan Press Ltd.

Matossian, Mary 1962: Ideologies of 'delayed industrialization': some tensions and ambiguities. In John H. Kautsky (ed.), *Political Change in Underdeveloped Countries*, New York: Wiley, 254–64.

Mazrui, Ali 1985: African archives and oral tradition. *The Courier*, UNESCO, Paris (February), 13–15.

Nairn, Tom 1977: *The Break-up of Britain*. London: New Left Books.

Raun, Toivo 1987: *Estonia and the Estonians*. Stanford, CA: Stanford University, Hoover Institution Press.

Renan, Ernest 1882: *Qu'est-ce qu'une Nation?* Paris: Calmann-Lévy.

Rickard, P. 1974: *A History of the French Language*. London: Hutchinson University Library.

Smith, Anthony D. 1986: *The Ethnic Origins of Nations*. Oxford: Blackwell.

Smith, Anthony D. 1991: *National Identity*. Harmondsworth: Penguin.

Smith, Anthony D. 1992: Chosen peoples: why ethnic groups survive. *Ethnic and Racial Studies* 15 (3), 436–56.

Smith, Anthony D. 1995a: Gastronomy or geology? The role of nationalism in the reconstruction of nations. *Nations and Nationalism* 1 (1), 3–23.

Smith, Anthony D. 1995b: The nation: real or imagined? Transcript of opening statement in a debate on nationalism with Ernest Gellner at the University of Warwick, 24 October.

Smith, Anthony D. 1996: Culture, community and territory: the politics of ethnicity and nationalism. *International Affairs* 72 (3), 445–8.

Viroli, Maurizio 1995: *For Love of Country: An Essay on Patriotism and Nationalism.* Oxford: Clarendon Press.

Vital, David 1990: *The Future of the Jews: A People at the Crossroads?* Cambridge, MA and London: Harvard University Press.

Weber, Max 1947: *From Max Weber: Essays in Sociology.* London: Routledge & Kegan Paul.

Wistrich, Robert 1995: Theodor Herzl: Zionist icon, myth-maker and social utopian. *Israel Affairs* 1 (3), 1–37.

Zenkovsky, Serge 1960: *Pan-Turkism and Islam in Russia.* Cambridge, MA: Harvard University Press.

3

The Nation: Invented, Imagined, Reconstructed?

Introduction

Imagery has always played a crucial role in politics and nowhere more so than in our understanding of nationalism. Nationalists have always pictured their chosen nation in florid, even glowing images, waxing lyrical over the beauties of the national countryside and the exploits of national heroes. Imagery has also played an important part in the creation of national consciousness: the figure of the French Marianne or British John Bull, the symbolism of the double-headed Tsarist eagle or Israeli Star of David, the appropriation of the ruins of Great Zimbabwe or the Great Pyramids of Egypt – all suggest the uses of evocation in constructing the modern nation.

Inventing the Nation

Lately, however, the 'uses of imagery' have come to occupy a pre-eminent place in attempts to *explain* the formation of nations and the spread of nationalism, especially among modernists. The modern nation is treated in these accounts as an abstract concept which emerges in specific historical circumstances, ones in which human agency and imagination play a pivotal role. The nation becomes a construct of the modern imagination and a historical invention on the part of particular categories or classes of

'The Nation: Invented, Imagined, Reconstructed?', *Millennium: Journal of International Studies*, 20/3 (1991): 353–68. Reproduced with the permission of the publisher.

modern societies. Such an approach marks the zenith of the reaction against an evolutionary determinism which regarded the rise of nations as inevitable processes, part of the 'movement of history' and a stage which was necessary (and generally beneficial) in the development of human society.[1]

The reaction against this kind of evolutionary explanation (of which nationalism itself represented one favoured account) began in the post-war era and was associated particularly with the idea of 'building' the nation. But the Deutschian concept of 'nation-building', though it breathed the language of political activism, was nevertheless fundamentally processual. It pointed to underlying socio-demographic processes – urbanization, mobility, literacy, communications – which set in motion, and fuelled, the growth of nations and the activities of nationalists.

For Karl Deutsch himself, 'nation-building' signified the mutual adjustment of the processes of social mobilization and cultural assimilation, to produce the necessary complementarity of social communication and the creation of linkages between centres and regions. The activities of nationalists within these cumulative processes were of limited importance and confined to the later stages of the formation of national communities.[2]

It was left to Deutsch's followers, notably political scientists like Lerner, Pye, Almond, Apter and Binder, to enlarge the scope of elite activities in the process of 'nation-building'. This could be done in several ways. One was to emphasize the role of personality types: a 'mobile personality' able to empathize with others was critical in Lerner's dramatic account of Middle Eastern nationalism. Alternatively, one could point to the role of communicators, political elites and intellectuals, as the analyses of the 'new states' in Africa and Asia by Pye, Almond, Apter and others suggested. In other accounts, ideology assumed a determining role; for Binder, as for Halpern, Islam and Arab nationalism were central to the understanding of the tortuous road to nation-building in the Middle East and North Africa.[3]

Historians, too, were beginning to re-emphasize the activities and beliefs of particular agents in the rise of nationalism and the growth of nations. In 1960, Kedourie had given a prominent place to certain European belief systems and movements in the genesis and spread of nationalism. In the early 1970s, he extended his emphasis on such activities; backward in time to medieval millennialism and outward in space to the receptive elites of Asia and Africa who were penetrated by colonial ideas and institutions – including the idea of nation.[4] By the mid-1970s, historians like Tilly and Seton-Watson were also looking to the state and its ruling classes for the initial impetus and framework of many nations. Tilly's stress on the place of warfare and Seton-Watson's on the role of nationalist 'design' and deliberation in the creation of so many new nations after 1815 underline both the modernity and the constructed nature of the nation and nationalism.[5]

It comes as no surprise, therefore, to find younger historians like John Breuilly regarding nationalism as a special, and successful, form of modern politics, used by elites to capture state power in opposition to ruling classes. Even though Breuilly accords less importance to ideology and hence intellectuals in his account, the activist tenor of his argument is clear: nationalism serves as a vital political discourse (or argument) able to mobilize different strata, uniting divergent social interests and legitimating their political aspirations. In other words, a political instrument of political factions, no more.[6]

The Invention of Nations

If nationalism is primarily a tool of political interests, what of the nation? Can it too be understood in Marxian terms: as the site and language of political and class interests and aspirations? Can we not analyse its appeal and stability in terms of the interests and social needs which it serves?

That is certainly one of the assumptions behind a relatively recent approach which seeks to understand national phenomena through the analysis of social engineering: the case of 'invented traditions'. For Eric Hobsbawm, Terence Ranger and their associates, much of what passes for nationalism and national consciousness may be regarded as the epitome of the most important and pervasive of such 'invented traditions' – the 'communitarian' ones which create and symbolize the social cohesion of the members of stable social groups like the nation. For Hobsbawm and his associates, such invented traditions are a peculiarly modern phenomenon. The term denotes a set of practices which are normally governed by overtly or tacitly accepted rules. The practices are of a ritual or symbolic nature and seek to inculcate certain values and norms of behaviour by repetition, automatically implying continuity with the past. 'In fact', Hobsbawm continues, 'where possible, they normally attempt to establish continuity with a suitable past,' as did the use of the Gothic style for the rebuilt British Parliament in the mid-nineteenth century.[7]

At this point, Hobsbawm distinguishes between the adaptation of genuine 'old' traditions to new situations and the conscious invention of essentially 'new' traditions to meet new needs. The former occurs in all societies, including those usually dubbed 'traditional'. The latter is found only in periods of rapid social change, especially in so-called modern societies. In such cases, the need to create order and community in an age of innovation becomes paramount. Hence, the importance of a created 'national community', one which secures the cohesion of its members in the face of fragmentation and disintegration engendered by rapid industrial change.

In a later chapter, Hobsbawm ties this general approach to a more specific period and set of circumstances, namely, Europe and America from 1870 to 1914. This he regards as the heyday of invented traditions and of the creation of nations. Why should this period be singled out? Largely because it was after 1870 that Europe and America witnessed a rapid *political mobilization* of the masses, which appeared to threaten the stability of the old orders. To counter the threat of mass democracy posed by the inclusion of the lower classes (and later women), the ruling elites sought ways to control the consequences of rapid social change, by channelling the aspirations and activities of the masses into collective ritual routines and repetitive behaviour governed by accepted rules.[8] Hobsbawm lists three main modes of inclusion and control: through the creation of institutions like festivals, sports, unions, etc.; by the invention of new status systems and modes of socialization, such as the hierarchical education system or royal ceremonial; and by the formation of a 'community' such as the nation, which establishes or symbolizes 'social cohesion or the membership of groups, real or artificial communities'.[9]

The latter is particularly pervasive and significant. Not only does nationalism make use of history to legitimate its innovations, much of its own contents rest on invented traditions. The latter are:

> highly relevant to that comparatively recent historical innovation, the 'nation', with its associated phenomena: nationalism, the nation-state, national symbols, histories and the rest. All these rest on exercises in social engineering which are often deliberate and always innovative, if only because historical novelty implies innovation.[10]

Thus, despite the historic and other continuities embedded in the concept of 'France' and 'the French', these concepts must themselves include a 'constructed' or 'invented' component. Hobsbawm continues:

> And just because so much of what subjectively makes up the modern 'nation' consists of such constructs and is associated with appropriate and, in general, fairly recent symbols or suitably tailored discourse (such as 'national history'), the national phenomenon cannot be adequately investigated without careful attention to the 'invention of tradition'.[11]

The Ethnic Past and its Uses

There is a sense in which the thesis of Hobsbawm and his associates is uncontroversial. After all, do not nationalists themselves claim that they are engaged in awakening the nation by reminding their co-nationals, through festivals and rituals, education and political struggle, of their common history and destiny? They might even describe their activities as exercises in reinventing lost traditions which they administer, like so many Prince Charmings, to their Sleeping Beauty.[12] But, in another sense, this idea of the nation, as composed in large part of so many consciously invented traditions, is quite foreign to the spirit not just of nationalism, but of more conventional scholarly accounts of the rise of nations. The very notion of an 'invented tradition' underlines the strongly instrumentalist nature of Hobsbawm's approach and the Marxist tradition of class manipulation from which it springs.

The picture presented by this perspective suggests a largely inert mass with a set of changing needs, which can be fulfilled only through repetitive symbolism and ritual behaviour. These needs are supplied by the ruling elites through conscious attempts to provide new traditions which will fill the gap left by the decline of old traditions. This, in turn, suggests that in eras of rapid 'social mobilization, people have an overriding need to feel that they belong to a community, hierarchy or belief system. There is also an overriding need, in such destabilizing circumstances, to mask the radicalism of social change with a veil of tradition and continuity with an assumed past, usually a national one. Certainly, it is in the interests of ruling classes or sub-elites to foster such a sense of continuity, in order to resocialize uprooted populations and inculcate new values of order and hierarchy. Only by these means can the ruling classes reassert their control over the dangerous and dislocating processes of rapid industrialization and political mobilization which threaten to overturn the existing class order. It follows that the 'superstructure', in the form of 'invented traditions', plays an unexpectedly crucial part in the creation and stabilization of modern societies and their class regimes.

There are several problems with this approach. To begin with, the term 'invented tradition', with its deliberately jarring connotations, covers a variety of possible relations between tradition and change. These run all the way from quite deliberate inventions and constructions by a single initiator (Hobsbawm cites the case of Baden Powell's Boy Scouts) to the changing traditions of the legal or parliamentary professions with their much slower evolution-cum-innovation, or the changing functions of universities. How shall we include all these within a single undifferentiated concept of 'invented tradition'? The difficulties are even more marked in

the case of the rise of national communities. Even if we try to confine ourselves to 'subjective' components of this complex process (by no means
an easy undertaking), we shall find it almost impossible to disentangle the
elements of pure 'invention' from those of a 'rediscovery', 'revival' or
'reconstruction' of pre-existing elements. It is quite true that we can date
various flags, anthems and ceremonial pieces to specific and often quite
recent moments of history, but are we to regard these as 'inventions'? Likewise, did their initiators think they were creating 'new traditions' for
posterity or simply symbolizing the cohesion or purpose that they and
their contemporaries felt at that moment of time? If the latter is correct,
is the concept of an 'invented tradition' only a retrospective judgement
of the historian?

Further, there is the problem of 'tradition' itself, a notoriously elusive
concept. Presumably, it signifies something that is 'handed down' from
generation to generation, thereby creating a respect, even veneration, for
the old ways – for precedent, for the communal past. As Hobsbawm concedes, traditions are adaptable; in fact, they can change almost as much as
can customs. Nevertheless, tradition always implies some continuity with
the past; an unbroken, if sometimes attenuated, link with earlier beliefs and
practices. But, when this link is broken, when the continuity is shattered,
does this mean that every attempt to revive the tradition and return to some
aspect of the past is factitious? Is every form of 'neotraditionalism', the
conscious attempt to return to the old ways, doomed whenever attempted
as an exercise in political manipulation? Can we adequately explain
the many fundamentalist revivals all over the world by such a simple
expedient?[13]

The problems of this kind of approach are not diminished when it is
applied to the relationship between modern nations and their presumed
pasts. The idea that the latter represent quarries from which might be
extracted and shaped those building blocks and materials through which
competing elites or ruling classes could instil order and control mass
mobilization raises a host of difficulties. Can such manipulations hope to
succeed beyond the immediate moment? Why should one invented version
of the past be more persuasive than another? Why appeal to the past at all,
once the chain of tradition is seen to be beyond repair? Putting nationalist self-conceit to one side, how much real weight can be assigned to the
historical and linguistic activities of the 'inventors' and 'designers' of
nations? To take an extreme case, the concept of 'Pakistan', an amalgam
in a single name of several ethnic provinces, nevertheless drew its mobilizing power from the collective sentiments of the Muslim masses of India.
Without the historical memories, heroic myths and ethno-religious ties of
the Muslim populations, no amount of conscious manipulation or invented

tradition could have brought the state of Pakistan into existence, or set it on the tortuous road of national formation.[14]

In the case of the 'old, continuous nations' of Europe, the links with their ethnic pasts are even closer. Though there is room for selection from, or elaboration of, those pasts, there is much less scope for the creation of a semi-fictionalized past, let alone outright forgery (though both have been tried, with temporary success).[15]

The late eighteenth-century reinstitution of the Welsh *Eisteddfodau* is a classic illustration of the complex relationship between attempts to revive ancient ethnic traditions and outright invention or 'fabrication'. Bardic contests of increasing technical and ritual elaboration date back to 1176 and were a common feature of medieval Welsh cultural life. By the late medieval era, they had become technically sophisticated and courtly occasions. But by the seventeenth century, they had fallen into abeyance, though their memory was preserved in the so-called 'almanack *Eisteddfodau*' held in taverns by local poets.[16]

It was only in the later eighteenth century that many middle-class Welsh exiles in London began to feel the need to revive aspects of earlier Welsh culture. In 1789, Thomas Jones and his friends reinstituted the first modern *Eisteddfod*, which became the model for those held after 1815. Prys Morgan comments on this revival: 'It was a triumph of professional organisation, and a perfect adaptation of a very ancient institution to modern circumstances.'[17]

In contrast, the introduction, in 1819, of the *Gorsedd* of Bards (throne of the Druids) into these poetry contests by the romantic intellectual, Iolo Morganwg (Edward Williams), was more akin to pure invention. Certainly, religious Druid processions had no place in the medieval bardic contests, nor was there any basis for Iolo's fantasies about the Druidic origins of the medieval Welsh bards. Here, undoubtedly, we have a pure 'invented tradition', based on a mistaken reading of Welsh history, but which was essential to Iolo's vision of the revived Welsh nation. The resonance and success of the *Eisteddfod* festival to this day is largely due to the need for Welsh cultural expression in terms of an old tradition of poetry and literary contest as well as in the colourful 'religious' Druidic procession which heralds the bardic ceremonies. While the organization of this cultural and ritual event is modern, it incorporates the main features of the old bardic institution. This is just as the modern coronation ceremonies of the British monarch, though fairly recent in their organization and elaboration, embody much more ancient memories and traditions which endow these events with a sense of venerated antiquity to this day.[18]

Typically, where the modern nation claims a distinctive ethnic past, as so often happens, 'invented traditions' turn out to be more akin to 'reconstruction' of aspects of that past. The latter acts as a constraint on 'invention'. Though the past can be 'read' in different ways, it is not any past, but rather the past of that particular community, with its distinctive patterns of events, personages and milieux. It is not possible to appropriate or annex the past of another community (French history by the British, or vice versa, despite the many inter-weavings of their pasts) in the construction of the modern nation. The reason is not just because the ideology of nationalism prizes historical authenticity, but because later generations of a particular community are formed in their collective life through the memories, myths and traditions of the community into which they are born and educated. If the concerns of a (ever changing) present shape, to some extent, our perceptions of the communal past, that past, as it is handed down from generation to generation in the form of subjective 'ethno-history', sets limits to current aspirations and perceptions. The communal past defines to a large extent our identity, which in turn helps to determine collective goals and destinies.[19]

The task, therefore, of those who set out to forge modern nations is more one of reconstructing the traditions, customs and institutions of the ethnic community or communities which form the basis of the nation, than of inventing new traditions. Of course, if by 'invention' we simply mean a novel recombination of existing elements, then the process of forming modern nations will certainly involve some 'invention'. What is much more debatable, and less frequent, is the fabrication and single-handed initiation of national traditions and national history as crucial components of nationhood. It is one thing to establish such traditions and 'discover' such history; it is quite another to ensure their lasting success and popular acceptance. Traditions, myths, history and symbols must all grow out of the existing, living memories and beliefs of the people who are to compose the nation. Their popular resonance will be greater the more continuous with the living past they are shown to be.

This means that 'manipulation' and 'reconstruction' can, and often do, coexist and reinforce the process of nation formation. For example, Tilak appealed to the cult of the Marathi hero, Shivaji, to mobilize Indians against the British in the early twentieth century and invoked the dread cult of Kali, goddess of destruction, against the partition of Bengal. (In modern anti-colonial terms, he reinterpreted the advice of Krishna in the *Bhagavad-Gita*.) In these efforts, he could undoubtedly be described as attempting to 'manipulate' the mass sentiments of the Hindu community.

At the same time, he was also 'reconstructing' that religious community as a unified *political* community – something it had rarely been. (The Ashokan empire was nominally Buddhist.) The success of the new national community depended on the nationalists' ability to mobilize the Hindu population. This, in turn, meant reconstructing, by recombining living traditions and potent myths and symbols, an existing ethno-religious Hindu community as the basis of the modern Indian nation. Given the power of religion and the diversity of languages, regions and castes on the Indian sub-continent, Tilak and his successors grasped the need for Hindu mobilization as the sole basis for a cohesive new Indian nation. Rather than 'invent' the nation and its traditions, the nationalists selected one of several alternatives and recombined and reinterpreted its myths, symbols, memories and traditions. This recombination and reinterpretation took place in the context of other processes conducive to the formation of nations world-wide and in an age of global nationalism.[20]

'Print-Communities' in Chronological Time

The image of the modern nation as an invented category, a construct of social engineering and a recent cultural artefact, forms the point of departure of another, equally influential, account of nations and nationalism: Benedict Anderson's *Imagined Communities*. His object of explanation, 'the *attachment* that peoples feel for the inventions of their imaginations – or . . . why peoples are ready to die for these inventions' suggests a similar intellectualist framework in posing the initial problem.[21] At the same time, Anderson is well aware of the powerful emotional dimensions of nationalism, as well as the material and political factors which facilitate the growth of nations. For Anderson, the nation is defined not as the object of an ideology but, like religion or kinship, as a form of community: 'it is an imagined political community – and imagined as both inherently limited and sovereign.'[22] There is nothing unusual about such imaginings; all communities larger than villages are imagined. What distinguish the nation from other imagined communities are: its size, which is generally large but always *limited* (there are always other nations beyond one's own); its sovereignty, which guarantees its freedom; and its powerful sense of fraternity which evokes so much self-sacrifice. The nation is an imagined community because its members will 'never know most of their fellow-members, meet them, or even hear of them, yet in the minds of each lives the image of their communion'.[23]

Under what conditions can such imagined communities arise? Anderson distinguishes general conditions from more specific historical factors. There are the great human fatalities which secular ideologies so often overlook: those of death and oblivion and of linguistic diversity. The nation as a community which links time immemorial to a sense of destiny and posterity has become one of the main routes for overcoming human suffering and death. The other fatality is the Tower of Babel: the irremediable linguistic diversity of humanity, and their general mutual incomprehensibility.

Of themselves, these fatalities are too general to 'produce' the growth of nations or the rise of nationalism; that requires more particular factors, negative as well as positive. Negatively, nations required a historical and geographical space which was vacated by those two great realms or cultural systems that had held sway till the sixteenth century: the great sacred scriptural communities and the equally high centres of sacred monarchy, which began their long decline in Europe in the seventeenth century. Behind the dissolutions of these sacred realms, however, lay a more fundamental change in the modes of apprehending the world: a revolution in conceptions of time. Instead of the old, medieval conception which situated events simultaneously in the present, past and future and in which the past prefigured the future through divine Providence, the modern conception places events in 'homogeneous, empty time' which is measured by clock and calendar. Henceforth, communities can be conceived as sociological organisms moving through calendrical, homogeneous, empty time, just as the solid community of the nation moves up or down history.[24]

Accompanying this revolution in the conception of time was another, equally powerful transformation: the emergence of 'print-capitalism'. From Gutenberg's invention, the book became capitalism's first mass-produced industrial commodity. It was followed in the eighteenth century by the newspaper, 'one-day best-sellers', which precisely dates the communal march through homogenous, empty time. Together, the book and the newspaper overthrew the dominance of Latin (the sacred elite language), helped to spread a dynamic Protestantism with an unprecedented rapidity, creating new mass reading publics, and hastened the spread of vernacular languages, including vernacular administrative languages.[25]

Perhaps these developments were only negatively significant. In a positive sense, what 'made the new communities imaginable was a half-fortuitous, but explosive, interaction between a system of production and productive relations (capitalism), a technology of communications (print), and the fatality of human linguistic diversity'. Anderson stresses that we are not speaking of particular languages and territories, but the '*interplay* between fatality, technology and capitalism'.[26]

By establishing vernacular 'print-languages' above the dialects and beneath Latin, by endowing these languages with a new fixity and by differentiating them in terms of status, the technology of 'print-capitalism' acted on the fatality of human linguistic diversity and created the possibility of imagining a new kind of limited, but sovereign community – what one might term the nation as 'print-community'. In the tropes of historical and sociological novels, as in newspaper reports, a new fictive realism creates an imagined time and space around the representative everyday hero or heroine, with whom we are induced to 'identify', even though we shall never meet or know the individuals portrayed. By means of a series of literary devices, the reading public created by print-capitalism is enabled to 'imagine' a sociological community 'narrated' by an author within the boundaries of given 'print-languages'.

These are, of course, fairly general causal factors, albeit ones located in a specific historical period (mainly, but not only, Europe from the sixteenth to early nineteenth centuries). They must be supplemented by more specific analyses of the 'modular' development of nations in particular culture areas. In Latin America, for example, it was the 'administrative pilgrimages' carried out by Creole sub-elites, with their inevitable political distortions, that fuelled the Creole-led independence movements of 1810 against a declining imperial Spain. In Europe, on the other hand, we must distinguish between the classic ethno-linguistic nationalisms in which a small class of literary intellectuals mobilized the masses through vernacular print-languages, and the attempts by ruling elites to annex nationalism as an official, even imperial, culture and ideology and to protect themselves from the effects of the mass-mobilizing, popular movements.[27]

A final wave of anti-colonial nationalisms in Africa and Asia, and instructively in multilingual Switzerland, draws from the experiences of previous kinds of nationalism, to 'model' the new territorial nation on the basis of both educational and administrative pilgrimages. Since the great imperial powers required educated native cadres to man and run their overseas colonies, they created that small, bilingual intelligentsia which proved able to adapt the earlier nation-building traditions to the varieties of multilingual and polyethnic territories which were created by the joint impact of expanding capitalism and the imperial state.[28]

Narrating the Nation

Two aspects of this fascinating and original account of nationalism require further examination. The first concerns Anderson's description of the *explanandum*: the nation as a community narrated in a particular print-language. Seen from this angle, the nation becomes a kind of modern 'text' and nationalism a form of political 'discourse', rather than an ideology. We are then invited to join in a 'reading' of text (and subtexts), as if the key to an explanation of the power of this form of discourse and text lay in a literary analysis of the meanings and devices employed by nationalists and others in their modelling of 'nation-ness'.

This immediately raises several problems. The first is methodological: analysis of the meanings imparted by, or found in, literary products of nationalism cannot substitute for causal explanation of the rise, content, form, timing, intensity and scope of a given nation and nationalism. Anderson himself does not confuse the two, as we shall see, but it is a short step to relegating causal analysis for the more exciting and apparently rewarding task of revealing how the nation has been/is being 'narrated' by its devotees.[29]

There is a related methodological problem. It is possible to exaggerate the role of specifically literary products in the processes of creating and narrating the nation. There is in fact a long tradition of such over-emphasis, traceable to Herder and his followers. Herder himself cautioned against it, citing the importance of other forms of cultural expression: folk ballads, ethnic dances, music, folklore. To this list, one might add the powerful imagery of the visual arts: not just of paintings and sculptures, but of furnishings, ceramics, metalwork and, above all, architecture. What more powerful image of the resurgent, but continuous, nation than the neo-Gothic buildings favoured by nationalist revivals, starting with Pugin's British Houses of Parliament, to the monumental creations and designs of the Hungarian millennial celebrations or those of the Neo-Slavic movement in *fin de siècle* Russia?[30]

It is interesting here to ask what these revivalists thought they were doing. Were they creating, or re-creating, a lost (submerged, neglected, oblivious) nation? One can certainly point to cases of deliberate and intentional creation which come close to Hobsbawm's 'invention'. However, in reviving a medieval style which they believed to be 'authentic', were they not also creating within self-imposed, but also communally given, limits? In *that* sense, we could agree that in *reviving* (albeit in changed form) an older communal style, they were also contributing to the 'reconstruction' of the nation out of pre-existing ethnic ties and traditions.

This leads to a more important point. There is a sense in which Anderson's print-languages breed 'print-communities' in transplantable, modular fashion (pirating the patent, as he puts it). This suggests that nations are *ultimately* inventions of the collective imagination and hence, in some sense, imaginary. It is easy to reach this conclusion, even if Anderson himself would deny it. But, equally important, Anderson's formulation ignores the question, *Who* is the nation? Why these and not other nations? Certainly, this cannot be answered, as he realizes, from his general theory. It requires consideration of historical cases, or groups of them. What Anderson's subsequent historical discussions tend to relegate is the presence or absence and nature of pre-existent ethnic ties – a lingering or vivid sense of community which the creators of the modern nation took as the basis of their work of 'reconstruction'. In general, the proliferation of what we may term the 'ethnic' model of the nation stems from both the influence and ideals of nationalist ideologies and from activation of larger segments of population to fulfil those ideals. This has posed severe problems for the civic and territorial political nationalisms which are based on the ex-colonial states and boundaries and that inspire the creation of many of today's African and Asian would-be nations. Creating and narrating territorial nations here may only serve to ignite a popular and vernacular *ethnie*-based nationalism, be it in the Punjab, Sri Lanka, Kurdistan or Eritrea.[31]

Capitalism and Print-Languages

So far I have concentrated solely on the way in which Anderson construes the nation as the object of explanation. From what has been said, it might appear that Anderson's approach is largely subjectivist: the nation as text to be deconstructed, a series of narratives of 'inventions of the imagination'. But this is only one side of a complex account. The other takes off from the question, Why do so many sacrifice their lives for the nation? The answer would appear to be, because 'print-capitalism' has forged them into solidary, fraternal communities of the imagination ready to endow the nation with a purity and disinterested nobility for which they willingly are ready to lay down their lives.

Here, Anderson returns to Marxist roots, even while he despairs of the ability of Marxism to face the challenge of nationalism in theory as well as practice. It is the restless quest for markets which 'chases the bourgeoisie all over the world' (in Marx's words) that, when allied to the new technology of print, has made the revolution in communications (perhaps as profound a revolution as capitalist industrialism) mould and spawn new communities of print-language in place of the old sacred scriptural communities like Islam, Buddhism or Christendom. These print communities are, in effect, the imagined communities of the nation.

Several questions come to mind. The importance of capitalism in creating the bourgeoisie and encouraging the growth of a wider educated 'middle class' is well known, as is the role of that class, or sections of it, in providing the initial leadership of many, but not all, nationalist movements. We need not insist on the penetration of capitalist relations of production into given areas of the globe to account for the rise of particular nationalisms. There was very little capitalism, let alone industry, in early nineteenth-century Serbia or the Ukraine or in early twentieth-century West Africa when their nationalisms emerged. It suffices that a tiny intelligentsia, often in European exile, should become bilingual in print-languages for the germ of the new nation to be planted.

But shall we look to capitalism for the birth of this indigenous intelligentsia? Is it not to be sought, as Anderson himself underlines, in the needs of the new 'state-at-war' which Charles Tilly and his associates have analysed? Besides, the modern state's activities antedate both print and expanding (rather than city-state) capitalism in Western Europe. Though the wealth created by the urban bourgeoisie extended the state's territories and operations, it was not responsible for the state-making and later nation-building activities of the ruling elites.[32] Again, the role of the intelligentsia in furnishing the leadership and concepts of the emergent nation is well documented. They do indeed provide many of the initial narratives and imagery of the nation, even if they do not invent them *de novo*. But, if they are to succeed politically and if their concepts and images are to assume concrete shape, they must be taken up by movements and be turned into institutions. For this, the intelligentsia requires either the organs of state or a popular base which can create its own social order. But the state and popular community typically reshape the intelligentsia's images and narratives to accord with *political* and/or *ethnic* imperatives. Hence, the bases of the nation that ultimately emerge are to be sought, not in print-languages primarily, but in the interplay between powerful political units and equally potent communal identities. In many cases, the resulting duality has not been resolved, to the profound detriment of the existing nation.[33]

This suggests a further important amendment to Anderson's account: the continuing role of both monarchs and priests, or more broadly states and churches. Anderson has charted the ways in which monarchs used nationalism to shore up their faltering dynasties. Their successors, the dynasts of the modern national state (the Nassers, Titos, de Gaulles and Stalins) have continued the old habit of using the organs of state to shape the nation, with or without regard for intellectuals and print-languages. Quite often, the language is a *lingua franca*, an administrative language of convenience, hardly a mother-tongue ennobled with print and literature of its own. Today, in many parts of Africa and Asia, it is the state itself, through its economic policies, its political patronage and mass education systems, that seeks, with varying success, to create and narrate the emergent nation. As for priests, they have proved more lasting than monarchs. Religious nationalism, or the superimposition (or uneasy coexistence) of mass religion on nationalism, has made a remarkable come-back, primarily in the Islamic world, but also on the Indian sub-continent and in parts of Europe and the Soviet Union. This is hardly surprising. World religions have long been divided into specific ethnic liturgies and traditions and have often come to serve not merely as badges, but as motors and repositories of popular myths, symbols and memories. Even in

Anderson's terms, the desire for immortality, both in the next world and in this one (through one's posterity), may coincide, with the two reinforcing that sense of individual-in-collective destiny which is so crucial to the nation.[34]

Conclusion

Central to the concepts of 'invention' and 'imagination' is the idea of a basic social transformation from generally stable societies with slowly changing customs and traditions to a modern epoch of rapid social change, which liberates human beings and allows them to shape and direct their destinies. Indeed, so far-reaching is this transformation that it impels us to try to control the rapidity of change through the construction of a new social order and new traditions. At the root of this new order, as Anderson emphasizes, is a new conception of linear time and, we may add, clearly demarcated space. It is this intellectual revolution of social consciousness that makes possible all the other changes that go into the making of nations and nationalism: class and politics, print and language, intelligentsia and invented tradition. It is this cultural revolution, too, that makes it possible to grasp the new world of nations as a constructed order – a world of imagined communities and invented traditions whose texts and logic the analyst must unmask and deconstruct.

Such a conception places *homo faber* at the centre of its concerns, ultimately denying the power of the past (of received structures) to determine the products of human agency. But, given the often vivid ethnic legacy from pre-modern times as the basis of relatively successful nations today, the role of intellectual narrators and artist-celebrators is far more circumscribed than the present approaches suggest. It would be absurd to talk of the intelligentsia 'constructing' Poland *tout court*, let alone 'inventing' the Polish nation. This is not to deny their central role in formulating the specifically *modern* concepts of Poland, as opposed to the older religioethnic community and realm, or in disseminating those concepts in the last two centuries. But, without the heritage of pre-modern ethnic ties (memories, myths, traditions, rituals, symbols, artefacts, etc.) that composed the evolving Polish community from the early medieval period, the modern 're-construction' of a Polish nation is inconceivable.

In a world in which statesmen and intelligentsias are seeking to create new 'territorial' nations in Africa and Asia, the appeal of approaches that emphasize the modular, modelling and inventing faculties and processes is self-evident. It would be an error, however, to accord the latter too much weight and allow them to deflect our attention from the central role of ethnic and political factors that have in the past and continue today to select, shape and inspire modern nations.

Notes

1 This was, of course, a theme to be found in Marx's writings – the notion of the 'leading' nations (France, England, Germany) of capitalism – and in neo-evolutionary 'modernization' theory. See, e.g., Neil Smelser, *Essays in Sociological Explanation* (Englewood Cliffs, NJ: Prentice-Hall, 1968).

2 There was no room for an initial, guiding 'blueprint' of the nation, which activists would then set out to 'realize', not at least in Deutsch's early formulations. As for the later 'nation-building', it signified more the construction of an infrastructure and the institutions of state than of the nation as such. See Karl Deutsch, *Nationalism and Social Communications* (New York: MIT Press, 1966); and K. Deutsch and William Foltz (eds), *Nation-Building* (New York: Atherton, 1963). For a critique, see Walker Connor, 'Nation-building or nation-destroying?', *World Politics* 24 (1972), pp. 319–55; and A. D. Smith, *State and Nation in the Third World* (Brighton: Harvester Press, 1983), ch. 1.

3 One might also cite here the reintroduction of elites into 'modernization' theory by Shmuel Eisenstadt, *Modernization: Protest and Change* (Englewood Cliffs, NJ: Prentice-Hall, 1965). See Daniel Lerner, *The Passing of Traditional Society* (New York: Free Press, 1958); and the critique in A. D. Smith, *Theories of Nationalism*, 2nd edn (London: Duckworth, 1983), ch. 5. For the political scientists' 'modernization' approaches, see Clifford Geertz (ed.), *Old Societies and New States* (New York: Free Press, 1963); Lucian Pye, *Politics, Personality and Nation-Building* (New Haven: Yale University Press, 1957); David Apter, *Ghana in Transition* (New York: Athenaeum, 1963); Leonard Binder, *The Ideological Revolution in the Middle East* (New York: John Wiley, 1964); and Manfred Halpern, *The Politics of Social Change in the Middle East and North Africa* (Princeton: Princeton University Press, 1963).

4 The prominence given by Kedourie to misguided youth in search of unattainable visions and their 'adaptation' (modelling) of the European concept of the nation to very different African and Asian milieux prefigures the current interest in the imaginings and inventions of secular intelligentsias. See Elie Kedourie (ed.), *Nationalism* (London: Hutchinson, 1960); and Kedourie, *Nationalism in Asia and Africa* (London: Weidenfeld & Nicolson, 1971), Introduction.

5 Of course, this is only one aspect of a much broader canvass. Neither Hugh Seton-Watson, *Nations and States* (London: Methuen, 1977) nor Charles Tilly, *The Formation of National States in Western Europe* (Princeton: Princeton University Press, 1975), have any doubt about the primacy of the structural processes, the conjunction of discrete causal chains and sequences, which led to the formation of the older, European nations.

6 Of course, there is a prior structural crisis, the growing split between state and society in Europe since the sixteenth century, which encourages the

specious reintegrative solution of the 'nation'; but it is the political goals and skills of nationalists that command Breuilly's attention. See John Breuilly, *Nationalism and the State* (Manchester: Manchester University Press, 1982).

7 Hobsbawm distinguishes such invented traditions from custom and from convention or routine, as in a bureaucracy or factory routine. See Eric Hobsbawm and Terence Ranger (eds), *The Invention of Tradition* (Cambridge: Cambridge University Press, 1983), pp. 1–3.

8 Eric Hobsbawm, 'Mass-producing traditions: Europe, 1870–1914', in Hobsbawm and Ranger (eds), *Invention of Tradition*, pp. 263–307, adds that even socialist groups found it necessary to 'invent' traditions which were nevertheless linked with older, popular festivals (May Day, instituted in 1890).

9 These types often overlap. The functions of the first 'flowing from a sense of identification with a "community" and/or the institutions representing, expressing or symbolising it such as a "nation"'. See Hobsbawm and Ranger, *Invention of Tradition*, p. 9.

10 Ibid., pp. 13–14. Hobsbawm cites the cases of Israeli and Palestinian nationalism or nations as necessarily novel, 'whatever the historic continuities of Jews or Middle Eastern Muslims', because of the novelty for that region of the 'very concept of territorial states'. Exactly here lies the problem. As Anderson reminds us, the novelty lies in the transformation of ancient Jewish religious aspirations into modern Israeli political ones.

11 Ibid., p. 1. Trevor-Roper's essay on the construction of Scottishness, notably the kilt and Highlands concept, provides a vivid illustration of this thesis; other later examples can be found in Eric Hobsbawm, *Nations and Nationalism since 1780* (Cambridge: Cambridge University Press, 1990), ch. 4.

12 This is the metaphor in Kenneth Minogue, *Nationalism* (London: Batsford, 1967); it is one of many (e.g., reviving, reawakening, regenerating) which nationalists use to describe their own role.

13 For attempts to define 'tradition' and 'traditionalism', see J. R. Gusfield, 'Tradition and modernity: misplaced polarities in the study of social change', *American Journal of Sociology* 72, 4 (1967), pp. 351–62; and Shmuel Eisenstadt, *Tradition, Change and Modernity* (New York: John Wiley & Sons, 1973). For an early set of analyses of fundamentalist movements, see the essays in Donald E. Smith (ed.), *Religion and Political Modernization* (New Haven: Yale University Press, 1974).

14 The extent to which 'Pakistan' was the product of elite interests and manipulations or of pre-existing mass ethno-religious sentiments is the subject of a debate between Paul Brass and Francis Robinson. See David Taylor and Malcolm Yapp (eds), *Political Identity in South Asia* (London: Curzon Press for the Centre for South Asian Studies, 1979).

15 One thinks of the vogue for Ossian, or the forged medieval Czech manuscripts, or the debate on the Song of Igor's Host in Russian nationalism. See H. Paskiewicz, *The Origin of Russia* (London: George Allen & Unwin, 1954).

16 For the details of this process, see P. Morgan, 'From a death to a view: the hunt for the Welsh past in the Romantic period', in Hobsbawm and Ranger,

Invention of Tradition, pp. 43–100, the very title of which suggests the continuing relevance of ancient Welsh traditions.

17 Ibid., p. 59. An old tradition was married to modern methods of mass organization, a common feature of neo-traditionalist movements. See Halpern, *Politics of Social Change*.

18 See D. Cannadine, 'The context, performance and meaning of ritual: the British monarchy and the "Invention of Tradition", *c*.1820–1977', in Hobsbawm and Ranger, *Invention of Tradition*, pp. 101–64. But the modern meanings are quite different in each generation.

19 See the analysis of 'blocking presentism' in J. D. Y. Peel, 'The cultural work of Yoruba ethnogenesis', in Elisabeth Tonkin, Maryon McDonald and Malcolm Chapman (eds), *History and Ethnicity* (London: Routledge, 1989), pp. 198–215 and the contrasting opening essay by Edwin Ardener, 'The construction of history: "vestiges of creation"', ibid., pp. 22–33.

20 For the uses of the past by early Indian nationalists, see the essays by Crane and Adenwalla in R. A. Sakai (eds), *Studies on Asia* (Lincoln: University of Nebraska Press, 1961); see also B. T. McCulley, *English Education and the Origins of Indian Nationalism* (Gloucester, MA: Smith, 1966). Such Hindu nationalism opened the way for a religio-national exclusivism which marks the sub-continent to this day.

21 The phrase 'inventions of the imagination', in the sense of creations, can be read in different ways, but the insistence throughout that language is the central category – print-language – underlines the prior cognitive dimension. We learn languages, but are born into communities of putative descent. See Benedict Anderson, *Imagined Communities: Reflections on the Origins and Spread of Nationalism* (London: Verso, 1983), p. 129, emphasis in original.

22 Ibid., p. 15. He considers the nation a cultural artefact of the late eighteenth century, an 'invention', but not in the sense of 'fabrication' or 'falsity', but of 'imagination' and 'creation'. It remains unclear why nations are seen as limited and sovereign communities, except that they emerged in an age of growing religious pluralism and of Enlightenment and Revolution.

23 Ibid., Why only 'imagined', why not also, even primarily for most people, 'felt'? Not only the image of communion, but also a profound emotional bond, unites and gives the members of the community life and purpose.

24 Ibid., pp. 20–31. Anderson uses Walter Benjamin's graphic phrase about 'homogenous, empty time' in contrast to the medieval 'messianic time', citing Benjamin's *Illuminations* (London: Fontana, 1973), pp. 263–5.

25 Ibid., pp. 38–9, 41–9. Though capitalism is given priority, the slow, uneven rise of state languages, predating print and capitalism, is accorded an independent status; but this is left undeveloped. Surely, the whole panoply of modern state operations and not just its linguistic unification policies form the framework within which capitalism, print and linguistic and religious homogenization had to operate; the competition of war-making states in Europe formed the matrix of nascent nations. See Andrew Orridge, 'Separatist and autonomist nationalisms: the structure of regional loyalties in the modern state', in Colin Williams (ed.), *National Separatism* (Cardiff:

University of Wales Press, 1982), 43–74; and Tilly, *Formation of National States*.

26 Anderson argues that language, like death, is a general human fatality: there is no likelihood of humanity's linguistic unification. True, but it is at least conceivable (as bilingualism on a global scale?). Whereas in the other fatality, mortality, capitalism finds a truly tenacious enemy, whose importance was always felt; hence the appeal of the great world religions and the many forms of ancestor worship. See Anderson, *Imagined Communities*, p. 46, emphasis in original.

27 Ibid., chs. 4–6. Despite the evidence he adduces in ch. 5, Anderson places the onset of Europe's nationalisms (they occurred at different times in various parts of the continent) at the close of the era of successful liberation movements in the Americas, i.e., around 1820. Hobsbawm, *Nations and Nationalism since 1780*, does the same no doubt because of the growing tide of printed dictionaries, philological treatises, grammars, etc. But this overlooks the pioneering role of Western European historians and artists. See Robert Rosenblum, *Transformations in Late Eighteenth Century Art* (Princeton: Princeton University Press, 1967); and Hans Kohn, *The Idea of Nationalism* (New York: Collier–Macmillan, 1967).

28 Anderson, *Imagined Communities*, ch. 7. But is it the last wave? Even when he penned his work, Anderson had witnessed the 'ethnic revival' with its spate of autonomy movements in the West, to be followed in the last few years by a wave of violent ethnic neo-nationalisms in the Soviet Union and Eastern Europe. Truly, as he says (p. 12), 'The reality is quite plain: the "end of the era of nationalism", so long prophesied, is not remotely in sight.' See A. D. Smith, 'The supersession of nationalism?', *International Journal of Comparative Sociology* 31, 1–2 (1990), pp. 1–31. It seems strange to bracket Switzerland with the truly modern creations of many African and Asian states (though some of these had, in parts of their domains, ethnic forbears); the Swiss state and nation may be nineteenth-century creations, but the latter was founded on long-held traditions, myths, symbols, memories and values, which acted as foci of 'liberty' for French and Italian neighbouring communities from the later eighteenth century. In other words, the 'ethnic core' of modern Switzerland, the Alemannic cantons (with a few additions), had political and military traditions of confederation in defence of local liberties, which gave political expression to their loose sense of ethnic kinship. Without these, a modern Swiss nation is inconceivable. See Jonathen Steinberg, *Why Switzerland?* (Cambridge: Cambridge University Press, 1976); and Georg Thürer, *Free and Swiss* (London: Oswald Wolff, 1970).

29 Such temptations are not always resisted in some of the essays on British/English national identities. See Raphael Samuel (ed.), *Patriotism: The Making and Unmaking of British National Identity* (London: Routledge, 1989); and Gerald Newman, *The Rise of English Nationalism: A Cultural History, 1740–1830* (London: Weidenfeld & Nicolson, 1987).

30 For the exhibition catalogues, see Eri Gyongyi and Jobbagyi Zsuzsa (eds), *The Golden Age of Hungary: The Art and Society in Hungary, 1896–1914*

(London: Barbican Art Gallery, Corvina, 1989); and *The Twilight of the Tsars* (London: South Bank Centre, Hayward Gallery, 1991). For Herder's cultural populism, see Isaiah Berlin, *Vico and Herder* (London: Hogarth Press, 1976). We should also underline, once again, the role of historians – Gibbon, Moser, Muller, Rollin, Villaret, Karamzin, Palacky, etc. See Paschalis Kitromilides, '"Imagined communities" and the origins of the national question in the Balkans', *European History Quarterly* 19, 2 (1989), pp. 142–92.

31 I have discussed this tension between newly created civic and territorial political identities and resurgent ethnic and genealogically based identities more fully in A. D. Smith, *National Identity* (Harmondsworth: Penguin, 1991), chs. 5–6.

32 Here the accounts of Tilly, *Formation of National States*, and Seton-Watson, *Nations and States*, ch. 2, seem to supplement and modify that of Immanuel Wallerstein, *The Modern World System* (New York: Academic Press, 1974); and A. D. Smith, *Theories of Nationalism*, 2nd edn (London: Duckworth, 1983), ch. 6.

33 The two routes of nation formation, those of bureaucratic incorporation and of vernacular mobilization, are more fully discussed in A. D. Smith, *The Ethnic Origins of Nations* (Oxford: Blackwell, 1986), ch. 6, and in A. D. Smith, 'The Origins of Nations', ch. 7 in this volume.

34 For examples of religious nationalisms, see Ali Banuazizi and Myron Weiner (eds), *The State, Religion and Ethnic Politics: Afghanistan, Iran and Pakistan* (Syracuse, NY: Syracuse University Press, 1986) and Pedro Ramet (ed.), *Religion and Nationalism in Soviet and East European Politics* (Durham, NC: Duke University Press, 1989).

4

Nationalism and Classical Social Theory

Many of the main concerns and assumptions of recent modernist theories of nations and nationalism stem from some of the main sociological traditions. Both the strengths and the weaknesses of modernism can be traced back to the evolutionary and Eurocentric postulates of classical sociological theories, and it is to their influence that I now turn. Any convincing theory of nationalism must, in addition to the usual scientific requirements of theory construction, combine three characteristics:

1 a clear-cut statement of the objectives of the theory, that is, which aspects of the broad group of 'nationalist phenomena' are being investigated, with an equally clear-cut definition of terms, which differentiates the phenomena in question from other related ones;
2 an 'internal' approach which involves a search for the springs of cultural identity and community, and draws on an empathic understanding of the meanings with which the participants endow their attachments and activities;
3 an 'external' approach which sets out from a broad comparative perspective and historical framework within which it locates and classifies the various local and individual manifestations of nationality and nationalism, in order to explain their role and features.

Given the state of theory construction in the social sciences as a whole, it is hardly surprising if few genuine theories of nationalism have

'Nationalism and Classical Social Theory', *The British Journal of Sociology*, 34/1 (1983): 19–38. Reproduced with the permission of the editors of *The British Journal of Sociology*.

emerged; and none has found general acceptance. In this respect, sociology is no exception. Indeed, for reasons shortly to be enumerated, the sociology of nationalism has laboured under special handicaps, not the least being the rather scant attention given to so central a topic of social investigation.

The argument I want to advance here takes the form of a series of statements, each of which modifies its predecessor and which together suggest directions for further research. There are three such assertions.

(1) If we look at the writings of classical sociologists from about 1800 to 1920 (and even of many sociologists thereafter), we find little explicit attention paid to problems of nationality and nationalism, as if the subject did not merit special, or separate, investigation; and concomitantly little interest in defining a separate set of questions and definitions in this area.

(2) On the other hand, deeper study of some of the classical social theorists reveals a tacit interest in important aspects of the whole field of 'nationalist phenomena', usually cloaked behind other concerns, but able to provide illumination and cues for theories.

(3) Yet, for all their suggestive power, these sociological perspectives and theories cannot encompass the many problems and dimensions of nationalism; they need to be integrated with aspects and findings of neighbouring disciplines – anthropology, political science, history and international relations, in particular – to provide adequate theories. The sociologist must, therefore, lean heavily on the work of scholars in these other disciplines and be ready to stray far from his conventional terrain, if he is to grasp the complex and often baffling nature of his object of study and come up with some testable propositions.

In what follows, I shall try to elaborate and illustrate these contentions and also propose a brief classification of the chief sociological perspectives on nationalism; and then conclude with some suggestions for further interdisciplinary investigations. My main concern throughout is with the classical social theorists of the nineteenth and early twentieth centuries. But the argument sometimes demands a consideration of eighteenth-century and mid-twentieth-century theories, especially in the first, rather general survey of the neglect of nationalism by sociologists. I should add that, in the space of an article, full justice cannot be done to theorists who have addressed themselves to our subject *en passant*; instead, attention will be focused on those who have given it more than cursory attention, or whose writings in adjacent fields could help to illuminate problems of nationalism.

Sociological Neglect of Nationalism

I want first to illustrate the general lack of attention given to nationalism throughout the history of sociological investigation until very recently, and to suggest some possible explanations for this remarkable neglect. This will help to locate the few classical theorists who did have something interesting to say about nationalism. For this purpose, we can divide the development of sociology into five periods: eighteenth-century 'precursors'; second, nineteenth-century evolutionism, including classical Marxism; third, the late nineteenth-century period of classical sociology stretching to the 1920s; fourth, the inter-war growth of American sociology, especially functionalism; and, finally, the contemporary phase of many paradigms ranging from 'micro-sociologies' to neo-Marxisms.[1]

Eighteenth-century writers were generally impressed with the power of patriotism and the state's ability to homogenize its populations into a compact body of citizens.[2] Both the French and the Scottish enlighteners accorded considerable value to the 'civic religion' of democratic societies. Montesquieu, of course, felt that the actuating principle of democratic republics was the 'virtue' of public spirit; he also differentiated between national cultures in terms of the 'spirit' of their peoples, which in turn was conditioned by their climates and geographical situations.[3] This was something that Hume, in his essay 'Of National Characters', which also appeared in 1748, disputed: he did not think 'that men owe any thing of their temper or genius to the air, food or climate'.[4] But at least both felt the subject merited some attention, and Montesquieu admits that 'This subject (sc. Laws in relation to the Principles which form the general spirit, the morals and the customs of a nation) is very extensive'.[5] Nor did it fall on infertile ground in Scotland: Ferguson felt that there are 'habits of thinking peculiar to nations, to different ages and even to individuals of the same nation and age';[6] and he argued for a national militia, to inculcate the virtue of republican Rome, since 'Institutions that fortify the mind, inspire courage and promote national felicity, can never tend to national ruin'.[7] In this respect, Ferguson was exceptional; most of the Scottish enlighteners followed Montesquieu's lead in thinking mankind basically peaceful, and excluding, as far as possible, war between nations from their schemes of progress.[8]

Although in many ways the 'spirit' of a nation and its laws is pivotal to Montesquieu's sociology, neither he nor the other *philosophes* developed their observations on national character into a coherent and comparative framework. Two partial exceptions at the end of the rationalist phase of the Enlightenment are found in Rousseau and Herder. Rousseau took an obvious delight, not just in national diversity as such, but in what he called the 'religion of the citizen' and we would term nationalism, praising Moses for having loaded the Jews with customs and prescriptions to keep them separate, and urging both Corsicans and Poles to cultivate their natural and national virtues and manners.[9] He also claimed that national institutions can mould the spirit and manners of a nation: 'Ce sont les institutions nationales qui forment le genie, le caractère, les goûts et les moeurs d'un peuple . . . qui lui inspirent cet ardent amour de la patrie.'[10] But, once again, there is no attempt at comparative sociological investigation of a phenomenon he so encouraged. Similarly with Herder. Despite his theory of the formation of language and its role in collective life, Herder's suggestive insights into national genius (especially in the arts) and national 'authenticity' never led to any attempt at systematic analysis of these peculiarities or the causes of national sentiment. In fact, Herder abhorred systems of any kind; he was himself an enthusiastic 'cultural populist' who believed in the organic unity of life and all life's experiences.[11] To him it was enough that 'Language expresses the collective experience of the groups': 'Let us follow our own path', he urged; '. . . let all men speak well or ill of our nation, our literature, our language: they are ours, they are ourselves, and let that be enough.'[12]

The nineteenth-century sociologists failed to follow up these suggestions. Their interest was riveted by the twin revolutions, the political in France and the industrial in England; and they signally failed to draw the consequences for nations and nationalism, despite the evidence around them.[13] Neither St Simon nor Comte devoted attention to the subject, despite their common interest in the new type of social order emerging in industrial societies; they tended to find in science itself the cure for any lack of consensus during the painful transition to industrialism.[14] Nor, on the other side of the Channel, did the typical Burkean conceptions of organic society, constitutionalism and union between past, present and future generations furnish any inspiration for the grandiose schemes of social change proposed by Spencer, Morgan, Tyler and the other social evolutionists; for their utilitarianism looked to co-operation between individual parts of a social aggregate as the necessary bond in society.[15] Despite, for example, Spencer's interest in the military aspects of society, issues of nationality and patriotism play an insignificant part in the vast corpus of his (or the other evolutionists') writings.

For all their universal concerns, the social evolutionists remained firmly anchored to their European context. Classical Marxist theory was similarly Eurocentric.[16] This was partly a function of its Europe-centred revolutionary aims, partly of its equally European Hegelian heritage. For Hegel, the Idea underwent successive material concretizations in different epochs and civilizations, and reached its fullest expression in modern European (Prussian) civilization. Similarly, each national genius is a part of the process by which the *Geist* realizes itself in history, and its supreme expression is the unitary nation-state. If the nation fails to realize its mission in the historical scheme, and fails to create its own state, it must decline and lose its world-historical status.[17] Other nation-states will emerge embodying new principles and a new spirit, for 'The most natural State is a State composed of a single national character'.[18] Defence is the supreme object of the state, and states therefore must tend towards expansion; and since the state is a supreme expression of the nation as a whole, 'war has the deep meaning that by it the ethical health of a nation is preserved and their finite aims uprooted . . . war protects the people from the corruption which an everlasting peace would bring upon it'.[19] Now, as Gallie points out, Marx and Engels formulated their own approach at a period of relative military quiescence; but this did not prevent Engels in particular from taking a strong interest in military relations between states. Both Marx and Engels were involved with particular strategies for socialist development in different European states, and both recognized the importance of warfare in general and of specific wars in cementing the sense of nationality.[20] Yet the theory of 'historyless peoples' that Engels, in particular, inherited from Hegel, prevented the founders of Marxism from formulating a comparative theory of nationalism in place of the normative 'great nation-state' emphasis of Hegel.[21] Hence their often-remarked disdain for the struggles of smaller East European nationalities then in progress all round them; and their heavy western bias.[22] More fundamentally, a deep suspicion always attached to nationalism in the minds of Marx and Engels; their approach remained strictly 'instrumentalist', for, since 'the working-class have no stake in the fatherland', all that mattered was the role of any nationalist movement in the furtherance or hindrance of socialist revolution.[23] Besides, despite its Hegelian heritage and Engels' understanding of the importance of interstate wars, the Marxist approach became more economistic, and placed its emphasis upon stratification *within* nations and upon economic alienation and development of classes rather than ethnic communities. This in turn meant a devaluation of culture, ideals and the state, precisely those elements without which no sociology of nationalism can be constructed. Economic interest came wholly to overshadow cultural affinity as the driving force of historical development.

Later Marxists did try to amend this hiatus in the canon, but with little success. Lenin certainly appreciated the power of nationalism, if only as a weapon of the bourgeoisie in Eastern Europe, or as an anti-colonial force in colonized territories in Asia and Africa; he even endorsed the principle of national self-determination.[24] But there was little attempt to fashion an overall theory of nationalism in his many writings; and even Stalin's essay of 1913, which does at least define the nation in both 'objective' and 'subjective' terms, hardly constitutes more than a sketch towards such a theory.[25] It was left to Renner and Bauer in Austria to provide the only systematic attempt by Marxists to come to terms with the 'national question'; Bauer's conception of a 'community of character' born of a 'community of fate' or shared experiences accorded with Renan's well-known lecture and tried to restore those elements of culture repudiated by classical Marxism.[26] This moves us some way towards an ethnic theory of nationality; but it remains reminiscent of eighteenth-century monocausal hypotheses, the 'one and the same effective force' from past history, which Bauer posited without much evidence.[27]

In the third phase, at the turn of the century, there was a partial break with the optimistic, ultra-rationalist, even scientistic schemes of social evolution, and a correspondingly greater interest in the sources of 'irrational' behaviour.[28] In the new cultural atmosphere, one might have expected that more attention would be paid to collective sentiments and ideals. Yet, the classical sociologists are only a little less disappointing than their predecessors, if we are to judge by the proportion of their total output devoted to nationalism or identity. True, Michels did devote a whole book to the subject, entitled *Der Patriotismus*; Pareto's attention was drawn by this example of non-logical action; and Durkheim wrote some passages and essays on the subject, especially under the impact of the Great War. But it was left to Weber, himself a German political nationalist like Hegel before him, to treat the subject rather more fully; and to Simmel, an outsider in German society, to draw some insights from his predicament for subjects like *Conflict* and *The Stranger*. Against this, we must set the fact that, in large parts of their work, the subject of nation-states and nationalism is not mentioned; and this needs to be borne in mind when we turn to the more detailed analysis of Durkheim's, Simmel's and Weber's few writings that bear on nationalism.

It may be useful to deal briefly with the last two phases of sociological history, to complete the picture. On the whole, the inter-war years and the immediate aftermath of World War II evinced a curious lack of interest in nationalism, despite some concern with fascism in Parsons' essays during the war.[29] Park, of course, like Thomas and Znaniecki, studied intensively processes of immigration and cultural assimilation, subjects adjacent to nationalism; but only Louis Wirth spared any time to consider the forms of nationalist movements and the nature of nations.[30] Otherwise, the period was dominated by a functionalism that returned to the grandiose conceptions of the evolutionists (despite its overt antagonism to laws of change) and had no place, not even a small principality, for nations or nationalism in its vast imperial domains. Neither Merton nor Levy nor Davis devote more than a passing thought to nationalism, and then only in the context of sources of social solidarity. Even Parsons, though latterly showing some sensitivity to ethnicity, tended to subsume the nation and nationalism within the broader categories of 'society' and its normative patterns.[31] All of these theorists take the American pattern of an overarching society composed of *fixed* social groups and institutions as normative; whereas the problem of nationalism lies exactly in the indeterminacy of these ethnic and political constituents and the fluidity of their boundaries and territories. Only in the work of some political scientists influenced by functionalism – Apter, Binder and Pye – and in the later theories of Smelser and Eisenstadt, is there some concern with problems of nationalism, especially in the Third World.[32]

Finally, since the 1960s, when the functionalist paradigm broke down and the field was opened to rival paradigms, there has been some renewal in certain quarters of the early interest in nationalism of the eighteenth-century pioneers. Not among the many 'micro-sociologies' which take history and structure as givens; not even among the so-called conflict theorists like Rex, Dahrendorf, Lenski and Coser;[33] but among some practical Marxists like Fanon and Debray, and more recent Marxian writers like Nairn and Hechter; among students of 'ethnicity' like Bell, Enloe and Walker Connor, working with post-Deutschian conceptions of modernization; and of course in the Deutschian school itself.[34] But these are still exceptions.

This is a sad catalogue of neglect and missed opportunities. And we may well enquire as to the reasons. Two types of reason can be distinguished: methodological and theoretical. Methodologically, nationalism presents great difficulties of definition, classification and explanation; it involves a vast historical and geographical field, requires knowledge of several languages, familiarity with many events, customs and sentiments, and an empathy with various situations and problems of identity. And there is no agreement even on basic definitions. Sociology faces special difficulties here. These are, first, the sheer range of ideas and concepts of the nation held by the participants (not to mention the analysts); as Weber puts it,

> In the face of these value concepts of the 'idea of the nation', which empirically are entirely ambiguous, a sociological typology would have to analyse all sorts of community sentiments of solidarity in their genetic conditions and in their consequences for the concerted action of the participants.[35]

And he adds, significantly: 'This cannot be attempted here.' And, second, sociology faces a particular difficulty in matching what I have called the 'internal' with the 'external' accounts of nationalism, with such perspectives as do exist tending towards one or the other extreme, usually the 'external' one. This is in turn a function of sociology's positivistic heritage and of its difficulty in grasping elements of uniqueness and incorporating them, without destroying their character, in an ordering framework of analysis.

This brings us to the more revealing theoretical reasons for sociology's neglect of nationalism. They all stem, at bottom, from the European origins of sociology and its largely Eurocentric outlook. Sociology arose, after all, in countries with a fairly firmly entrenched sense of nationality, which was both clear-cut and dominant within the state apparatus and polity. Interestingly, it was in Germany and Italy, where that sense was less firmly entrenched, that sociologists turned some attention to questions of nationalism; whereas in England and France, the subject was hardly ever raised. In America, whither sociology was transplanted early in our century, the situation was almost unique: a continent rather than a country or nation, consisting of many 'states' and immigrant ethnic communities, and divided by the parallel issue of 'race'. The special problems of this continent tended to inhibit a comparative approach which would include a framework for studying nations and nationalism.

Its historical context apart, sociology has always been preoccupied with horizontal or class divisions; and these have overshadowed other, ethnic or national, lines of cleavage. This concern may again be traced to the effects of the twin Revolutions at the end of the eighteenth century which made the European course of development so unique. European sociology has naturally been taken up with the contrast between pre- and post-industrial/capitalist society and the transition to modern, politically inclusive societies. So modernization, industrialism and class conflict have come to provide the classical 'site' of modern macro-sociology, emphasizing socio-economic structures.

Third, the main impetus behind sociological theory and investigation was a concern with the evolutionary 'laws of change', or order and change. But nationalist doctrine is also essentially evolutionary and concerned with the laws of national development; while, at the same time, the growth of nations and nationalism is often viewed by sociologists and others as part and parcel of the evolutionary laws of change.[36] It is, therefore, as if its own thoroughly evolutionist background and impetus made sociology, as the study of the laws of social order and social change, unable to distance itself sufficiently from its own basic premises, which are also those of nationalism, and from so essential an aspect of the modern laws of change, i.e. the growth of nations. If this is the case, then it would go far in explaining why nations and nationalism were so long accepted as a sociological 'given'; and why the study of society was always *ipso facto* the study of the nation, which was never disentangled as a separate dimension or issue. It would also help to explain the popularity of 'methodological nationalism', in which basic social data are always collected and evaluated in terms of large-scale entities called 'nation-states'.[37]

In short, the difficulty for a discipline so impregnated with the selfsame assumptions as those held by its object of study, to stand back and realize its historical peculiarity, has prevented sociologists till quite recently from devoting the attention to that object which it clearly deserves; with the result that the growth of nations and nation-states, and of their ethnic core from which most sociologists are normally recruited, are topics and features of society 'taken-for-granted'; they are part of the basic furniture of the mind carried as much by students of society as by any others of its members.

Sociological Perspectives on Nationalism

And yet, this negative verdict is only a part of the overall picture. Since the war, several distinguished sociologists have begun to study ethnicity and nationalism, and they are drawn from a variety of theoretical persuasions. Their concern has, of course, been prompted in the main by recent political developments, especially in the Third World; but the inspiration behind their analyses can be traced back to the fundamental interests and images of classical sociology. What I want to argue here is that, although classical sociology had little to say directly on the subject, its main perspectives nevertheless have a good deal to offer the student of nationalism by way of general approach and illumination. I shall consider here three main approaches – developmental, communitarian and conflictual – with special emphasis on the outlooks of Durkheim, Simmel and Weber.

1 Developmental perspectives   Recently, nationalism has figured in two types of developmental approach: the modernization theories of Smelser, Eisenstadt, Shils, Bendix, Lerner and Karl Deutsch; and the uneven development theories of Hechter, Tom Nairn and Samir Amin. In the first, nationalism becomes a more or less essential part of the process by which traditional societies disintegrate and transform themselves into modern ones. For the 'neo-evolutionists' like Smelser, Levy, Eisenstadt and even Shils, nationalism is a product of the period of disturbance and strain through which modernizing societies must pass.[38] By far the most complex and interesting of these accounts is that given by Karl Deutsch, who singles out the processes of social mobilization and cultural assimilation as the twin motors of the growth of nations.[39] In his use of quantitative indicators like trade flows, exposure to mass media, urbanization and the like, and his broad tracing out of universal trends, Deutsch stands in the tradition of the nineteenth-century evolutionists, with their interest in gross temporal sequences and structural changes. Similarly, the recent parallel analyses of Hechter and Nairn, who trace the uneven development of capitalism over the globe, to explain the rise and incidence of ethnic nationalism, owe much to the Marxist variant of evolutionism, with its historicist outlook and concern for qualitative leaps in social change.[40] All these theories and models are premissed on certain basic ideas of social development held by the classical evolutionists and Marxists, above all the belief that the causes of social change lie within the unit or process under consideration – be it a given society, or capitalism, or modernization.[41] In other words, they all adopt an 'endogeneous' approach, even if they locate the origins of nationalism, geographically, in the West and see it being imposed elsewhere through the operations of the laws of capitalism or modernization or social mobilization. At the same time, all these accounts are, in another sense, 'external' ones: they do not start out from the nation or nationalism under consideration, nor do they usually reach into it, as it were, from the outside. They rarely concern themselves with the quality of national culture or nationalist movement, except in very schematic terms. Even the social groups and institutions involved in creating nations receive rather sketchy and mechanical treatment. They are really only interested in uncovering the 'law' which will explain the near-ubiquity of nationalism in the modern world, rather than with penetrating into the inner world of nationalism and ethnicity. In that respect, they have remained true to their positivist and evolutionary pedigree.

2 Communitarian approaches In contrast to the developmental approaches which are the heirs of the Enlightenment and the twin Revolutions, communitarian approaches partake of two traditions: an enlightened, radical one stemming from Rousseau and Montesquieu, and a post- and counter-revolutionary tradition associated with Burke in England and Bonald and de Maistre in France. In the former, as we saw, the 'spirit of the nation' and the love of country form the only true bases for a democratic society; to Rousseau, especially, the self-sacrificing love of city-state characteristic of ancient Sparta and republican Rome was the exemplar of social cohesion and fraternity in a community such as Corsica or Poland.[42] Likewise, it was community, not society, that the French counter-revolutionaries were bent on re-creating after the revolutionary upheaval; above all, the sacred hierarchy and order characterizing any truly organic society.[43] The key to society was authority, and the root of all social authority was religion. Take away religion, and you remove the one sure foundation of social order and individual happiness. Only religion could ensure community between heterogeneous men and women; only a full assent to its supernaturally backed values and norms could give everyone the sense of belonging, of solidarity, which was man's basic need.[44]

Curiously, some of these themes reappear in quite recent theories of social cohesion in Third World countries. Both sociologists like Shils and political scientists like Binder and Apter have dwelt on the need for civil bonds in societies undergoing rapid change; and they have sought to characterize the fervent nationalism of several African and Asian states today as cases of 'political religion'.[45] Some of these accounts treat the qualities of nationalism in countries like Syria or Ghana in considerable depth; but their rather functionalist explanation lacks an essential historical dimension, and springs again from a grand 'external' schema, into which nationalism, or particular cases of it, are inserted.[46] The source of change is, once again, held to be internal to the political unit under study – in that respect, functionalists are heirs to classical evolutionism – but in regarding the presence of nationalism as a sign of strain during the era of modernization, or as a therapy for the disturbances it occasions, these accounts remain largely 'external' to the phenomenon they seek to understand. They do not, and cannot, supply what Weber termed a *verstehende soziologie*, in which a phenomenon is rendered sociologically intelligible through an analysis of the meanings with which the participants in a national community or movement endow their actions.[47]

The one great sociologist from whom such an account, based on the communitarian approach, might be drawn is, of course, Emile Durkheim; and some of his concerns have obviously inspired the formulations of the post-war sociologists and political scientists. Though Durkheim wrote little directly about nationalism or nationality problems, he became increasingly interested in the subject, and not only with the drift towards world war.[48] There were also theoretical grounds for his interest, going back to his early studies of the writings of Comte and such German sociologists as Schäffle.[49] They clustered round Durkheim's conceptions of the *conscience collective* and the nature of 'mechanical solidarity'. Three aspects can be distinguished here. First, there is the description of that kind of solidarity as ethnic or tribal in nature. As early as his first major work, *The Division of Labour in Society*, Durkheim was writing:

> What brings men together are mechanical causes and impulsive forces, such as affinity of blood, attachment to the same soil, ancestral worship, community of habits, etc. It is only when the group has been formed on these bases that co-operation is organised there.[50]

The result of these mechanical causes and impulsive forces is a sense of solidarity or community based upon shared beliefs and sentiments, and a close resemblance between its members. In such societies, the collective conscience of the entire group is expressed in its traditions, which change only very slowly, because 'what comes from the past is generally the object of a very special respect'.[51] The second aspect concerns the role of these ethnic or communal traditions today. Though the collective conscience and the 'mechanical' type of solidarity gradually decline under the impact of urbanization, secularization and specialized labour, they are never eliminated. When Durkheim, speaking specifically about modern societies, claims that every society is a moral society, and that individuals today have as strong a sentiment of dependence on society as in past ages, he is foreshadowing a common theme in the recent literature on the ethnic revival in the West.[52] This is that the sense of ethnic community has not been eroded by modernization or social mobilization; on the contrary, it has, if anything, been strengthened, and men and women today still require the sense of belonging and the shared sentiments of earlier, small-scale communities.[53]

In one sense, Durkheim's account of the survival of the sense of community falls short of recent accounts: it lacks a specifically historical and comparative character, and has an almost timeless quality. But this defect is compensated for by the depth of his analysis of the roots of community and identity, the third aspect of his conception of the collective conscience. For Durkheim, the content of traditional beliefs and sentiments was religious; it embodied a system of beliefs and practices or rites, relative to sacred and profane things, and was renewed constantly by the group constituted as worshippers. Now Durkheim goes on to claim that, even in modern times, though science may erode traditional beliefs, yet 'religion' in the broad sense remains at the heart of any community. Similarly, modern societies need rites; for '. . . before all, rites are means by which the social group reaffirms itself periodically'.[54] Modern societies, too, need this periodic regeneration; Durkheim twice cites the patriotic fervour of the French Revolution (in *The Elementary Forms of the Religious Life*) as an example of society setting itself up as a god, or creating its own gods:

> At this time, in fact [he continues] under the influence of the general enthusiasm, things purely laical in nature were transformed by public opinion into sacred things: these were the Fatherland, Liberty, Reason. A religion tended to become established which had its dogmas, symbols, altars and feasts.[55]

And he goes on to argue that there is no real difference between Christian or Jewish festivals, and a 'reunion of citizens commemorating the promulgation of a new moral or legal system or some great event in the national life'.[56] Durkheim claims that 'there is something eternal in religion' which will survive all changes in symbolism, because 'There can be no society which does not feel the need of upholding and reaffirming at regular intervals the collective sentiments and the collective ideas which make its unity and its personality.'[57] And it is only through assemblies and reunions of citizens that this 'moral remaking' can be achieved, since they alone allow men to reaffirm their common sentiments.

In many ways, Durkheim's analysis fits the case of nations and nationalism rather better than the often supernatural religions he sought to encompass.[58] When Durkheim, for example, argues that 'before all else, a faith is warmth, life, enthusiasm, the exaltation of the whole mental life, the raising of the individual above himself',[59] and that a society is above all 'the idea which it forms of itself', his ideas bear directly on the functions of nationalism for an ethnic community conscious of its identity. Moreover, his detailed discussion of symbols of totemic religion can be applied with far less strain to the symbolism of the nation; in fact, his analogy of the soldier dying for his flag rather than his country, because sight of the flag rekindles his collective emotions, fits his thesis far more naturally than does the case of totemic symbols.[60] Moreover, in later life, his belief in the need for new social gospels and rites also focused on patriotism, in order to cement professional groups and give warmth and a greater feeling of proximity to an otherwise remote state. National regeneration, along with professional ethics, was required to combat excessive individualism and the anomie of modern industrial societies.[61]

Lacking an adequate sociology of specific cultures and of politics, however, Durkheim stopped short of applying his ideas directly to modern nations and their secular faiths. Nor was he able to give an account of the genesis of nations and nationalism; his wholly 'internal' analysis addresses itself to the functions of collective symbolism, ritual and ideals. It has been left to recent theorists like Ernest Gellner to take up some of his suggestions – notably those about anomie and the decline of tradition – and formulate new hypotheses about the role of communication and culture in creating nations and nationalism.[62]

3 Conflict approaches Some of the omissions of the communitarian approaches are made good in the third main sociological perspective, with its emphasis on social and political conflict. In fact Simmel sees in conflict itself a prime cause of social cohesion. Enmity sharpens group boundaries and mobilizes the members of a group, so that they become aware of their ethnic or national unity; he cites the cases of France, Spain, the USA, Holland and Switzerland, among others, as examples of nations achieving unity and identity only through wars with outside powers which threatened their existence.[63] On a more general level, competition and conflict represent for Simmel essential elements in the process by which individuals are bound together; their conflicting interests and values ensure a high level of social interaction.[64]

Conflict is also regarded by Max Weber as a necessary and universal attribute of social life. Only with Weber it is predominantly the conflict of irreconcilable and unique values, because man is ultimately a cultural being, that is, a bearer of specific values.[65] In choosing and bearing some values, he automatically excludes, or denies, others. Life, for Weber, 'knows only of an unceasing struggle of these (sc. Olympian) gods with one another. Or speaking directly, the ultimately possible attitudes towards life are irreconcilable, and hence their struggle can never be brought to a final conclusion. Thus it is necessary to make a decisive choice.'[66] This is true not only for individuals, but also for groups; they too become bearers of specific values, they too choose certain values and thereby compete with others. The natural locus for the cultural values of the group is a nation; its culture, as conveyed in its art, literature, manners, beliefs and character, endows the nation with its individuality (*Eigenart*), and 'The significance of the "nation" is usually anchored in the superiority, or at least irreplaceability, of the culture values that can only be preserved and developed through the cultivation of the individuality (*Eigenart*) of the community.'[67]

Whence springs this cultural individuality? Weber reviews in turn many possible sources: physical type, common religion, shared customs, above all, community of language. Any or all of these may become 'culture values' for the members of the ethnic or national community, but none of them alone suffices to define a 'nation', and none constitutes a necessary condition of the sense of nationality. In each case, the transition from an ethnic or culture group to a 'nation' requires political action, often of a military nature. Both the Swiss and the Alsatians illustrate the insufficiency of language; in both cases, the sense of common and unique customs derives from shared political and military memories. Of the latter, Weber has this to say:

Many German-speaking Alsatians feel a sense of community with the French because they share certain customs and some of their 'sensual culture' (*Sinnenkultur*) . . . and also because of common political experiences. This can be understood by any visitor who walks through the museum in Colmar, which is rich in relics such as tricolors, *pompier* and military helmets, edicts by Louis Philippe and especially memorabilia from the French Revolution; these may appear trivial to the outsider, but they have sentimental value for the Alsatians. This sense of community came into being by virtue of common political and, indirectly, social experiences which are highly valued by the masses as symbols of the destruction of feudalism, and the story of these events takes the place of the heroic legends of primitive peoples.[68]

More generally, Weber regards the political community and political action as the primary inspiration and basis for the 'belief in common ethnicity', which in turn always rests on a sense of common origins. This belief in common descent, along with shared customs, underlies the notions of both ethnicity and 'nation', and, says Weber, 'All history shows how easily political action can give rise to the belief in blood relationship, unless gross differences of anthropological type impede it'.[69]

But the 'nation' is something more than a belief in common descent and shared customs, or ethnicity. The concept of the 'nation' means, above all, 'that one may exact from certain groups of men a specific sentiment of solidarity in the face of other groups'.[70] But this is still rather vague, and Weber ultimately places the idea of the nation in the realm of politics. 'A nation', he writes, 'is a community of sentiment which would adequately manifest itself in a state of its own; hence, a nation is a community which normally tends to produce a state of its own.'[71] This tendency towards autonomous statehood distinguishes 'nations' from other communities with sentiments of solidarity; but it does not explain why this political type of community, the 'nation', should emerge and become the norm for legitimating states in the modern world.

It is clear that Weber, a strong German nationalist himself, accepted the nation as a prime cultural value, a collective manifestation of his heroic commitment to pluralism and individualism; at the same time, this ready acceptance may have deflected his attention away from trying to deal with the many problems raised by the advent of nations and nationalism.[72] Notes on the relevant chapter of the third part of *Economy and Society* indicate that Weber intended to deal with the idea and development of the national state in history. As things stand, Weber's all too brief contributions touch on many important aspects of nationalism, like the key role of political memories, the intelligentsia and the national mission, but they only indicate his basic 'political' approach.[73] This comes out most forcefully in his discussion of the close relationship between the very different ideas of nation and state. Weber sees the nation as a community, while the state is a rational association; both however need each other in the modern world, for the state, as a power-based entity, requires the legitimation and direction of the nation for its popular support, while the nation requires the state to protect its unique cultural values in the general struggle of value-bearing communities. And similarly, the bearers of the concept of the state like bureaucrats and officers, and the artists, teachers and writers who are the 'specific bearers of culture and the idea of the nation', need each other, despite their competing claims.[74] Only a state can ensure the survival of the many cultural values unique to nations, large and small, that Weber so approved of as a guarantee against the soulless and mechanical rationalization which threatened to engulf the world.[75]

Beyond the Sociology of Nationalism

This brief discussion of the main sociological perspectives on nationalism gives some idea of both their strengths and limitations. Weber's contributions, especially, reveal something of the range of problems raised by a study of nationalism – in defining clearly the objects of investigation, in uncovering the sources of cultural identity and community 'internally', and in providing a broad 'external' comparative framework for causal explanation. But they remain too fragmentary to provide a coherent account, which can match the 'internal' and 'external' requirements convincingly. And he has had no successor, at least among sociologists. Those that have recently turned their attention to the topic have generally failed to give due attention to the inner springs of identity, and especially the historical roots of communal sentiments; so their schemas are difficult to apply to individual cases. Nor have they followed Weber's recommendation to tie the analysis of nations and nationalism closely to that of the state and its military and bureaucratic needs. Their work, therefore, often lacks a genuine political dimension – an obvious failing in the case of such a politically saturated phenomenon as nationalism. This is particularly true of the many sociologists who have been influenced by communitarian approaches and by functionalism; modernization theories like those of Deutsch, Lerner and Gellner make very little reference to the central role of the modern bureaucratic state.[76] Besides, the sociology of nationalism, such as it is, suffers from a more general failure to evolve a convincing sociology of culture – despite the considerable work of men like Karl Mannheim, Edward Shils and Ernest Gellner. Most theorists concede the central role of culture values in nationalism, and of the intelligentsia as their bearers and disseminators. And many case studies document that role.[77] Yet, only rarely has it been accorded its due in any general approach or theory of nationalism.

Even an 'underlabourer' conception of the tasks of a sociology of nationalism would, therefore, have to consider at least four main areas for further analytic enquiry. These are:

1   the social composition, and mobility profiles, of both the leadership and
    the followers of nationalist movements – a key topic on which data are
    either lacking, or unsystematized;[78]
2   the institutional foci of the formation of nations and the rise of nation-
    alism – such as armies, churches, universities and the bureaucracy – as
    well as the question of urban versus rural, and traditional versus secular,
    bases;[79]
3   the main patterns of communication and integration of social units,
    especially their settlement patterns, defence networks, trade flows and
    language clusters, which underpin a community's individuality and
    unity, as Deutsch and his school have shown;[80]
4   the social origins and functions of national symbols, myths and
    traditions, their uses by nationalist leaders to attract a mass base and
    effect political change, and their inner meanings for the respective
    participants.[81]

Each of these areas – as well as the material and ideal interests of each
community and its strata – has received some attention; and each can be
illuminated by the general classical approaches within sociology that I
have enumerated. Yet much more remains to be done, both in basic analysis and in subsequent synthesis.

Even more needs to be done, if we opt for a more ambitious conception of the role of any sociology of nationalism. But a truly synthetic
approach, which aims at higher-level theory, must forsake the normal dis-
ciplinary confines of sociology (indeed of any academic discipline) and
forge links with research in neighbouring disciplines. Inevitably, with a
subject which has so many aspects and ramifications, and which straddles
so many disciplines and lines of enquiry, a sociology of nationalism that
eschews other aspects must be partial and misleading. It was this point that
the conflict approach most clearly grasped. You cannot study a given
nationalism or nation in isolation from others; for nationalisms, like
nations, are born out of the interplay and conflict with each other and with
other exogenous factors. A sociology of nationalism will need to look
more closely at the findings of anthropology if it is to grasp the nature of
ethnic identities in town and country, the uses of ethnic symbolism, or the
interplay of competing ethnic loyalties; and turn to political science to
understand the relations between states and nations, between different
nations in multinational states, or competing ideologies within plural
states. In both cases, it will thereby strengthen its own 'internal' and 'external' accounts of nationalism. Similarly, by looking to the historians for
their periodization of the growth of nations in the modern world, and for
discrepancies between an actual historical record of any community and

its nationalist leaders' versions or popular myths of that history, the sociologist is able to ground his own perspective more strongly in a given temporal milieu and in individual cases of nationalisms. Finally, to create a broader 'external' framework in which to locate his investigations, the sociologist must take up the challenge of the whole interstate system in which nations have been formed and inserted – together with the associated problems of nuclear stalemate, foreign policy, regional conflict and sovereignty and dependency studied by researchers in international relations.

It is perhaps in this last respect that a sociology of nationalism is most deficient. There is very little in the way of a systematic sociology of international relations; even the topic of warfare has merited less attention than it deserves. Sociologists make little attempt to work 'outwards' from social to geopolitical facets; and conversely, hardly ever think it necessary or worthwhile to work 'inwards' from the global interstate system to the rise of nations or nationalism, either in general or in specific cases. It may, of course, be claimed that that would go far beyond a sociology of nationalism; if so, then an adequate approach to a subject like nationalism must transgress academic frontiers and recognize the limitations of classical sociology in this important respect. But, as with the sociology of underdevelopment, so with that of nationalism; both require a global context, and both can only be grasped within the framework of a much broader perspective.[82]

Notes

1   On the contemporary phase of sociology, cf. H. Martins, 'Time and theory in sociology', in J. Rex (ed.), *Approaches to Sociology* (London: Routledge & Kegan Paul, 1974).

2   Most eighteenth-century writers accepted the *fact* of nation-states and nationality, even if many deplored it, as shown in the survey by A. Kemilainen, *Nationalism: Problems Concerning the Word, Concept and Classification* (Yvaskyla: Kustantajat Publishers, 1964).

3   R. Aron, *Main Currents in Sociological Thought* (Harmondsworth: Penguin, 1968), on 'Montesquieu'.

4   D. Hume, *Of National Characters* (1748), cited in P. Gay, *The Enlightenment: An Interpretation* (London: Weidenfeld & Nicolson, 1970), vol. 2, p. 329.

5   D. de C., Baron de Montesquieu, *The Spirit of the Laws*, trans. T. Nugent (New York and London, 1966), book 19; and Aron, *Main Currents*, pp. 45–6, who finds in this book a 'synthetic conception of society', with a preliminary attempt to relate various moral and material causes of the 'general spirit of nations'.

6   Adam Ferguson, *Principles of Moral and Political Science*, 2 vols, cited by W. C. Lehmann, *Adam Ferguson and the Beginnings of Modern Sociology* (New York: Columbia University Press, 1930), p. 75.

7   Adam Ferguson, *Essay on the History of Civil Society* (1767), p. 343, cited in D. Kettler, *The Social and Political Thought of Adam Ferguson* (Ohio State University Press, 1965), p. 209, also pp. 88–91, 287; also Gay, *Enlightenment*, pp. 336–43.

8   Aron, *Main Currents*, p. 56; and Gay, *Enlightenment*, pp. 339–40.

9   On Rousseau's nationalism and remarks on the Jews and Corsicans, see S. Baron, *Modern Nationalism and Religion* (New York: Meridian Books, 1960), pp. 24–9; and A. Cohler, *Rousseau and Nationalism* (New York and London: Basic Books, 1970).

10 J.-J. Rousseau, *Political Writings of Rousseau*, ed. C. E. Vaughan (Cambridge: Cambridge University Press, 1915), vol. 2, p. 431; Gay, *Enlightenment*, pp. 532–3.

11 I. Berlin, *Vico and Herder* (London: Hogarth Press, 1976).

12 Ibid., p. 182; and F. Barnard, *Herder's Social and Political Thought* (Oxford: Clarendon Press, 1965).

13 On these revolutions and their consequences for social thought, cf. R. Nisbet, *The Sociological Tradition* (London: Heinemann, 1966).

14 On this, see Gouldner's Introduction to E. Durkheim, *Socialism and St Simon* (New York: Collier Books, 1962).

15 Some of these schemes are discussed by J. Burrow, *Evolution and Society* (Cambridge: Cambridge University Press, 1966), and R. Nisbet, *Social Change and History* (Oxford: Oxford University Press, 1969).

16 See the critique by Avineri in S. Avineri (ed.), *Karl Marx on Colonialism and Modernization* (New York: Anchor Books, 1969), Introduction.

17 R. Rosdolsky, 'Friedrich Engels und das Problem der "Geschichtsloser Völker"', *Archiv für Sozialgeschichte* 4 (1964), pp. 87–282, assesses the influence of Hegel's ideas on Engels' outlook.

18 G. Hegel, *Ideas towards a Philosophy of History of Mankind* (1785), cited by V. R. Mehta, *Hegel and the Modern State* (New Delhi: Associated Publishing House, 1986), p. 83.

19 G. Hegel, *Philosophy of Right* (1821), sec. 324, cited in Mehta, *Hegel and the Modern State*, p. 87.

20 W. B. Gallie, *Philosophers of Peace and War* (Cambridge: Cambridge University Press, 1978), ch. 4, esp. pp. 75–9.

21 Rosdolsky, 'Friedrich Engels'; and H. B. Davis, *Nationalism and Socialism* (New York and London: Monthly Review Press, 1967), chs 1–3.

22 I. Cummins, *Marx, Engels and National Movements* (London: Croom Helm, 1980). Cummins also shows how this bias affected their judgement of non-European developments, and how it was partly a result of their fear of an absolutist and reactionary Tsarism.

23 This and other remarks on nationalism, scattered throughout Marx's and Engels' writings, are collected and analysed by Davis, *Nationalism and Socialism* and Cummins, *Marx Engels, passim*.

24 V. Lenin, *Theses on the National and Colonial Questions* (1920), collected in *Lenin on the National and Colonial Questions* (Peking: Foreign Language Press, 1967).

25 J. Stalin, *Marxism and the National and Colonial Question* (London: Lawrence & Wishart, 1936).

26 O. Bauer, *Die Nationalitätenfrage und die Sozialdemokratie*, 2nd edn (Vienna: Brand, 1924), p. 135.

27 See the criticism in K. Deutsch, *Nationalism and Social Communication*, 2nd edn (Cambridge, MA: MIT Press, 1966), pp. 19–20.

28 H. S. Hughes, *Consciousness and Society* (London: MacGibbon & Kee, 1959).

29 T. Parsons, *Essays in Sociological Theory* (New York: Free Press, 1964), chs 6–7.

30 L. Wirth, 'Types of nationalism', *American Journal of Sociology* 41 (1936), pp. 723–37.

31 T. Parsons, 'Some theoretical considerations on the nature and trends of change of ethnicity', in N. Glazer and D. Moynihan (eds), *Ethnicity: Theory and Experience* (Cambridge, MA: Harvard University Press, 1975), 53–83.

32 Cf. nn. 36 and 46 below; and G. Almond and J. Coleman, *The Politics of the Developing Areas* (Princeton: Princeton University Press, 1960); and N. Smelser, *Theory of Collective Behaviour* (London: Routledge & Kegan Paul, 1962).

33 Conflict theory remained wedded to class and authority issues, but L. Coser, *The Functions of Social Conflict* (London: Routledge & Kegan Paul, 1956), does take up Simmel's concern with cohesion through social strife.

34 Deutsch, *Nationalism and Social Communication*; pp. 141–74; Bell's essay in Glazer and Moynihan, *Ethnicity*; C. Enloe, *Ethnic Soldiers* (Harmondsworth: Penguin, 1980).

35 H. Gerth and C. Mills (eds), *From Max Weber* (London: Routledge & Kegan Paul, 1948), pp. 175–6.

36 Notably in the work of recent 'neo-evolutionists' like Smelser and Eisenstadt and Levy; cf. S. N. Eisenstadt (ed.), *Readings in Social Evolution and Development* (Oxford and London: Pergamon Press, 1970).

37 E. K. Scheuch, 'Cross-national comparisons with aggregate data', in R. Merritt and S. Rokkan (eds), *Comparing Nations* (New Haven: Yale University Press, 1966).

38 On their approaches, cf. A. D. Smith, *The Concept of Social Change* (London and Boston: Routledge & Kegan Paul, 1973).

39 Deutsch, *Nationalism and Social Communication*.

40 M. Hechter, *Internal Colonialism* (London: Routledge & Kegan Paul, 1975); T. Nairn, *The Break-up of Britain* (London: New Left Books, 1977).

41 For a discussion of this, cf. Nisbet, *Social Change and History*.

42 A. Cobban, *Rousseau and the Modern State*, 2nd edn (London: Allen & Unwin, 1964).

43 On this tradition, cf. R. Weiss, *Conservatism in Europe, 1770–1945* (London: Thames & Hudson, 1977).

44 Cf. the analysis of de Maistre in I. Berlin, 'The hedgehog and the fox' in *idem, Russian Thinkers* (London: Hogarth Press, 1978).

45 E. Shils, *Political Development in the New States* (New York: Humanities Press, 1964); D. Apter, 'Political religion in the new nations', in C. Geertz (ed.), *Old Societies and New States* (New York: Free Press, 1963).

46 L. Binder, *The Ideological Revolution in the Middle East* (New York: Wiley, 1964); and D. Apter, *Ghana in Transition*, rev. edn (New York: Athenaeum, 1963).

47 M. Weber, *The Methodology of the Social Sciences*, ed. E. Shils (New York: Free Press, 1949).

48 Coming from Lorraine and a Jewish community, he could hardly be unaware of the problem; cf. S. Lukes, *Emile Durkheim: His Life and Work* (New York: Harper & Row, 1972).

49 On which, cf. A. Giddens, *Capitalism and Modern Social Theory* (Cambridge: Cambridge University Press, 1971), ch. 5.

50 E. Durkheim, *The Division of Labour in Society*, trans. G. Simpson (New York: Free Press, 1964), p. 278.

51 Ibid., p. 291.

52 Ibid., pp. 228, 398.

53 Cf. M. Esman (ed.), *Ethnic Conflict in the Western World* (Ithaca, NY: Cornell University Press, 1977), *passim*.

54 E. Durkheim, *The Elementary Forms of the Religious Life*, trans. J. Swain (London: Allen & Unwin, 1964), p. 387.

55 Ibid., p. 214.

56 Ibid., p. 427.

57 Ibid.

58 On the difficulties of Durkheimian and functional definitions of religion, cf. M. Spiro, 'Religion: problems of definition and explanation', in M. Banton (ed.), *Anthropological Approaches to the Study of Religion* (London: Tavistock, 1966).

59 Durkheim, *Elementary Forms*, p. 425.

60 Ibid., p. 220.

61 E. Durkheim, *Professional Ethics and Civic Morals* (New York: Free Press, 1958).

62 E. Gellner, *Thought and Change* (London: Weidenfeld & Nicolson, 1964), ch. 7.

63 G. Simmel, *Conflict and the Web of Group Affiliations* (Gleucse, IL: Free Press, 1964), esp. p. 100.

64 Ibid., esp. pp. 88 ff.

65 Weber, *Methodology of the Social Sciences*, p. 81.

66 Gerth and Mills (eds), *From Max Weber*, p. 152 (Science as a Vocation).

67 M. Weber, *Economy and Society*, trans. G. Roth and C. Wittich (New York: Bedminster Press, 1968), pt III, ch. 3, p. 926.

68 Ibid., pt I/2, ch. 5, p. 396.

69 Ibid., p. 393.

70 Gerth and Mills (eds), *From Max Weber*, p. 172.

71   Ibid., p. 176.
72   Cf. the discussion in D. Beetham, *Max Weber and the Theory of Modern Politics* (London: Allen & Unwin, 1974), ch. 5.
73   Cf. Gerth and Mills (eds), *From Max Weber*, pp. 171–9, 448, n. 6; also Weber, *Economy and Society*, pt I/2, ch. 5.
74   Gerth and Mills (eds.), *From Max Weber*, p. 176.
75   On rationalization, cf. ibid., Introduction; D. Wrong (ed.), *Max Weber* (Englewood Cliffs, NJ: Prentice-Hall, 1970).
76   On this, cf. A. D. Smith, *Theories of Nationalism* (London: Duckworth, 1971), chs 5–6, 10.
77   Cf. the essays by Shils, Benda and Matossian and J. H. Kautsky in J. H. Kautsky (ed.), *Political Change in Underdeveloped Countries* (New York: John Wiley, 1962); P. C. Lloyd (ed.), *The New Elites of Tropical Africa* (London: Oxford University Press, 1966); and some essays in I. Wallerstein (ed.), *Social Change: The Colonial Situation* (New York: John Wiley, 1966).
78   Cf., e.g., W. Bell (ed.), *The Democratic Revolution in the West Indies* (Cambridge, MA: Schenkman Publishing Co., 1967).
79   Cf. M. Halpern, *The Politics of Social Change in the Middle East and North Africa* (Princeton: Princeton University Press, 1963); L. Tivey (ed.), *The Nation-State* (Oxford: Martin Robertson, 1980).
80   Cf. C. Tilley (ed.), *The Formation of National States in Western Europe* (Princeton: Princeton University Press, 1975).
81   Cf. D. Taylor and M. Yapp (eds), *Political Identity in South Asia* (London: SOAS, Curzon Press, 1979).
82   I am grateful to Dr N. Mouzelis for his comments on an earlier draft of this paper.

Part II

History

5

Were there 'Nations' in Antiquity?

In Part I, I examined the theoretical bases of various forms of modernism and their failure to give due weight to the antiquity of nations. I turn now to some of the more concrete issues of nationhood and ethnicity, which reveal the historical and sociological rootedness and antiquity of certain aspects of nationhood. I start by asking whether we can speak of 'nations' in the ancient world.

Did the ancient Egyptians constitute a 'nation', and was ancient Egypt an early form of 'nation-state'? This question, rarely raised by Egyptologists, let alone by modern historians and social scientists schooled in the post-war modernist orthodoxy of the study of nations and nationalism, is, nevertheless, one that is worth posing for the questions of conceptualization and comparison that it raises: that is, the problem of the nature of our conceptual categories of human community and identity, and their historical and sociological applicability. Certainly, it is in that spirit that the question is posed here.

Nevertheless, we do well to start with the case in hand, because of its special features. After all, the designation 'ancient Egypt' refers to a population subsisting over at least 3,000 years in a particular location, one that possessed a collective proper name and self-definition, and whose territory, at once compact and straggling on both banks of the Nile, known to the inhabitants as *Kemet*, the 'Black Land', undoubtedly helped to preserve the special character of an Egyptian culture and religion, despite periodic incursions of neighbours from south and east. Add to this the uniqueness of language and of hieroglyphic script, the distinctive repertoire of myths, symbols and memories, and the peculiar position of the head of the Great House, or Pharaoh, as god-king on earth, who, together with a centralized bureaucracy ruled most of Egypt from a single place for long periods of time, and a *prima facie* case for embryonic nationhood becomes apparent. But, in what sense of nationhood? Can it be useful to compare an ancient Egyptian nation with a modern French or Polish nation? And, if so, in what respects? And why does it matter?[1]

The problem is not simply the vexed question of definition, though that is part of it. Nor simply of the status of particular theories: in this case, the various versions of the modernist paradigm of nations and nationalism, discussed in Part I, which tend to rule out the possibility of nations existing before nationalism, and of nations before modernity. More important, the question about Egypt forces us to enquire into the nature of forms of human community and categories of association that are cross-cultural and cross-temporal, and raises the problem of whether we can and should speak of different types or forms of the concept of the nation. That is why an examination of the evidence for the existence of a concept of nation, and of the corresponding form of collective cultural identity, in the ancient world, is pertinent.

In what follows, I shall concentrate on the question of the presence or absence of nations in antiquity. I shall not address questions of ethnic or national continuity beyond late antiquity; nor will I deal with the ideology of nationalism itself (see Chapter 9 below). My view on this latter issue is the opposite of the late Adrian Hastings's thesis. Nationalism, he argued, is a reaction of a nation under threat, and as such can be found long before modernity – among the later Anglo-Saxons, for example. The theory of the nation may be modern, he concedes, but theory is unimportant. I take the view that, though nationalism is more than a theory or even an ideology, it is a modern phenomenon, emerging in the eighteenth century and coming to fruition under the aegis of Romanticism's cult of authenticity. What Hastings terms 'nationalism', I regard as a more or less fervent 'national sentiment', and hence always particularistic, even solipsist; whereas modern nationalism is, by definition, universalistic as well, since in its perceptions there are always other nations.[2]

The Western Model and its Uses

If nationalism is at one level a modern ideology and movement which marries ethno-cultural unity to popular sovereignty in an ancestral homeland, what of the nation whose cause it seeks to promote? The nation, surely, is also modern, a territorial and legal community of participant citizens with membership by birth and residence and a distinctive public culture. Indeed, in the modernist paradigm, there can be no nations before nationalism because they are creations of nationalists and the state. In Eric Hobsbawm's words: 'Nations do not make states and nationalisms but the other way round.'[3]

It is worth spelling out the features of the modern nation in more detail, in order to clarify the differences between it and comparable pre-modern collective cultural identities. In this widely held view, the nation refers to an ideal-type of a named human community with the following features.

1 The nation is a geographically bounded community, with clear and recognized borders, within which the members reside, and with a clear centre of authority.
2 The nation is a legal community: that is, its members have common rights and duties as members under a single law code.
3 As a result, the nation is a mass participant community, with all classes participating in politics and society.
4 The culture of the nation is equally a mass, public culture, with culturally distinctive elements inculcated through mass educational institutions.
5 The nation is an autonomous community, and the members are accordingly citizens of a national state.
6 The nation and its state are part of a wider inter-national system of national states, of which they are sovereign members.
7 The nation is a human community that owes its conception and legitimation to nationalism, the ideology.

Of course, individual cases differ in certain respects from this ideal-type, to which they approximate; but the above provides a summary of the main features of the concept of a nation as a modern phenomenon.

Now, measured against the yardstick of this ideal-type, ancient Egypt clearly fails to qualify as a nation. Not only does it lack many of the features of the ideal-type nation, it also exhibits features that are not part of that type – for example, a theocratic and dynastic ideology in place of nationalism. It lacks legal rights and duties common to all members of ancient Egyptian society, since they were specific to particular classes, and we cannot speak of mass participation of all classes except in the corvée and army. Egyptian culture, albeit quite distinctive and very public, could hardly be described as a mass culture and education system, and though there were diplomatic relations with other states, certainly at the time of the New Kingdom, it is doubtful how far we can speak of political membership in an 'international system,' even in the Tell-el-Amarna epoch of the second millennium BC.[4]

The same might be said of the ancient Persians. It is true that the Persians had a clear sense of themselves as a distinct community of language and religion, as much as did the Egyptian elites, and that on the staircase of the Apadana in Persepolis we may still see the sculptured reliefs of various peoples of their empire bearing gifts for the Persian New Year. But the Persians too were class-divided; there was no sense of popular participation in politics, no common rights and duties for all Persians, and no nationalist legitimation. Nor is it clear where the borders of the community ran, both before and after the acquisition of an empire by the Achaemenids, even after their migration from the Iranian plateau.[5]

Much the same can be said about the Hittites and other peoples of antiquity. True, the Old Kingdom of the Hittite nobles had its centre in the bend of the Halys river, and Hittite kings consulted a *pankush*, or assembly of notables; but this is hardly evidence of common rights and duties, let alone of mass participation. As with many other early peoples of the ancient Near East like the Elamites or the Kassites, the record is insufficient to allow any inference about the intensity or diffusion of a sense of collective cultural identity beyond a very small ruling class. There is slightly more evidence for the sentiments and conduct of city-states like those of the Sumerians, Phoenicians and Philistines, but earlier theories of a primitive form of Sumerian democracy seem to have been misplaced, and the fierce rivalries of many of these city-states seem to have prevented any attempt or even desire to give unitary political expression to their sense of common ethnicity based on myths of common origin, language and customs, though Nippur did serve as a religious centre for the Sumerians, and the Philistine lords did manage to field joint armies against external foes.[6]

I shall not run through the gamut of possible candidates for nationhood in the ancient world, but it would hardly do to omit from this preliminary survey those peoples whose legacies to medieval and modern Europe, and hence to nationalism, are so well recorded. In dismissing the idea that ancient Greece constituted a nation, Moses Finley made use of the familiar distinction advanced by Friedrich Meinecke between a *Staatsnation* and a *Kulturnation*, a distinction that made sense in nineteenth-century Germany. Only there, unlike in Greece (unless you consider Bismarck's Prussia the analogue of Philip's Macedon), many of the German-speaking principalities did in the end manage to unite and become a *Staatsnation*. In ancient Greece, the pan-Hellenic dreams entertained by a small minority around Isocrates continually stumbled on the rock of loyalties to the *polis*, with the result that cultural identity centred on Hellas or its ethnolinguistic subdivisions (Ionians, Dorians, Aeolians, etc.) remained, for the most part, apolitical. Of course, most Greeks did recognize that there was a political dimension to Hellas; Pericles' Funeral Oration can be read, *inter alia*, as an Athenian bid for political as well as cultural leadership of 'all-Greece'. But, even under dire Persian threat, some *poleis* medized; and if Edith Hall is right, the idea of Hellas really only gained currency as a result of the Persian Wars.[7]

On the other side, a marked sense of Greek cultural unity encompassed many spheres. Greece could clearly be described as a cultural network of activities and institutions linked by its distinctive religious rites centred on the Olympian pantheon under Zeus. Its city-states were closely connected through a distinctive Greek language-group, the pioneering forms of its vernacular literature, its recurring festivals and Games reserved for Greeks, its colonies with their ties to the motherland, its own calendars, customs, architectural styles and art, however much was owed to earlier civilizations in the East. All of this combined to delimit Greek culture and society sharply from those of its neighbours and instil in Greeks a sense of cultural superiority, even disdain, to non-Greek-speaking *barbaroi* outside the homeland.[8]

So, in terms of the ideal-type, with its strong emphasis on political power, ancient Greece may not qualify as a nation. It never produced a single centre of authority, nor a unifying law code, only customary rights, for all Greeks. But it clearly approximates to another ideal-type, that of the *ethnie*. By an *ethnie*, I mean a named human community whose members share common myths of ancestry and memories, elements of common culture, and some measure of solidarity, at least among the elites. The shared memories often include a link with a specific territory. The poems of Homer and Hesiod provided the Greeks with both their ancestry myths and their shared quasi-historical memories, as well as a territorial location for heroic exploits. Moreover, despite many local variations and dialectal and cultural subdivisions with political overtones, Greeks also shared many religious and linguistic elements of culture, and in many cases a sense of common ethnic and cultural identity as Hellenes.[9]

If Hellas cannot be described as a nation, what about the *polis* itself, especially the larger *poleis* to which the members were so fervently devoted? Recently, this very case has been argued for ancient Athens. Athens, argues Edwin Cohen, following Aristotle, is a clear example of a nation on account of its extent across Attica and the size of its population. Though political rights were confined to an elite, the really important social status was that of the *astos*, or resident, which was open to women and metics. Hence we have a much greater level of social participation in a clearly demarcated territory, allied to a strong sense of Athenian patriotism and a set of fifth-century myths about native kings and autochthonous ancestors, fabricated in true constructionist style. But, as Cohen fails to supply a clear definition of the concept of nation, and hardly addresses

ethnic and cultural dimensions, the argument lacks conviction. Suffice it
to say that the Greeks did not distinguish *ethnies* from nations in their
language; that Athenian culture, like Athenian ancestry myths, was hardly
distinctive, being a variant of Ionian Greek culture and ethnicity; that Attic
borders were more permeable than Cohen suggests, and that participation and political rights were still carefully graded. Certainly, in terms of
the ideal-type, Athens could hardly qualify as a nation, though, like Sparta,
it might be taken as an exemplar of patriotic solidarity many centuries
later.[10]

It is not usual to find in ancient Rome the lineaments of nationhood, but
the patriotism exhibited, or remembered, from the time of Scipio and Cato,
in the face of the Carthaginian menace, and the imperial Roman mission
proclaimed by the *Aeneid* and in Augustus' circle, have prompted some
scholars to reconsider the question of the growth of a national identity in
late republican Rome. Erich Gruen, in particular, has focused attention on
the origins of the Aeneas legend as a new Roman foundation myth, whose
function it was to assert a specific Roman and Italian national identity
which, by selecting Greece's classical enemy as its forbear, was both part
of, and opposed to, the Greek cultural world. But, while in this instance
we are clearly dealing with an identity and ancestry myth that is both political and cultural, not to mention a distinctive, public culture, the absence
of clear borders for Rome, the narrow patrician circumscription of rights,
and the lack of an ideology of nationhood, all indicate that Rome and
Latium fail to conform to the ideal-type of the modern 'nation'.[11]

Which leaves the ancient Jews. Sometimes regarded as the prototype of
the nation, the ancient Judahites after the united monarchy and before the
Roman destruction of Jerusalem in AD 70 appear to possess many of the
attributes of nationhood. These include clearly laid down borders (from
Dan to Beersheba), common rights and duties for all males prescribed in
the Torah, a distinctive, public religious culture around the sabbath and
festivals, and in some periods a kingdom of their own existing in the
context of the regional interstate systems of the Near East – not to mention
a fierce belief in their own collective election and special mission.[12]

Yet, in terms of the above ideal-type, it is doubtful whether the ancient
Jews can be regarded as a nation. Though they enjoyed common rights and
duties, most Jewish males were excluded from political participation in the
Temple hierarchy, which was the key political and economic institution;
though we can at times speak of ancient Judea as a religious-political
and legal community, notably under Josiah and later again under the
Hasmoneans, and in a rather different way under Judah HaNasi and the
rabbis in the Talmudic epoch. Yet, even though the Jews did at various
time enjoy different degrees of political autonomy, it is difficult to discern
a specific nationalist ideology of a Jewish nation. The Maccabean upris-

ing was an offshoot of a religious and cultural struggle between Hellenizers and pious traditionalists; and, as for the oft-cited case of the Zealot minority and its war of liberation from Roman oppression, the assertion that the land belonged to the Judeans hinged on the prior religious belief that Eretz-Israel was the possession of God and hence could not be alienated to Caesar.[13]

Towards an Alternative Definition

It is exactly at this point that doubts creep in. We recall that Puritan beliefs about seventeenth-century Holland and England, and about God's chosen Englishmen and the Dutch New Israel, provided a launching pad for nationalist ideologies in the subsequent century. We have also been forcefully reminded recently of the religious revival in many lands and the spate of 'religious nationalisms'. This can hardly allow us to draw much comfort from the thought that secularism created a sharp dividing line in the eighteenth century and is intrinsic to the very definition of nationalism. At one level, nationalism may indeed be described as a secular ideology; but that hardly exhausts its multifaceted character, nor its persistent emotional appeal. The links between the modern ideology of nationalism and its sacred sources are more complex and obscure.[14]

But let us for the moment accept the argument that ancient Judea lacked any truly nationalist ideology of Eretz-Israel, and that there was little mass political participation or idea of citizenship among the Judeans under Alexander Jannaeus, let alone Herod. Does the absence of nationalist ideology and of mass political participation invalidate a claim to the status of nationhood – as opposed to that of ethnicity? And must we agree with Ernest Gellner that the ancient world has no trace of, and no place for, nations?[15]

That conclusion seems to be altogether too categorical and too neat. It assumes that the ideal-type I have delineated is a pure analytic construct, whereas it is clearly the product of a particular ideology and milieu. That ideology is a specific version of nationalism, the civic-territorial version, and the milieu is eighteenth- and nineteenth-century Western Europe. Hence, what we have right from the outset is not a general definition of the nation, but a partial one: a modern, Western, civic-territorial nationalist, ideal-type of the nation. There are three points to note about this particular definition. The first is the pivotal nature of one particular feature, that of mass participation. Nationalism, as Walker Connor repeatedly avers, is a mass phenomenon; it appeals to 'the people'. But so, he continues, is the nation. If that is the case, if we cannot speak of nations until the great majority of their populations participate in their political life, which in democracies means voting rights, then we cannot really describe them as nations until at least after the First World War, because women were only enfranchised in Europe and the USA after 1918. What then shall we call the societies of these states before that liberating dawn? Must we dismiss their national self-appellations as no more than wishful rhetoric? Can't people feel they belong to a 'nation' without participating in its political life? What, in this context, constitutes, a great majority? What of the many classes of second-class citizens, denizens, asylum-seekers, and the like? Shall we say that because a significant minority of the population fail to be given equal citizenship rights, we cannot describe the community as a nation?[16]

The second point is one we have touched on: namely, the very Western and Eurocentric nature of the civic-territorial nationalist version of the ideal-type of the nation. As Stein Tönnesson and Hans Antlöv have pointed out, in the introduction to their *Asian Forms of the Nation*, other, non-Western forms do not fit easily into this Western model. In the Asian cases of the nation, the emphasis falls less upon territory and residence, legal community, mass citizenship and civic culture, though these are important, than upon fictive genealogical ties, vernacular culture and religion, nativist history and popular mobilization. A similar theme has been developed by Yasir Suleiman, who has sought to show that Western conceptions of the nation do not square with Arabic ideas of an Arab nation, with its emphasis on high linguistic culture, Islam and classical Islamic history. The effect of such critiques is to underline the specificity of the modern Western nationalist model of the nation, both in time and place, and its lack of easy applicability outside that context.[17]

The final point is more controversial. But we cannot overlook the fact that concepts of the nation, like those of *ethnie*, have a long history of usage prior to its specific, modern nationalist meaning. I am thinking not so much of the ways in which the term *natio* was used to designate geographical subdivisions of medieval church councils and universities, but of its frequent use in Latin and vernacular European languages in the Middle Ages and early modern epoch, including in translations of the Bible. These purveyed the rough-and-ready division between *am* and *goyim* in the Hebrew Old Testament text, and of *laos* and *ethnē* in the Greek New Testament text to distinguish Jews and Christians from the Gentiles. This must alert us to the importance of the pre-nationalist history of usages of the concept to refer to certain pre-modern collective cultural identities, and this raises the possibility that some of these collectivities might be described as 'nations', at least in some sense of that elusive term.[18]

But, in what sense? Clearly, not in the sense demanded by the Eurocentric and nationalist ideal type of the nation, with all its biases and limitations. Can we perhaps frame a different ideal-type, one that is not embedded in nationalist ideology, and that might therefore be free of its Western limitations? If not, we are doomed forever to judge and measure every other cultural collectivity by the yardstick of a conception peculiar to a particular place and time, and find each and every case doubly lacking: first, in one or more of the features intrinsic to the time-specific ideal-type, and second, in the peculiar power and dynamism that the presence of these features ensures and which we associate with the concept of 'nation'. The result, as Bruce Routledge argues, is to create the past as an implicit or explicit 'mirror' of the present, that is, of Western modernity, usually by way of contrast, and fail to argue the case on its own merits and in its own context.[19]

I am more optimistic in this regard. I think we can, and should, try to offer different ideal-types of the nation, at least in some respects. What distinguishes them from the Western type is their dissociation from the world-view of nationalism; yet their features when combined produce a similarly powerful effect.

I start from the premiss that the nation, unlike the state, is a form of human community which is conceptually a development of the wider phenomenon of ethnicity, and that particular nations originated as specialized and politicized subvarieties of one or more ethnic categories, networks and communities (or *ethnies*). The latter, in turn, may have derived from smaller clan-based groupings, but by the time they become ethnic networks or communities, they have lost any earlier kinship elements, except in their myth of origin and descent. *Ethnies*, as we saw, approximate to the ideal-type of a named human community, with myths of common descent, shared memories and one or more elements of common culture such as language, religion and customs, and a sense of solidarity, at least among the elites. While they are often linked to specific territories, *ethnies* may, as diaspora communities attest, continue to function outside any homeland, and remain resilient over centuries.[20]

Though the concept of the nation shares certain elements with that of the *ethnie*, the emphasis falls elsewhere. For example, fictive descent myths play a much diminished role in nations, except in the nationalist rhetoric of blood and perhaps in times of extreme danger. Instead, nations are distinguished by a panoply of shared memories, myths, symbols and traditions, including foundation myths; but the cultivation of shared memories, myths and symbols is only one of the processes of nation formation that endow it with such power. Conversely, where a link with a given territory may have been present in the case of the *ethnie*, if only symbolically, that link turns into occupation and possession of a homeland and comes to occupy centre stage in the concept of the nation.[21]

Here, I can only briefly enumerate the main processes of nation formation, processes that constitute the elements of an alternative ideal-type
which, as the nation is a 'moving target', are better conceived as generic
processes of nation formation. They include:

1 the discovery and forging of a common self-image, including a collective proper name, which symbolizes 'us' as opposed to others around us;
2 the cultivation of distinctive shared memories, myths, symbols and
   traditions of the historic culture community formed on the basis of one
   or more ethnic categories and communities;
3 the occupation, residence in, and development of a common ancestral
   homeland with clear and recognized borders;
4 the creation and diffusion of a distinctive public culture for the members
   of the collectivity;
5 the observance of distinctive common customs and the framing of
   common laws for the members.

Of course, these processes vary in duration and extent, and their development can be reversed. Collective self-definition, myth-and-memory cultivation, territorialization of ancestral memory, creation and diffusion of
public culture, and development of law and custom; these are the essential processual elements of nation formation, and they are simultaneously
subjective and objective, a mixture of unplanned development and conscious intervention. Analytically separate, they develop historically in different ways and at varying rates, depending on a host of economic, political
and cultural circumstances. If and when they combine to an observable
extent, the result is the creation of what we term 'nations' out of pre-existing ethnic and cultural elements. Ideal-typically, then, a nation would be
a named and self-defined human community whose members cultivate
shared memories, myths and symbols, occupy and develop an ancestral
territory, create and spread among themselves a distinctive, public culture,
and observe common customs and are bound by common laws. It is to this
pure type that given instances of communities termed 'nations' (by
themselves or others) approximate.[22]

Nationalities and *Ethnies*

With this simpler, and more generic, ideal-typical definition of the nation,
let us return to the initial question of the relations between 'nations' and
the various kinds of collective cultural identity found in the ancient Near
East and the classical world.

Steven Grosby, in a series of stimulating articles now collected in a book entitled *Biblical Ideas of Nationality*, is concerned to distinguish the various types of cultural collectivities in the ancient world, including tribal confederations, city-states, empires and what he calls 'nationalities'. Though he does not supply a definition of this latter term, he finds that the three vital characteristics of national communities are: first, a stable spatial extent that is at once translocal and bounded, and possesses a clear centre; second, the presence of a single cult and pantheon headed by a supreme deity, with a common law for members; and third, a sense of collective self, of the unity of the collectivity against outsiders. Of course, there may be other features in the case of particular national collectivities; in fifth-century Armenia, for example, Grosby stresses the importance of a separate language and script for the demarcation and self-consciousness of the community. As for a myth of common origins and descent, Grosby concedes its importance, but argues that it derives from the belief in a bounded territory and in birth in that territory.[23]

It is clear from Grosby's account that nationalities are not simply cultural categories or ethnic networks, as in the case of Hellas. They are centres of what Herder called *Kraft*, combining what we would term 'political will' with cultural intimacy. Grosby supplies a primordialist explanation for their power: that people attribute to their national collectivity life-enhancing functions connected with the soil and its nurturing products. We need not follow him in this to recognize that in laying emphasis upon the widespread belief in the close connection of peoples with their ancestral lands and the 'god of the land', Grosby has drawn attention to a powerful nexus of beliefs and attachments in all epochs. Speaking of these beliefs, Grosby contends that 'The existence of the nation, whether ancient Israel or the modern nation-state, is predicated upon the existence of a collective consciousness constituted by a belief that there is a territory which belongs to only one people, and that there is a people which belongs to only one territory'[24]

Grosby attributes much importance to self-definition and self-assertion, and they are clearly vital elements of collective cultural identity. But we should be cautious about over-emphasizing collective self-affirmations, not only because voluntaristic definitions bring us close to Renan's 'daily plebiscite', but because they tell us little about the cultural collectivities that affirm themselves as nations, and which could in principle include other kinds of cultural collectivity, like city-states and tribal confederations. Hence the importance of his other characteristics, such as a growing attachment to a stable, bounded, translocal territory, and to a single cult, god and law code. To these, we should add the development of a distinctive public culture and education system, and the cultivation of a corpus of shared memories, myths, symbols and traditions peculiar to that group of people.

How far were these processes developed in the ancient Near East? And to what extent were they combined such that we may begin to speak of nations in antiquity? Grosby examines three such cases: Edom, Aram and Armenia. All three appear in our extant sources as translocal, bounded units. As regards the first, in the book of Numbers (20: 21), we read: 'Thus Edom refused to give Israel passage through his border', and a little later we meet the phrase (20: 23), 'at the border (*gebul*) of the land (*eres*) of Edom'; and much later Edom was conquered by the Hasmonean kings.[25]

It is also possible that Edom had become a monolatrous society under its local god, Qaush, by the late eighth century, as had Judah under Yahweh. But we know nothing of other relevant processes: no myths of origin or historical memories, no distinctive public culture or laws and customs, only references in the Hebrew Bible to *kol-Edom* (all Edom) and *edomi* (the Edomites).[26]

The case of Aram is more complex and intriguing. The treaties inscribed on the Sefire Stele of *c*.745 BC contain the following clauses:

> and the treaty of KTK with [the treaty of] Arpad; and the treaty of the lords of KTK with the treaty of the lords of Arpad; and the treaty of the un[ion of . . .]W with *all Aram* and with <the kings of> Musr and with his sons who will come after [him], and [with the kings of] *all Upper-Aram and Lower-Aram* and with all who enter the royal palace.[27]

After an involved discussion, Grosby concludes that, with the city-kingdom of Arpad at its head, Aram was in the process of nation formation:

> This common designation of 'Aram' in the terms 'all Aram', 'Upper Aram' and 'Lower Aram' would appear to indicate the developing sociological uniformity of a collective self-consciousness of a nation. An element of this uniformity may also be seen in the fact that Hadad appears to have become the leading god of the Aramean pantheon.[28]

This conclusion is supported by the wide diffusion of the Aramaean language throughout its city-kingdoms and a probable sense of common ethnicity, expressed in the very names of the Aramaean states: the Bible speaks of Aram-Naharaim, Aram-Zobah, Aram Beth-Rehob and Aram-Damascus, and Tiglath-Pileser III speaks (in Stele IIIA from Iran) of 'The kings of the land of Hatti (and of) the Aramaeans of the western seashore'.[29]

Do we have here another *Kulturnation*? Grosby is unhappy with the term, and with Benjamin Mazar's 'ethnic-territorial' collectivity, as neither term can distinguish between empire, nation and city-kingdom and their different territorial referents. But can we accept his own designation of 'all-Aram' as a 'nation'?[30]

My own preference here would be to treat the Aramaeans as a large-scale ethnic network, divided, in the manner of Hellas, into a series of rival, but culturally similar, city-kingdoms whose jurisdiction waxed and waned, as a result of intra-ethnic wars and of encounters with external powers, notably Assyria. In this, they conformed to a well-known pattern of development with a long history in the area, including the Phoenician, Philistine and Canaanite city-kingdoms whose members shared elements of culture like language and religion, but retained separate political identities. The isolation of this pattern allows us to discriminate between looser ethnic city-kingdoms and confederations with shared culture and more compact *ethnies* and ethnic-territorial kingdoms in which processes of nation formation begin to be visible, in which we can also observe the links between such ethnic networks and *ethnies*, on the one hand, and the formation of nations, on the other hand.[31]

Nation Formation in Antiquity

Steven Grosby's third example, Armenia in the fourth and fifth centuries AD, may help us to clarify the distinction and illuminate some of the processes involved.

The period commences with the conversion to Christianity of Trdat III and his family by Gregory around AD 314, and sees a remarkable flowering of religious activity, language reform, art and epic history writing. The self-definition of Armenia and Armenianness was no longer purely ethnic – stressing the myth of Haik and early Armenian migration – nor purely territorial-political – a relatively autonomous province of Achaemenid Persia and then Parthia, with a temporary period of greatness as an independent state under Tigranes the Great in the first century BC. Now the emphasis shifted to culture, and more specifically to the Gregorian version of Monophysite Christianity and the Armenian language, the latter soon to be reinforced by the invention in the fifth century of a separate script by Mesrop Mashtots both for internal cohesion and for external missionary purposes. Missionary activity in Iberia and Albania to the north by Gregory and his successors stimulated the parallel growth of the Georgian church and kingdom, and compensated in no small measure for the depressing political situation of Armenia, with the mountain kingdom being a regular battleground for Roman and Sasanid Persian armies. By 387, the Armenian kingdom had been partitioned, but this did not end the succession of revolts followed by repression or the constant need to invoke Roman Byzantine aid against the Sasanid threat.[32]

In many ways, Armenia possessed an orientalizing culture, much influenced by Persian Zoroastrianism, and her social structure mirrored that of Sasanid society. But, as Nina Garsoian points out, the conversion to Christianity, perceived as a Western, Roman religion, together with unbending Sasanid hostility, pushed Armenia towards Rome and the West, though never to the point of accepting the Chalcedonian position adopted by Byzantium in 451. The myth of Armenia as the 'first Christian nation', and in time the one truly Christian nation, became a source of pride for subsequent generations, as did its missionary record.[33]

Equally important for self-definition was the glorious defeat of Avarayr in the selfsame year of 451. In fact, the defeat was not comprehensive, and was one of a series of battles with the Sasanids, much like the battle of Kosovo Polje against the Ottomans. But, because like King Lazar, the Armenian commander, Vardan Mamikonian, and many nobles with him fell heroically on the field, it has been commemorated throughout the centuries as a saints' day, and has continued to inspire resistance in battle. Even more potently, it was quickly embedded in the collective historical memory retailed in the flowering of epic histories from the fifth to the eighth centuries, from the histories of Agat'angelos and Paustos Buzand to those of Elishe and Mouses Xorenatsi. Thus Paustos' *Epic History* proclaims that the 'pious martyrs [who] strove in battle . . . died so that iniquity should not enter into such a God-worshipping and God-loving realm . . . [so] let every one preserve continually the memory of their valour as martyrs for Christ for . . . they fell in battle like Judah and Mattathias Maccabei'.[34]

By the fifth century, Armenian elites were provided with a providentialist reading of their history and situation, through the cultivation of myths, symbols and memories. Equally important, that reading placed the ancestral homeland, *erkir Hayoc'* (land of Armenia), at the centre of their self-understanding, and it is clear that for the Christian historians its boundaries were well known. For example, Agat'angelos's *History* recounts in great geographical detail the missionary travels of Gregory throughout the length and breadth of Armenia. There is also a much greater cohesion in terms of a distinctive public culture. This is partly the result of the adoption of a unique script, but even more because of the influence of a particular religious culture and its theological concepts. Through the institution of the Church and its scriptures, liturgy and clergy, Armenians became party to a covenant with Christ, and thus subject to its laws and regulations. Here, too, we find some movement towards a greater legal uniformity and cohesion, at least in theory.[35]

At the same time, this process should not be exaggerated. Armenia was a semi-feudal peasant society, divided into regions dominated by great noble families, or *Naxharars*, as well as lesser nobility, or *azats* – even the Church was a feudal appanage. Armenia was also divided into Roman Lesser Armenia and partitioned Greater Armenia, so that the picture of unity given by the Christian historians was considerably idealized. Nevertheless, there was a supreme noble family, that of the royal dynasty, to which the Church leaders in fact belonged, which acted as a restraint on the *Naxharars*. Moreover, the spirit of martyrdom for the holy covenant of the Armenian Apostolic Church united the aristocracy to a clear conception of the Christian nation of Armenia – Lazar P'arpeci's sixth-century *History* speaks of the valiant princely men 'who gave themselves in countless numbers to martyrdom on behalf of the covenant of the holy church'.[36]

Elishe, too, according to Robert Thomson, argues that the reason for the covenant, which he thinks was modelled on the *brit qodesh* of the Maccabees, was to the preserve the Armenians' 'ancestral and divinely-bestowed *awrenk*', a term that embraces more than religion to include customs, laws and traditions, a whole way of life that characterised Armenians as Armenians'.[37] In other words, though the fragmented social structure appeared to deny the possibility, the conception of nationhood was certainly present and received expression in the distinctive institution of the Armenian Church and its covenant. This is something more than the vague relationship of 'all-Aram', or the separate territory of Edom. There are even references in Paustos' *Epic Histories* to the gathering of an Armenian 'council (*zolov*)', which included 'even [some/many?] of the *ramik* (ordinary people) and *sinakan* (peasantry)', though we should not make too much of this.[38]

Once again, the evidence for processes of nation formation is uncertain and conflicting. Centrifugal and unifying elements appear side by side. But for students of modern nations, this should come as no surprise. Well into the nineteenth century, the aristocracy dominated political life and assemblies, even in Western national states, even when their estates no longer afforded a base for separate political activity and large sections of the population remained disenfranchised into the twentieth century, and with little protection from the law. Instead, we should look for parallels in an earlier period: Armenia was closer to early modern nations in absolutist states, with their great nobles competing with the Court and bureaucracy, but with a clear sense of a shared origin and history, the growth of a distinctive public culture, a growing attachment to an ancestral land, and the appearance of laws and customs specific to the inhabitants of that land.[39]

Similar centrifugal and centripetal forces can be discerned in ancient Israel and Judah. Leaving aside the ongoing debates about early Israelite tribal assemblies reflected in the relatively egalitarian laws of the Mosaic code or the lack of evidence for a strong united monarchy, there is little doubt that by the eighth century BC, clear self-definitions of 'Israel' and 'Judah' as related sociological communities had taken hold among many people in both the northern and the southern kingdoms. But, despite the efforts of certain prophets like Amos and Hosea, following in the traditions of Elijah and Elisha, to insist on the exclusive worship of Yahweh and popular obedience to his laws, the ruling elites of the more materially advanced northern kingdom of Israel were much more powerfully influenced by the pagan Phoenician and Aramaean cultures than were the rulers of its poorer southern neighbour. For all that, the destruction of the kingdom of Israel by the Assyrians in 721 BC and the deportation of its elites did not entail the destruction of the northern religious traditions. Rather, they seem to have been incorporated into the Deuteronomic, and other editings, of the much older Israelite laws, histories and prophecies that may have achieved their present biblical form in Judah and Babylon from the seventh to the fifth centuries.[40]

For Steven Grosby, the Judahites of the time of King Josiah in the later seventh century BC possessed the characteristics of a 'nationality'. By that time, they appear to have had a clear self-designation and a sense of their collective existence as a people under threat, as well as an exclusive devotion to a single God of the land. They were also in the process of collating the many traditions, memories and myths of their ancestors, in a fixed religious centre, Jerusalem, and they had a clear attachment to the God-given land of Eretz-Israel, which they held to have fixed boundaries and which they were intent on reoccupying in the wake of the Assyrian withdrawal. But the extent to which the reforms of kings Hezekiah and Josiah, and the laws of the Deuteronomic code, were observed and accepted by non-priestly segments of the Judean population, is uncertain. The fact that pagan *asherot* had to be destroyed in the high places throughout the land, that a Book of the Law was 'discovered' in the Temple around 621 BC, and that it had to be publicly promulgated in the purified Temple by Josiah, suggests that we are witnessing the beginning of a process of observance of common laws:

> And the king went up into the house of the Lord, and all the men of Judah and all the inhabitants of Jerusalem with him, and the priests, and the prophets, and all the people, both small and great; and he read in their ears all the words of the book of the covenant which was found in the house of the Lord. And the king stood by a pillar, and made a covenant before the Lord, to walk after the Lord, and to keep his commandments and his testimonies and his statutes with all *their* heart and all *their* soul, to perform the words of this covenant that were written in this book. And all the people stood to the covenant. (2 Kings 23: 2–3, AV)[41]

In respect of this pact, Grosby argues that the saliency of the belief in the god of the land and hence of a *lex terrae* corresponds in some measure to the modern conception of citizenship, since it entailed membership in a community of religious law, with corresponding common rights and duties. While correct in itself, the comparison glosses over considerable differences between the two, not least in their philosophical underpinnings. More important, it is unnecessary and misleading. Once again, comparison through similarity or contrast makes the ancient practice or belief a mirror-image of Western modernity, rather than a phenomenon of its own space and time, and hence in its own historical right.[42]

On the other hand, socialization in a distinctive public religious culture, which carried with it some idea of god-given rights and duties, was a feature of several communities in the ancient world. This, at least, seems to have been the intention of the Deuteronomic code and associated histories, even if the subsequent destruction of the kingdom of Judah by the Babylonians cut short their diffusion and implementation. It was left to the exiles, both in Babylon and after their return to Jerusalem, to implement the Mosaic code in the Persian province of Judea, especially after the reforms of Ezra and Nehemiah.[43]

Whatever the reasons, a restored Judean community committed to the worship of Yahweh and the observance of his laws, at least in principle, and centred on Jerusalem and the Second Temple, seems to have been able to persist first under Persian, and later under Ptolemaic and then Seleucid, protection. Though there were schisms – between Hellenizers and traditionalists and subsequently between Sadducees, Pharisees and Essenes – they do not appear to have undermined the sense of a separate Judean ethnicity, or the boundary introduced by the exclusive worship of Yahweh, the importance of the Sabbath and the annual festivals or the observance of the Mosaic law code throughout the whole community, though more especially its male population, right into the period of Hasmonean and Roman rule. Indeed, it may be that, as Shaye Cohen has so fully and vividly documented, it is in the Hasmonean and Roman period that the creation of a Jewish ethnicity *vis-à-vis* Edomites and others can be traced.[44]

But does all this allow us to characterize ancient Judea as a 'nation' in this period? For Doron Mendels in his provocatively titled *The Rise and Fall of Jewish Nationalism*, the Jews are indeed a nation, and one of many cases of 'nationalism' in the Hellenistic and early Roman world. This term, Mendels makes clear, actually signifies 'ethnicity'; it is quite unlike the modern usage of the term. But, then, says Mendels, historians of antiquity frequently make use of anachronistic terms like 'imperialism' and 'utopia'. In fact, Mendels is really concerned with the *ethne* (peoples) of the Hellenistic world, though he is happy to speak of nationalist feelings or nationalistic traits like 'language, territory, history, culture, and religion'.

Indeed, on the same page, we read that Alexander the Great, for all his ideas of the unity of mankind, failed to abolish the existence of nations, just as Napoleon, with similar 'universalist' ideas, actually aroused nationalistic feelings among some of his subjects.[45]

Confusing as this conflation of terms may be, it relates only to a cultural nationalism of ethnic nations, and this is how, Mendels claims, the ancient historians and ethnographers themselves, from Hecataeus and Manetho to Berossus and Polybius, Strabo and Josephus, write about the division of their world into territories, peoples and cultures. However, Mendels's real interest is in the symbols of the 'political nationalism' that they also describe – that is, the symbols of 'the temple, territory, kingship, and the army', and more especially the political aspects of these symbols in Palestinian Judaism. Now, for Mendels, the adjective 'political' signifies the quest for sovereignty and independence, such as was achieved for Judeans in the Hasmonean state of the later second century BC. In this respect, the Judeans of the Hellenistic and Roman periods who constituted just one of many ethnic nations of the time, including Egyptians and Babylonians, Libyans and Arabs, all of whom managed to preserve their own 'national identities', were even more 'nationalistic' than their neighbours.[46]

All this sounds very much like a case of 'retrospective nationalism', of a piece with S. G. F. Brandon's thesis that the Zealot revolts against the Romans of the first century AD were an example of 'nationalist' guerilla warfare, and with Menahem Stern's view of the Maccabean revolt as an example of fervent religious nationalism. But, from the biased pages of Josephus it is difficult to reconstruct a clear view of the content of Zealot political aims, beyond the liberation of Eretz-Israel from Roman oppression and a desire for autonomy (*autonomia*). How were the inhabitants of this land conceived, non-Jews as well as Jews? And what kind of rule was to be instituted? If nationalism's primary object is indeed the autonomy of the nation, what was the nature of the Jewish nation on whose behalf, supposedly, the Zealots were waging war? And similar questions can be posed about the revolt of the Maccabees.[47]

I am not sure that such questions can be answered. But, even if we grant, as I shall go on to argue, the formation of a Jewish nation at this stage, we cannot go on to maintain that the defence of this nation merits the title 'nationalism' – but rather an intense, defensive 'national sentiment' of a kind that is frequently found in modern and pre-modern epochs. After all, the ideology of nationalism seeks the autonomy, unity and identity of the proposed nation as part of a world-view which holds that

1   the world is divided into nations, each with its own character, history and destiny;

2 political power stems solely from the nation;
3 to be free, the individual must belong to a nation, to which he or she gives primary loyalty;
4 nations must have maximum autonomy and self-expression;
5 world peace and justice demands a plurality of free nations.[48]

And crucial to this world-view are the twin cults of authenticity and cultural diversity to which Romanticism was wedded, and which find little or no echo in the ancient world. Certainly, there is no evidence of nationalism in this sense in Maccabean and Zealot circles.[49]

All this seems to me to be a far cry from the careful sociological enquiry of Steven Grosby into the presence or absence of constitutive elements of nationality in Judah and other collectivities in the ancient world. On the other hand, one must admit that Mendels's choice of epoch is a more likely milieu for the generation of nation-forming processes in Judea. It is doubtful whether and to what extent the Mosaic code had a deep impact in the seventh or sixth centuries BC. But it clearly became much more widely observed in the late Second Temple epoch, as well as in the Mishnaic period when, as Jacob Neusner documents, a much more participant synagogal Judaism had replaced the Temple hierarchy, and when the rabbis sought to create a largely self-governing community, mainly in Galilee, based on the needs and circumstances of the *Am-haaretz*, the common man of the land. Here, I would argue, we have the nucleus of a nation operating according to its own religious laws, even though it was at the time under Roman and Byzantine occupation and suzerainty. In this respect, we should recall that not all nations have sought outright independence, even in the modern world, as the cases of Scotland, Catalonia and perhaps Quebec remind us, but have nevertheless exhibited all the processes of nation formation that I enumerated earlier.[50]

Both in Armenia and in Judea, the emergence of a national community took place in the crucible of pre-existing states, in which political action was the main factor in ethno-genesis. In other words, kingdoms helped to forge nations by providing the arena and impetus for those processes of self-definition, memory cultivation, territorial development, the diffusion of public culture and legal standardization that together constitute the bounded sociological and cultural community we call the nation. But this is only one aspect of the matter. Though it has obviously played a significant role in many cases, political action, and the state, cannot be credited with sole responsibility for subsequent nation formation. We need also to consider other, non-political factors of shared origin myths, historical memory and culture (mainly language and religion), that in these and other cases created a vivid sense of common ethnicity – indeed, on occasion a sharply demarcated *ethnie*. In both Judea and Armenia, these factors, and especially those of religious belief, sacred law and clerical institutions, were able to 'carry' the sense of common ethnicity and the memory of nationhood into exile and diaspora. While it is possible to argue that, unlike most ethnic categories, networks and communities in antiquity, Judea and Armenia exhibited a balance of state and nation, and this was significant for survival, it was ultimately the strong territorial attachments, distinctive scriptures and messianic beliefs of their members that enabled these ethnic communities to survive the vicissitudes of diaspora and nurture over the *longue durée* the dream of collective territorial restoration to an ancestral homeland.[51]

Conclusion

With Armenia and Judea in mind, we can return to our original question. In some ways, ancient Egypt exhibited the processes of nation formation. After all, it had a clear name and self-definition, a consciousness of being a separate community and a suspicion of outsiders like the Nubians and the Hyksos. When King Kamose of Thebes around 1570 BC exclaims:

> I should like to know for what purpose is my strength. One prince sits in Avaris, and another in Nubia, and here sit I with an Asiatic and a Nubian, each having his slice of Egypt. I will grapple with him, and rip open his belly. My desire is to save Egypt which the Asiatics have smitten. Your counsel is wrong and I will fight with the Asiatics . . . Men shall say of me in Thebes: Kamose, the protector of Egypt.[52]

he is surely referring to a wider collectivity than Thebes or Upper Egypt. There is also much evidence of territorial attachments, as in the Song of Sinuhe, who had fled Egypt and become prosperous in Palestine (Upper Retenu), but felt a foreigner and desired to be buried 'in the land wherein I was born'. There was also, of course, a rich corpus of myths and symbols, including creation myths, widely disseminated by priests and scribes and enacted in temples, together with a considerable repertoire of historical memories recorded in both inscriptions and papyri. We may also discern the growth of a distinctive religious public culture perpetuated in powerful priesthoods and scribal institutions, in whose culture all upper-class Egyptians were educated. Finally, there is little doubt about the high degree of legal regulation by the well-developed state bureaucracy and its penetration of the countryside.[53]

But this is where the problem lies. We can certainly point to a relatively powerful, and enduring, Egyptian state and its culture, but can we equally speak of a sense of Egyptian nationhood? I am not sure. In terms of common rights and duties, Egypt was a very unequal society, even if there were links and pathways from commoners to scribes and even nobles; but then that is true of a great many other, modern societies. Still, the problem of the degree of inclusion of the commoners remains; there was nothing like a pact or covenant between the Pharaoh and his people that we have seen in the case of fifth-century Armenia or first- and second-century Judea. It is difficult to know to what extent Egyptians were imbued with the scribal culture or were inculcated with its values. The public culture was that of the state and the priesthoods. So, when Kamose claims the title of 'protector of Egypt', is it the nation he desires to liberate, or the state and its territorial integrity? It may be difficult, given the nature of the sources and the dynastic monopoly on inscriptions, to go behind royal propaganda, but we should attempt to ask these questions, if only to clarify our own conceptual categories and test the limits of comparison.

In this connection, it is interesting that, while a clear sense of common Egyptian identity persisted through the Saite and Persian periods (witness the serious revolts against Assyrians and Persians) into the Ptolemaic and Roman periods, and resurfaced subsequently in more than one period, it was less marked than that of Armenians and Jews in their diasporas, before the modern epoch. It may be that the processes of nation formation had gone much further among ancient Jews and Armenians, and that while all three cases had been formed in the chrysalis of the state, an emergent Egyptian sense of nationhood was entirely dependent upon the success of an all-powerful and all-pervasive bureaucratic state. Its fragmentation signalled the reversal of nation-forming processes among the Egyptians.

But, in the absence of sufficient data, all this is speculative. What I hope this brief and necessarily schematic enquiry into the presence or absence of 'nations' in antiquity shows, is the possibility of distinguishing categories of collective cultural identity, in all periods of human history, through the use of the ideal-type method; and of differentiating other types of collective identity from ethnic and national types, and discovering the ways in which often fluid ethnic identities are related to more compact and clear-cut national communities.

Here, I have tried to give some examples of this fluidity and the processes involved from Near Eastern antiquity, through the use of general or pure types to which given examples more or less approximate. In particular, I have tried to separate the ideal-type of nation from the specific framework of nationalist ideology, which seems preferable to the common practice of embedding the concept of nation in the modern epoch and the Western world, thus leaving in outer darkness all those cases that formed in quite different milieux and circumstances. To rule these out as not conforming to the modern, Western type, appears arbitrary, if not myopic.

Notes

1 See A. Rosalie David, *The Ancient Egyptians: Religious Beliefs and Practices* (London, Boston and Henley: Routledge & Kegan Paul, 1982), pp. 4–5.

2 See Adrian Hastings, *The Construction of Nationhood: Ethnicity, Religion and Nationalism* (Cambridge: Cambridge University Press, 1997). On ideologies of nationalism, see Anthony D. Smith, *Nationalism: Theory, History, Ideology* (Cambridge: Polity, 2001), chs 1–2.

3 Eric Hobsbawm, *Nations and Nationalism since 1780* (Cambridge: Cambridge University Press, 1990), p. 10.

4 For the social structure and history of ancient Egypt, see B. G. Trigger, B. J. Kemp, D. O'Connor and A. B. Lloyd, *Ancient Egypt: A Social History* (Cambridge: Cambridge University Press, 1983).

5 See Richard Frye, *The Heritage of Persia* (New York: Mentor Books, 1966); and J. M. Cook, *The Persian Empire* (London: J. M. Dent & Sons, 1983), esp. ch. 1 for theories of Persian migration.

6 For the Hittite *pankush* (the 'whole assembly' was confined to the nobles and priests), see Sabatino Moscati, *The Face of the Ancient Orient* (New York: Anchor Books, 1962), ch. 5; and O. R. Gurney, *The Hittites* (Harmondsworth: Penguin, 1954), pp. 78–9. On the Sumerian city-states, see Samuel Kramer, *The Sumerians* (Chicago: University of Chicago Press, 1963). On the Philistines and other peoples, see D. J. Wiseman (ed.), *Peoples of the Old Testament* (Oxford: Clarendon Press, 1973).

7 See Moses Finley, *The Use and Abuse of History* (London: Hogarth Press, 1986), ch. 7; and Edith Hall, *Inventing the Barbarian: Greek Self-Definition through Tragedy* (Oxford: Clarendon Press, 1992).

8 On these elements of unity, see R. Schlaifer, 'Greek theories of slavery from Homer to Aristotle', in Moses Finley (ed.), *Slavery in Classical Antiquity* (Cambridge: Heffer and Sons, 1961); and Hall, *Inventing the Barbarian*. For the ethnic subdivisions of the Hellenes, see J. H. M. Alty, 'Dorians and Ionians', *Journal of Hellenic Studies* 102 (1982), pp. 1–14. For pan-Hellenist ideas in Greece, see Fondation Hardt: *Grecs et Barbares, Entretiens sur l'Antiquité Classique* VIII (Geneva, 1962).

9 There is a vast literature on the concept of 'ethnicity' and its related concepts of ethnic identity and ethnic community (or *ethnie*). See esp. Nathan Glazer and Daniel Moynihan (eds), *Ethnicity: Theory and Experience* (Cambridge, MA: Harvard University Press, 1975); Anthony D. Smith, *The Ethnic Origins of Nations* (Oxford: Blackwell, 1986), ch. 2; Elisabeth Tonkin, Maryon McDonald and Malcolm Chapman (eds), *History and Ethnicity* (London and New York: Routledge, 1989); Thomas Eriksen, *Ethnicity and Nationalism*

(London and Boulder, CO: Pluto Press, 1993); Edwin Wilmsen and Patrick McAllister (eds), *The Politics of Difference: Ethnic Premises in a World of Power* (Chicago and London: University of Chicago Press, 1996); John Hutchinson and Anthony D. Smith (eds), *Ethnicity* (Oxford: Oxford University Press, 1996).

10   Edwin Cohen, *The Athenian Nation* (Princeton: Princeton University Press, 2002); cf. Alty, 'Dorians and Ionians', on the sense of Ionian ethnicity cleverly manipulated by the Athenians in the Peloponnesian War.

11   Erich Gruen, *Culture and National Identity in Republican Rome* (London: Duckworth & Co., 1993), especially chs 1–2. See also J. V. P. Balsdon, *Romans and Aliens* (London: Duckworth & Co., 1979). Rousseau was only one of many French intellectuals who looked to Rome and Numa Pompilius' laws as evidence of nationhood; see on this, David Bell, *The Cult of the Nation in France, 1680–1800* (Cambridge, MA: Harvard University Press, 2001), ch. 2.

12   On the ethnic beliefs of ancient biblical religion, see Yehezkel Kaufmann, *The Religion of Israel*, trans. Moshe Greenberg (London: George Allen & Unwin Ltd., 1961). For the Covenant and the belief in ethnic election, see Michael Walzer, *Exodus and Revolution* (New York: Harper Collins, Basic Books, 1985); Ernest Nicholson, *God and his People* (Oxford: Clarendon Press, 1988); and Anthony D. Smith, *Chosen Peoples: Sacred Sources of National Identity* (Oxford: Oxford University Press, 2003), ch. 3.

13   On the Zealots as a nationalist guerilla movement, see the controversial account in S. G. F. Brandon, *Jesus and the Zealots* (Manchester: Manchester University Press, 1967), ch. 2; and Hyam Maccoby, *Revolution in Judea* (London: Ocean Books, 1974). On the struggles between Hellenizers and *hasidim* and the Maccabean revolt, see Victor Tcherikover, *Hellenistic Civilisation and the Jews* (New York: Athenaeum, 1970). On the parallels between biblical laws and those of Egypt and Mesopotamia, see Leon Epsztein, *Social Justice in the Ancient Near East and the People of the Bible*, trans. John Bowden (London: SCM Press Ltd, 1986); see also Irving Zeitlin, *Ancient Judaism* (Cambridge: Polity, 1984), esp. ch. 3.

14   On English Puritan national sentiment, see Liah Greenfeld, *Nationalism: Five Roads to Modernity* (Cambridge, MA: Harvard University Press, 1992), ch. 1; also Brendan Bradshaw and Peter Roberts (eds), *British Consciousness and Identity: The Making of Britain, 1533–1707* (Cambridge: Cambridge University Press, 1998). On the nature and rise of a Dutch Puritan national consciousness in the United Provinces, see Simon Schama, *The Embarrassment of Riches: An Interpretation of Dutch Culture in the Golden Age* (London: William Collins Sons and Co. Ltd., 1987), esp. ch. 2. On the resurgence of religious nationalisms, see Mark Juergensmeyer: *The New Cold War? Religious Nationalism Confronts the Secular State* (Berkeley and Los Angeles: University of California Press, 1993).

15   See Ernest Gellner, *Nations and Nationalism* (Oxford: Blackwell, 1983). On the secular character of nationalism, see Elie Kedourie, *Nationalism* (London: Hutchinson, 1960).

16   See Walker Connor, *Ethno-Nationalism: The Quest for Understanding*
     (Princeton: Princeton University Press, 1994), ch. 8; for a discussion, see
     Anthony D. Smith, *Nationalism and Modernism: A Critical Survey of Recent
     Theories of Nations and Nationalism* (London and New York: Routledge,
     1998, 161–5). On Connor's criterion, neither ancient Athens nor Judea would
     constitute nations, but neither also would some modern states like Switzer-
     land till well after the Second World War.
17   Stein Tønnesson and Hans Antlöv (eds), *Asian Forms of the Nation*
     (Richmond, Surrey: Curzon Press, 1996), especially Introduction. On the
     special place of the Arabic language in Arab national identity, see Yasir
     Suleiman, *The Arabic Language and National Identity* (Edinburgh: Edin-
     burgh University Press, 2003).
18   The distinction between *am* and *goyim* was not as clear-cut as that between
     populus (Romanus) and *natio* (distant, barbarous tribes) in Latin authors, as
     Patrick Geary, *The Myth of Nations: The Medieval Origins of Europe* (Prince-
     ton and Oxford: Princeton University Press, 2002), ch. 2, appears to think;
     see Steven Grosby: *Biblical Ideas of Nationality: Ancient and Modern*
     (Winona Lake, IN: Eisenbrauns, 2002), p. 15. On classical usages, see under
     ethnos in H. G. Liddell and R. Scott (eds), *A Greek–English Lexicon*, 6th edn
     (Oxford: Clarendon Press, 1869); and under *natio* in C. T. Lewis and C. Short
     (eds), *A Latin Dictionary* (1879) (Oxford: Clarendon Press, 1955). See Fred-
     erick Hertz, *Nationality in History and Politics* (London: Routledge & Kegan
     Paul, 1944).
19   Bruce Routledge, 'The antiquity of nations? Critical reflections on the ancient
     Near East', *Nations and Nationalism* 9, (2) (2003), pp. 213–33.
20   On 'state' and 'nation', see Connor, *Ethno-Nationalism*, ch. 4; and more nor-
     matively, Maurizio Viroli, *For Love of Country: An Essay on Nationalism
     and Patriotism* (Oxford: Clarendon Press, 1995). On the definition of *ethnie*,
     see Smith, *Ethnic Origins of Nations*, ch. 2. On the kinship basis of ethnic-
     ity, see Donald Horowitz, *Ethnic Groups in Conflict* (Berkeley and Los
     Angeles: University of California Press, 1985), chs 1–2, and Pierre van
     den Berghe, 'Does race matter?', *Nations and Nationalism* 1, 3 (1995), pp.
     357–68. On diasporas, see John Armstrong, 'Mobilized and proletarian
     diasporas', *American Political Science Review* 70 (1976), pp. 393–408, and
     the essays in Gabi Sheffer (ed.), *Modern Diasporas in International Politics*
     (London: Croom Helm, 1986).
21   On territory and nation, see David Hooson (ed.), *Geography and National
     Identity* (Cambridge, MA, and Oxford: Blackwell, 1994), and Mark Bassin,
     'Russia between Europe and Asia: the ideological construction of social
     space', *Slavic Review* 50, 1 (1991), pp. 1–17; and Eric Kaufmann and Oliver
     Zimmer, 'In search of the authentic nation: landscape and national identity in
     Switzerland and Canada', *Nations and Nationalism* 4, 4 (1998), pp. 483–510.
22   For fuller discussion of these processes, see Anthony D. Smith, 'When is a
     nation?', *Geopolitics* 7, 2 (2002), pp. 5–32; also Gordana Uzelac, 'When is
     the nation? Constituent elements and processes', *Geopolitics* 7, 2 (2002), pp.
     33–52, and other essays in the same special issue. For some measures of these

processes of ethnic and national formation, see Eric Kaufmann, 'Modern formation, ethnic reformation: the social sources of the American nation', *Geopolitics* 7, 2 (2002), pp. 99–120.

23 Grosby, *Biblical Ideas of Nationality*. Whether his criteria derive ultimately from his reading of modern nationality, or are grounded in ancient Near Eastern contexts, is a moot point.

24 Ibid., p. 27. On primordialism, see Smith, *Nationalism and Modernism*, ch. 7.

25 Grosby, *Biblical Ideas of Nationality*, p. 124. On the later conquest and forced conversion of the Edomites, see Shaye Cohen, *The Beginnings of Jewishness: Boundaries, Varieties, Uncertainties* (Berkeley, Los Angeles and London: University of California Press, 2000), ch. 4.

26 Grosby, *Biblical Ideas of Nationality*, p. 124, citing, e.g., 2 Samuel 8: 14.

27 Ibid., p. 127 (emphasis original), citing Sefire Stele I, face A (ll. 3–6).

28 Ibid., pp. 135–6.

29 Ibid., p. 135, citing Stele IIIA of Tiglath-Pileser III from Iran.

30 It is interesting that in these passages Grosby equates the concepts of 'nation' and 'nationality'.

31 See the critique by Routledge, 'Antiquity of nations?', and for the Canaanites, Philistines and others, Wiseman, *Peoples of the Old Testament*.

32 For a detailed history of early Armenia, its myth of origins and its conversion to Christianity, see Anne Redgate, *The Armenians* (Oxford: Blackwell, 2000), esp. chs 1, 4–6. On the dating of the conversion, the debates about Chalcedon and the missionary efforts, see Vrej Nersessian, *Treasures of the Ark: 1700 Years of Armenian Christian Art* (London: The British Library, 2001), chs 1–3. On early Armenian literature and script, see David Lang, *Armenia: Cradle of Civilization* (London: George Allen and Unwin Ltd., 1980), ch. 7. For a more general discussion of pre-modern Armenian ethnicity, see Razmik Panossian, 'The past as nation: three dimensions of Armenian identity', *Geopolitics* 7, 2 (2002), pp. 121–46.

33 Nina Garsoian, *Church and Culture in Early Medieval Armenia* (Aldershot: Ashgate Variorum, 1999), ch. 12.

34 Ibid., p. 128, citing Paustos Buzand, *Epic Histories* III, xi, 80–1.

35 On the boundaries of Armenia at the time of the missions, see Nersessian, *Treasures of the Ark*, ch. 1. On the religious culture of Christian Armenia and its combinations with earlier Sasanid Zoroastrian beliefs and rituals, see Redgate, *The Armenians*, chs 6–7. On the Armenian Monophysite religion and Church, see A. S. Atiyah, *A History of Eastern Christianity* (London: Methuen, 1968), IV, and K. V. Sarkissian, 'The Armenian Church', in A. J. Arberry (ed.), *Religion in the Middle East: Three Religions in Concord and Conflict*, vol. 1: *Judaism and Christianity* (Cambridge: Cambridge University Press, 1969).

36 Garsoian, *Church and Culture*, p. 128, citing Lazar P'arpeci's *History* (LPI, ii, 2 (34)).

37 Robert Thomson (ed.), *Elishe: History of Vardan and the Armenian War*, trans. R. Thomson (Cambridge, MA: Harvard University Press, 1982), p. 10.

Thomson's introduction places Elishe's *History* in the context of the wars and martyrdom, and of the new history writing of the period.

38   Grosby, *Biblical Ideas of Nationality*, p. 145, citing Buzand's *Epic Histories* III, xxi, and indicating the parallel with Josiah's council in 2 Kings 23. Once again, I am sceptical of the powers and composition of such councils, as we saw in the case of Sumer or among the Hittites. It is rather in the enduring institution of the Armenian Church and its regulative influence that we may perhaps discern a movement towards nationhood.

39   For national sentiment in early modern Europe, see the essays in Orest Ranum (ed.), *National Consciousness, History and Political Culture in Early-Modern Europe* (Baltimore: Johns Hopkins University Press, 1975).

40   On early biblical history, see *inter alia*, Martin Noth, *A History of Israel* (London: A. & C. Black, 1960); G. W. Anderson, *Tradition and Interpretation* (Oxford: Clarendon Press, 1979); Zeitlin, *Ancient Judaism*; Gosta Ahlstrom, *Who Were the Israelites?* (Winona Lake, IN: Eisenbrauns, 1986); and from an archaeological perspective, Israel Finkelstein and Neil Asher Silberman, *The Bible Unearthed: Archaeology's New Vision of Ancient Israel and the Origin of its Sacred Texts* (New York: Free Press, 2001).

41   See Grosby, *Biblical Ideas of Nationality*, pp. 95–8, citing 2 Kings 23: 3, and ch. 1 on the question of clear conceptions of the extent of Eretz-Israel (on which see Numbers 34, cited in ibid., p. 23). On Josiah's reformation, see Finkelstein and Silberman, *Bible Unearthed*, ch. 11. For the territorial aspect in Jewish thought, see W. D. Davies, *The Territorial Dimension of Judaism* (Berkeley, Los Angeles and London: University of California Press, 1982).

42   See Routledge, 'Antiquity of nations?'.

43   See, e.g., the codes of Urukagina, Hammurabi and Numa Pompilius. For the post-Exilic implementation, see *Cambridge History of Judaism* (Cambridge: Cambridge University Press, 1984), vol. 1, chs 7, 10.

44   See Cohen, *Beginnings of Jewishness*, esp. chs 3–4; also Martin Hengel, *Jews, Greeks and Barbarians*, trans. John Bowden (London: SCM Press Ltd, 1980), pts II and III.

45   Doron Mendels, *The Rise and Fall of Jewish Nationalism* (New York: Doubleday, 1992), p. 14.

46   Ibid., pp. 1, 38. Interestingly, Mendels's claim is echoed by Geary, *Myth of Nations*, ch. 2; but, unlike Mendels, Geary accuses the ancient authors of objectifying, schematizing and ranking ethnic groups which were much more fluid, unranked and subjectively conceived – apparently, by Herodotus. But, does not the near-consensus of ancient authors on this subject tell us something vital about the ways in which ethnic communities were conceived and felt by many people in the ancient world? Yet, that does not mean that we have to follow Mendels in categorizing these cultural communities as 'nations'.

47   See Brandon, *Jesus and the Zealots*, ch. 2; and Menahem Stern, 'The Hasmonean revolt and its place in this history of Jewish society and religion', in H. H. Ben-Sasson and S. Ettinger (eds), *Jewish Society Through the Ages* (New York: Schocken Books, 1971), pp. 92–106.

48 On this world-view, see Anthony D. Smith, *National Identity* (Harmondsworth: Penguin, 1991), p. 74.

49 On Herderian Romanticism, see Isaiah Berlin, *The Roots of Romanticism* (London: Chatto and Windus, 1999).

50 See Jacob Neusner, *Max Weber Revisited: Religion and Society in Ancient Judaism* (Oxford: Oxford Centre for Postgraduate Hebrew Studies, 1981).

51 On the importance of institutions in 'carrying' ethnicity and ensuring its persistence, see John Breuilly, 'Approaches to nationalism', in Gopal Balakrishnan (ed.), *Mapping the Nation* (London: Verso, 1996), pp. 146–74. For the Armenian case, see Ronald Suny, *Looking towards Ararat: Armenia in Modern History* (Bloomington and Indianapolis: Indiana University Press, 1993), and Panossian, 'The past as nation'. For the case of the Greek diaspora and the Orthodox *millet* and Church under Ottoman rule, see G. Arnakis, 'The role of religion in the development of Balkan nationalism', in Barbara and Charles Jelavich (eds), *The Balkans in Transition* (Berkeley: University of California Press, 1963). For a critique, see Paschalis Kitromilides, ' "Imagined communities" and the origins of the national question in the Balkans', *European History Quarterly* 19, 2 (1989), pp. 149–92. On national restoration movements among Greek, Armenian and Jewish diasporas, see Anthony D. Smith, 'Zionism and diaspora nationalism', *Israel Affairs* 2, 2 (1995), pp. 1–19.

52 Grosby, *Biblical Ideas of Nationality*, citing A. Kirk Grayson and Donald B. Redford (eds), *Papyrus and Tablet* (Englewood Cliffs, NJ: Prentice-Hall, 1973), p. 22.

53 Grosby, *Biblical Ideas of Nationality*, p. 31. On Egyptian myths, see David, *Ancient Egyptians*, and J. A. Wilson, *The Burden of Egypt* (Chicago: University of Chicago Press, 1951).

6

War and Ethnicity

One of the most powerful factors in the creation of both nations and ethnic communities in every period of history has been warfare in its various forms. Although there is a vast literature both on ethnic groups and on warfare, scholars have devoted little systematic attention to their interrelation. Even in the recently expanding field of the effects of war on society, the factor of ethnicity is hardly mentioned. I think this serious omission stems not only from the inherent difficulty of generalizing about so vast a historical and sociological field, but also from the tacit prevalence of a particular view of the interrelation, a view that is only now receiving a partial scrutiny.[1]

In what follows, I should like to challenge the prevalent view which sees warfare as largely the product of society and of its out-group hostilities, and to argue instead for the view that war has been a powerful factor in shaping, not society or ethnicity *per se*, but certain crucial aspects of ethnic community and nationhood. The influence of war has, however, been uneven; it has affected some aspects of ethnic community more than others. Moreover, that influence has been both direct and mediated; and in some ways, the indirect influences have been both more interesting and more pervasive.

'War and Ethnicity: The Role of Warfare in the Formation, Self-images and Cohesion of Ethnic Communities', *Ethnic and Racial Studies*, 4/4 (1981): 375–97. Reproduced with the permission of the editors. (<http://www.tandf.co.uk/journals/routledge/01419870.html>)

Theory

Group aggression

The simplest and most general form of the prevalent view may be termed that of 'group aggression'. In the more psychological versions this posits a belief in what McDougall called the 'instinct of pugnacity'. According to McDougall, this instinct had indeed changed its 'modes of expression . . . with the growth of civilisation'; but there 'is no reason to think it has grown weaker among ourselves under centuries of civilisation'.[2] And he cited various earlier examples of the way in which tribal–ethnic organization favours warfare and success in combat. The point is that 'pugnacity' or aggression is really a function of in-group solidarity, which 'naturally' favours a hostile attitude to out-groups. At the other end of the historical spectrum too, we find theories of the authoritarian personality attempting to explain militarism in terms of ethnocentrism: so, for example, American fears of Russia in the 1950s, its suspicion of the powerful out-group, promoted the classic twin forms of American nationalism, isolationism and imperialism, together with an enemy annihilation picture of the world.[3]

Anthropological and sociological formulations of the 'group aggression' view tend to emphasize the concepts of 'tribalism', nationalism and fascism in the genesis of war. Indeed, for liberal philosophers like Popper, fascism and nationalism are simply reversions to the atavistic and primitive urges and appetites of 'tribalism' in the generic sense.[4] It was, of course, Sumner who traced war to the hostility of out-groups, though he was careful to point out that some of the least developed tribes are peaceful. He argued, nevertheless, that though an in-group might not coincide with a tribe, group competition is the source of conflict and war.[5] The more intense that competition, the greater the likelihood of violence and armed conflict. Kedourie, too, sees this as one of the chief causes of modern warfare. He attributes to nationalism the modern equivalent of the universal 'need to belong', an inherent aggression, which in ethnically mixed areas is bound to lead to war. After all, nationalism, as a doctrine of the Will, exalts the cultural group and emphasizes its exclusiveness and superiority; it is therefore bound to exacerbate existing tensions and create new ones.[6] Wirth and Akzin, too, lean to the view that nationalism tends to promote conflict, Wirth by defining nationalism as 'conflict groups', Akzin by noting how modern urban economic competition for scarce facilities feeds on ethnic antagonisms.[7] Finally, social psychologists relate ethnic aggression even more closely to the needs of the group. Thus Barbu argues that where ethnic identity has been damaged or threatened, as in revolutionary France or Weimar Germany, militant aggression against outsiders and minorities is necessary to overcome the crisis of confidence and the ensuing social divisions.[8]

There are several flaws in the prevalent 'group aggression' view. To begin with, the instinct of 'pugnacity' must be inferred from the frequency of war, and here it becomes apparent that most wars can be attributed to other factors like mass migrations, religious or other movements, natural disasters, colonization and, above all, state formation. Nor need hostility be confined to tribal groups. It may manifest itself among clans, in family feuds, and between villages, city-states or empires.[9] Third, competition need not always resolve itself into overt armed conflict, or warfare. There are several methods short of war for resolving disputes between small or larger groups, as there are between individuals. It is only in a highly inter-dependent world such as we find today that ethnocentrism may contribute to a more hostile climate.

There are several other objections. Modern nationalisms, and even such a fascism as Franco's, may not induce overt hostilities. Indeed, some nationalist movements, like the Czech one, have tried to pursue their objects by wholly peaceful means; and where they have failed in this inten-tion, the cause must be found in their overall situation rather than in any inherent militaristic tendencies.[10] Nor can it really be said that nations have been more prone to conflict than any other political group. A large number of history's wars have been fought by multicultural empires or kingdoms, often across the territories of small ethnic groups which became pawns in their conflicts. Such wars were fought in a pre-ideological era, when doc-trines of popular will and identity were unknown, and there is no need to invoke a crisis of identity and confidence in such cases. And while inter-nal crises in modern nations may provoke a search for scapegoats, warfare or overt external armed conflict requires several other pre-conditions, including the institutionalization of warfare itself and the existence of a conflict relation with a polar nation.

In fact, most of these errors and difficulties stem from the unilateral attempt to derive war from 'society' generally; whereas it can be equally well urged that 'societies' – that is to say, given ethnic or other communi-ties – owe much of their form and solidarity to the exigencies of war. Not only does the latter view accord better with the historical facts, but it opens up more fruitful avenues of inquiry, which have till now been overlooked or blocked by the prevalence of blanket 'group aggression' assumptions.

Reference groups and military elites

Before considering this alternative view, however, we need to assess two other factors, which are sometimes proposed separately, and sometimes in conjunction with the two main theories.

The first is the notion that war is a product of negative reference groups, and that the violence of the conflict is determined by the intensity of their mutual images. According to this view, wars are polar conflicts with a traditional enemy: Frenchmen against Germans, Vietnamese against Khmers, Arabs against Israelis. The self-image that each develops is a product of this polar situation, and similarly with their stereotypes of the enemy, both receiving their definitive stamp from the war experience itself.

This spiral situation is reinforced by the second factor, the role of military elites. With the growth in military professionalization, followed by mass military participation, the military's self-image and its stereotypes of the enemy assume disproportionate importance. In so far as the ideology of the military is necessarily ethnocentric or nationalistic, in view of their security function, the negative reference is reinforced on both sides, and becomes generally aggressive and stereotyped.[11]

At this point, reference group theory may be harmonized with the assumption of the 'group aggression' view. The ideology of the military elites, the polar conflict situation and the negative mutual images and positive self-images, can be derived from the inherent aggression of in-group sentiment. And yet, the fact that in many new states, role and image disassociation which follows decolonization may be quite peaceful, and that the nationalist images of the elites of new states, even of their military, does not always generate conflict or overt war, shows that these reference group processes are dependent on factors other than inherent group aggression. If the handover to independence has been peaceful, the beneficiary community may even incorporate elements of the colonial benefactor's life-styles and ideals.[12]

Actually, both factors, stereotypes of reference groups and the role of the military, can be better understood in the context of inter-state relations and the institutionalization of warfare. Among simpler tribes, warfare tended to occur between what Malinowski termed 'tribe-states', with their centralized authoritative power and the corresponding organization of force.[13] 'Tribe-nations', the units of cultural co-operation, tend to be peaceful, especially towards strangers, while conflict thrives in the smallest groups like the household. In modern times, too, aggression against other nations defined as 'enemies' is largely a function of inter-*state* hostilities arousing ethnic sentiments rather than vice versa. The main source of nineteenth-century Franco–German enmity was not some innate group hostility or aversion, but the clash of interest between the French and Prussian states in the Napoleonic era or earlier, and its expression in overt wars. Equally, the inflamed nationalism and exaggerated influence of the military in both France and Germany after 1870 was the direct result of the public policies of Napoleon III and Bismarck, of the Franco–Prussian War itself, and of the dispute over Alsace.[14]

Reference group analysis is, therefore, more profitably related to the alternative view: namely, that it is external conflict which shapes ethnic community, and more especially its images. Besides, we should not forget that reference groups, positive or negative, are often multiple or serial. The ancient Egyptians had to fight Nubians as well as Hittites and Assyrians. Romans and Arabs fought successive powers, from whom they imbibed one or more elements in their own self-images. In the Hundred Years War, the infant English state had to fight on two fronts, against the Scottish as well as the French kingdom, a fact which affected the 'yeoman' imagery of the average English combatant.[15] And recently Germans and Poles have had to face a succession of enemies on different fronts, making the tracing of self-images and stereotypes a complex and often baffling study.

The 'cohesion' thesis

In radical opposition to the prevalent 'group aggression' view, the 'cohesion' thesis contends that all internal group solidarity is a product of external armed conflict, or the imminent threat thereof. In a crisis, in the heat of battle, old divisions are laid aside, and the nationalist dream of ethnic fraternity becomes a momentary reality. It is war itself which creates any sense of belonging and community. As Renan observed, 'la nation est une grande solidarité constituée par le sentiment des sacrifices qu'on a fait et de ceux qu'on est disposé de faire encore'.[16]

The classic formulation of this view is to be found in Simmel's study of *Conflict*. His main theme there is that conflict is a possible form of sociation, and that hostility sharpens group boundaries. He also claims that war requires a 'centralistic intensification of the group form, and this is best guaranteed by despotism'.[17] Not only does conflict accentuate the cohesion of an existing unit; it also mobilizes its members, bringing together persons who have otherwise nothing to do with each other. Simmel cites medieval France and Spain as examples of ethnic kingdoms that owed their national unity 'only' to their respective wars with the English and the Moors. And he goes on:

> The United States needed the War of Independence; Switzerland, the fight against Austria; the Netherlands, rebellion against Spain; the Achaean league, the struggle against Macedonia; and the founding of the new German Empire furnishes a parallel to all these instances.[18]

It is true that Simmel qualifies this argument when he observes that war also articulates 'the latent relationship and unity', and is 'more the occasion of unifications that are required internally than it is the purpose of these unifications'.[19] The question still remains, however, how far wars can be said necessarily to foster social cohesion. Clearly, it depends on a number of circumstances, including the type of war, the incidence of success, and the general climate of ideas. For example, some distant incursions have actually broken up ethnic states, as did the Mongol invasions of Kievan Russia and the Arab sultanates. More recently, Anglo–French incursions in the Middle East or China helped to disrupt their regional or ethnic unity for a time; and not all anti-colonial 'wars of liberation' have promoted ethnic unity in such new states as Indonesia, Zimbabwe or Angola. Besides, modern forms of intensive warfare can often strain internal solidarity and throw into relief existing divisions, discrepancies and alienations, as Simmel also noted.[20]

The trouble with the 'cohesion' thesis is not only an error of oversimplification, however. The real danger is that it deflects attention away from the other ways in which war moulds ethnic community. I have in mind here its role in (a) the formation of ethnic communities and (b) the growth of their self-images and stereotypes. It was, in fact, Weber who drew attention to the primary role of political action, including inter-state wars, in the formation of ethnic groups and their imagery, though he also emphasized the part played by memories of early mass migrations.[21] What I should like to do is to develop his approach, stressing here the role of wars in the shaping of ethnicity and its attendant imagery, as well as in fostering and also undermining ethnic cohesion.

Of course, I am not arguing that warfare is actually responsible for the initial 'ethnic *categories*'. For there to be the possibility for an ethnic community at all, there will normally exist some visible cultural differences or 'markers', which might help to divide populations into fairly well-defined groupings or ethnic categories.[22] What I am claiming is that the historic consciousness that is so essential a part of the definition of what we mean by the term 'ethnic *community*', is very often a product of warfare or the recurrent threat thereof, even where the war concerns third parties. The important difference between an 'ethnic category' and an 'ethnic community' can be illustrated by the case of the Slovaks and Ukrainians. In the eighteenth century, it would have been possible for the perceptive observer to distinguish the populations of certain East European valleys and plains from neighbouring populations by their different dialects, religious observances and possibly antecedents. It was only in the early nineteenth century that scholars, poets, priests and later journalists among these populations began to convince wider strata that the population who spoke these dialects and possessed these customs and antecedents constituted an 'ethnic community' because they possessed a common origin, history and culture; and hence that they belonged together in virtue of their common roots in time and place.[23] Later, they began to define their communities as 'nations', that is, ethnic communities, who also possess, or should possess, a common territory with geographical mobility throughout, a common self-contained economic system, and common political rights of citizenship. In doing so, the nationalists were blending very real, and often ancient, cultural realities with abstract ideals and aspirations. Hence the 'nation', unlike the 'ethnic community', is in part a construct of the nationalist; but, again unlike the ethnic community, this abstract entity, the nation, partly for this very reason possesses a dynamic character expressed in an institutional programme, and a sense of ideological destiny, that the ancient ethnic formations usually lacked. Perhaps, also, that is why the 'nation' is an essentially modern phenomenon. It is a product of a secular, ideological era, in which social categories like class and race can furnish political ideals and social programmes.[24]

History

Empires and ethnicity in antiquity

With these distinctions in mind, I want now to look at the impact of different kinds of wars and warfare on the formation, imagery and cohesion of some ethnic communities in three historical eras. The first era is pre-ideological and predominantly religious in symbolism, the pre-Roman ancient world in the eastern Mediterranean in the first millennium BC. In the second, Europe in the revolutionary and Napoleonic period, ideologies like liberalism, democracy and nationalism are beginning to spread; while the third, our century of total warfare, marks in many ways the apogee of these secular ideologies.

Although several factors, some of them obscure, contributed to the creation of the earliest Near Eastern civilizations,[25] the sense of ethnic belonging which began to grow among the Sumerians and Egyptians during the third millennium BC owed much to their defensive needs in the face of marauding tribes, and to the unification of the area through conquest.[26] Similarly, the shock of invasion by partly Indo-European peoples like the Hittites, Hurrians and Kassites in the second millennium bred a renewal of ethnic consciousness among the chief Semitic-speaking kingdoms of Babylonia and Assyria, as did the Hyksos invasion of Egypt.[27] When the native Pharaoh Kamose of Thebes declares:

> One prince rules in Avaris, another in Ethiopia, and here I am, associated with an Asiatic and a Negro. Each has his slice of Egypt, dividing up the land with me. . . . None can rest in peace, despoiled as all are by the imposts of the Asiatics. I will grapple with them, and cut open their belly! I will save Egypt and overthrow the Asiatics![28]

and succeeds in driving the Hyksos out of Egypt, he is formulating a new ethnic concept of an undivided Egypt to be ruled only by indigenous princes. His successors of the New Kingdom, however, were more interested in giving that ethnic sentiment imperial expression in distant lands.[29]

Possibly the most remarkable case of ethnic imperialism is furnished by the spectacular rise of the Assyrian kingdom in the later second millennium BC. Assyrian resistance to Hurrians, Hittites and Kassites furnished the spur to this development, and their economic needs for metals and timber led them to conduct raids into faraway territories. But perhaps the chief unifying force among Assyrians was their tradition of military kingship built up in the course of these wars, and especially during the long-drawn-out contest with the northern kingdom of Urartu around Lake Van.[30] General military success enabled the kings to create a stable bureaucratic state and an army machine widely feared for its ruthlessness and effectiveness. Not surprisingly, the Assyrians came to see themselves as tough, disciplined and terror-inspiring warriors first and foremost, with their war-god, Assur, chief of their pantheon. By contrast, foreigners were depicted as effeminate and submissive prey.[31] Assyria, however, was not free from internal dissensions, both within the noble stratum and between them and the conscripted peasantry, but military success managed to check their expression. Only Ashurbanipal's later failures in battle eroded royal control and ethnic cohesion, paving the way for eventual capitulation to the Medes and Babylonians in 612 BC.

Of all the Assyrians' victims, ancient Israel furnishes the clearest evidence of the decisive impact of war on ethnicity, and affords an interesting parallel, and contrast, with Assyria. Both were war-formed peoples *par excellence*, the Israelite confederation of northern and southern tribes emerging into history during their conquest of part of Canaan, and possessing traditions of enslavement in Egypt and military deliverance from Pharaoh's host through divine intervention.[32] The contrast lies in the fact that in the Assyrian case of 'tribe-state', the collapse of the military state spelt the dissolution of the people, whereas in the Judean case, destruction of the kingdom and captivity actually permitted the ethnic community to emerge and survive, as it has done to this day.[33] Among the early Israelites, in fact, two traditions of community and imagery fought for ascendancy from the outset. The first was that of charismatic heroes, called Judges, like Samson and Gideon, which led to the creation of kingship and the royal state under Saul and David. In this tradition, God is viewed as a lord of hosts, a god of war, destroying Israel's enemies.[34] The other tradition was priestly and prophetic in character, and it stressed the holiness of God and his people, a conception that elevated the community as such.

Solomon's rule marked in many ways a new phase. He involved his kingdom in a network of political alliances, notably with Hisham of Tyre, and thus brought the northern kingdom of Israel, which soon split away, into confrontation with first the Syrians and then the Assyrians. This meant that rather than fight analogous tribal confederacies, the Israelites had to involve themselves with highly organized empires and their military machines. Continual wars combined with Phoenician cultural erosion sapped the northern kingdom's identity and cohesion; despite warnings by Elijah and Amos, the 'prophets of doom', Israel failed to evolve its own communal ethos and a specifically Yahwist priestly cult, able to endow it with an ideal self-image. With the fall of Samaria in 722, the ten northern tribes were assimilated, and disappeared.

The smaller, southern kingdom of Judah adopted the alternative ethnic self-conception and a strategy of greater withdrawal from political entanglements, and survived long enough to crystallize a greater sense of ethnic solidarity and identity. The decisive factors were Judah's crucial geopolitical position across the great trade and battle routes of antiquity, which resembled that of the medieval Swiss;[35] and its unique response to this situation, which was heavily influenced by the Temple priesthood in Jerusalem and the associated prophetic movement of Isaiah, Micah and Jeremiah.[36] Weber, indeed, went so far as to assert that 'Free prophecy developed only with the rising danger to the country and the royal house. . . . Except for the world politics of the great powers, which threatened their homeland and constituted the message of their most impressive oracles, the prophets could not have emerged.'[37]

The case of Judah also illustrates the point that, in a pre-ideological era, the ethnic consciousness of smaller communities is often called into existence by the wars of great military states utilizing small communities as pawns in their struggles, and waging their wars in the territories of the smaller tribes. But whether such an ethnic consciousness can survive the surrounding turbulence will depend on the leaders' ability to steer clear of foreign involvements and on the interpretation they put on adverse political events. That, in fact, was the political role of the prophets: to interpret the blows inflicted by a Sennacherib or a Nebuchadnezzar as so many divine punishments for the sins of the ethnic community.[38]

So, although Judah too proved unable to withstand determined assault and remained politically divided, its ethnic consciousness was enhanced by adversity. In captivity in Babylon, the educated deported strata could now develop the alternative tradition of self-images which stressed holiness and quietism. In Deutero-Isaiah and Ezekiel, there arose the vision of a reborn Israel, a holy people, their dry bones awakened to life, a 'suffering servant' who would become 'a light to the Gentiles' – images of comfort and hope for a depoliticized people.[39]

From the moment that Cyrus permitted the exiles to return to Jerusalem, the Jewish state was replaced by a Jewish religious and ethnic community, soon to be buttressed by Ezra's ban on intermarriage. But the political impulse was not dead. After Alexander's conquests, Palestine became once again the battlefield of his rival successors, the Ptolemies and Seleucids, and economic and cultural opportunities began to divide the Jewish community into Hellenizers and Tsaddikim ('Pious Ones'). The attempts by the Hellenizing Seleucid monarch Antiochus IV Epiphanes to substitute Greek deities and rites for Jewish ones, even in the Temple, sparked off a religious revolt in 165 BC.[40] Led by the Maccabean priestly family, and employing guerilla tactics, the Tsaddikim managed ultimately to drive out the Syrians, and through an astute alliance with the rising Roman power succeeded in setting up an independent Hasmonean kingdom, thereby transforming religious fervour into a rekindled ethnic sentiment filled with potent military self-images.[41]

Yet the very zeal of the enterprise and its political success helped to reopen deep divisions within the Jewish community – family feuds, priestly rivalries and religious schisms – all of which provided the Romans with an excuse to intervene a century later. But their policies, too, proved unacceptable. Heavy taxation and insensitivity to Jewish religious susceptibilities provoked a renewed cycle of revolt after Herod's death.[42] This time, the leaders were a priestly family belonging to the Zealot persuasion, a political offshoot of Pharisaism which was bent on the restoration of a theocracy in Judaea.[43] The Zealot guerilla war, aided by messianic uprisings and anti-Roman sectarians in the desert, rekindled Jewish ethnocentrism, especially in Galilee, and renewed the military imagery of the Maccabees.[44] But as we have seen, heightened ethnic consciousness and ideal self-images of political superiority do not necessarily contribute to internal cohesion. At the moment of supreme trial, the great Jewish War of 66–73, Zealot fanaticism in the face of overwhelming odds brought into the open the simmering social and sectarian divisions within Palestinian Jewry, and hastened the final demise of the Jewish Temple and state.[45]

A similar paradox can be found among that other ethnic exemplar of antiquity, the ancient Greeks. Here, too, heightened ethnic consciousness and self-images of superiority were accompanied by minimal internal cohesion at the pan-Hellenic level. There were several bases of ethnic consciousness: a common Olympian pantheon of gods, interrelated dialects, myths of common origins, acknowledged sacred sites, especially at Delphi and Dodona, the Homeric canon, and various festivals and games.[46] When in the eighth century BC colonies were planted from Odessa to Marseilles, they remained outposts of a common Hellenic culture overseas. Other factors, however, militated against ethnic unity: the peculiar mountainous geography of mainland Greece, which allowed the city-states to flourish; wars between these city-states; the ethno-linguistic split between Ionians, Dorians and Aeolians; above all, the lack of real external threats in the formative period.[47] The resulting Greek consciousness was therefore uneven and cross-cut by *polis* loyalties. We can see this in the way that the Athenians responded to the appeals of their fellow-Ionians in their revolt against Persia, and in the way in which some Greek states, and the Delphic oracle, were prepared to medize in the Persian wars.

How far, then, did war, or its memory, shape a pan-Hellenic consciousness and its imagery? Of the earliest days we cannot be sure, although the tale of Troy and the myth of the Heracleidae associated with the Dorian invasions point to its role as an initial stimulus and a storehouse of images and myths. The Persian threat is more instructive. In the crises of Marathon and Thermopylae, a considerable number of *poleis* were prepared to put aside their quarrels, though only for a short time. At the level of ethnic cohesion, war actually militated against unity, because the wars between the city-states became serious precisely when innovations in military technology brought the hoplites to power in each city-state.[48] The demands of hoplites, and later rowers, for power were based on their services to the *polis* against other *poleis*: and it would take an external power, employing superior military tactics, to downgrade the social and military forces that had so long undermined pan-Hellenic cohesion.

But that is only part of the story. The Persian threat remained on the horizon, and became a pretext for ethnic solidarity. That call for unity, such as Pericles uttered at the Peace of Callias, was not just a pious sentiment, or a clever tactic in the intra-Greek power struggle.[49] It echoed a clear ethnic sentiment, which made Greeks feel superior to 'barbarians' and prize their valour and liberties above the material comforts of the Great King's 'slaves'.[50] In the fifth century, the Greeks came to see themselves as 'civilized' because of their communal discipline, a discipline learnt in the hoplite formation, and contrasting with Oriental luxury and numbers. In Aeschylus' *Persae*, in the metopes of the Parthenon, in the pan-Hellenism of Isocrates, this superiority and these contrasts are vividly expressed.[51] Hence the protracted wars with the Persian Empire, though they signally failed to bring a pan-Hellenic cohesion, did clarify and heighten a latent, if patchy, all-Greek ethnic consciousness, and endowed it with a sense of superiority and a host of vivid self-images and stereotypes.

Revolution and ethnic revival

In the ancient pre-Roman world, ethnic communities played a vital role in both cultural life and politics. In early modern Europe, by way of contrast, the ethnic factor was generally muted and submerged. It is true that from the fourteenth century on, ethnically homogeneous states were gradually forming in parts of Western Europe, and later in Sweden and Russia.[52] But ethnic sentiment and imagery played a minor role until the sixteenth century.[53] Even in the seventeenth and early eighteenth centuries, it was either dormant or so finely integrated with the dynastic state as to be barely discernible in its own right. The *philosophes* naturally assumed the existence of national characteristics, but it is interesting that the cases they had in mind – French, English, Spaniards, Swiss, Dutch, Russians, Swedes – were all sovereign dynastic states, capable of waging limited wars.[54]

Then in the late eighteenth and early nineteenth centuries there was an ethnic explosion all over Europe, in the name of national self-determination. As a sentiment, nationalism had been gathering force since at least the sixteenth century; but as an ideological movement for identity, autonomy and cohesion for a social group deemed to constitute an actual or potential 'nation', it was the product of the late eighteenth century, when it appeared in the wake of liberalism and popular democracy.[55] Starting in England and France, the new ideologies which included nationalism were taken up in Corsica, Poland, Switzerland, Holland and the United States, to be followed soon by movements in Germany, Italy, Hungary, Serbia, Greece, Spain and Ireland.[56]

The rapidity and success of this ethnic revival and of its associated nationalisms are usually attributed to the twin influences of the French Revolution and German Romanticism, coming in the wake of religious decline.[57] The Revolution was certainly crucial, if only because it unleashed a highly centralized and militarist nationalism within France itself, which her victorious armies quickly exported by example and propaganda. But the sense of national unity which the Revolution revealed so vividly was itself the product of centuries of increasingly centralized administration in a relatively well-defined territory. In England, too, the absolutist and bureaucratic island state had succeeded in crystallizing a strong historical sense of Englishness;[58] even though the 1688 Revolution had interrupted the development of the centralized state, it had welded the English educated classes together sufficiently to give rise in the eighteenth century to a strong national sentiment that found expression in the writings of Bolingbroke and Burke, in the revival of Milton and Shakespeare, and in the medievalizing art of Horace Walpole, Blake, Flaxman and

Fuseli, a historicizing movement continually reinforced by external wars with Continental powers.[59] In France, centralizing and homogenizing trends went even further, despite aristocratic resistance; and the popular demand by Siéyès and the *Cahiers* for a unified France of bourgeois citizens was hardly surprising.[60]

How did the nature and incidence of warfare contribute to this ethnic revival? Broadly speaking, its impact before 1792 was indirect, and after 1792 direct. Here we must recall that the age of 'enlightened despotism' was also the era of highly professional warfare incorporating advanced military technology, notably artillery, and that wars were part of the dynastic competition and fought for limited advantages. For this reason, wars were partial and undemocratic. As Andreski remarks:

> It is significant that never in the history of European armies was the chasm between officers and men deeper than in the eighteenth century; and that was precisely the time of limited wars, mildly conducted for insignificant stakes. As the wars became more ferocious, the armies became more egalitarian.[61]

The wars of these dynastic states were fought by armies maintained and equipped by a bureaucratic and 'scientific' state, which allowed the development of advanced military technology, an interrelationship which Howard sums up:

> The development of state power and organisation made such professional forces possible; but the development of military practice and technology made them, functionally, almost essential.[62]

By strengthening a stable network of territorial states, the professional army indirectly fostered a loyalty and cohesion in the demarcated population, which helped to erode local allegiances and encouraged the belief in an all-powerful bureaucratic state and its standardized culture. So when after 1750 a declining royal regime tried to instil in Frenchmen a return to the martial and stoic virtues of the *Grand Siècle* and of antiquity, while France continued to fare badly in the Seven Years War, it was increasingly able to evoke a radical response from the rising educated strata in the towns.[63] Here Rousseau's call for a civic patriotism and simple virtues, taken up by Diderot and others, found a ready ear.[64] By the 1780s, the new ethnic historicism, which looked back with Rousseau and David to Sparta and Rome, and with Villaret and d'Angiviller to French medieval heroes, had taken on radical and even republican implications, which the crown was powerless to halt, and which paved the way for the revolutionary nationalism of 1789 and 1792.[65]

Before 1792, then, limited professional warfare between territorial states tended to make a relatively homogeneous population conscious of its origins and common history, through the agency of the bureaucratic and centralizing state. As that state came to dominate society and required well-trained, loyal civil servants, the rising secular intelligentsia naturally gravitated to the centre in search of office and status. Their increasing leadership in, and commitment to, the territorial state fostered a bureaucratic nationalism awaiting the call of *la patrie*.

That call came, for Frenchmen, in 1792. Prolonged, increasingly savage and comprehensive wars now began to fuel and shape the ethnic revival directly, and not only in France. Within France, the Revolution reduced the long-standing gulf between state and army, and society, and so could release the tide of patriotic sentiment. In the great *fêtes*, the tricolour, anthem and *levées en masse* under the Jacobins, French national consciousness gained classic expression.[66] The need to defend and export the Revolution threw up a whole new patriotic imagery of France as the home of republican virtue and liberty, and later, under Napoleon, of the great nation in arms, an imperial liberator and civilizer.[67]

France's enemies, too, were soon compelled to adopt counter-images and a new ethnic self-consciousness, especially where defeat compelled them to resort to conscription, as with Prussia after Jena. Prussia, indeed, was fairly successful in keeping democracy at bay by appropriating the symbols of a Germanic ethnicity, which its military success and hierarchical structure merely served to inflame.[68] In polyethnic empires like Russia and Austria, resistance to Napoleon's incursions and the subversive ideas of the Revolution merely served to foster dissidence among subject ethnic communities, and especially their excluded and suspect intelligentsias.[69] The syndrome is inevitable in an ideological era, where regimes must count on the exclusive loyalty of their armies and bureaucrats, and where they will therefore tend to reserve the top posts for members of the ruling ethnic community; and conversely, the Westernized and excluded intelligentsias of the subject communities will increasingly blame their exclusion on 'ethnic discrimination'.

Apart from these indirect effects, the wars of the Revolution and Napoleon were themselves of an entirely different order from the gentlemanly professional contests of the eighteenth century. They were more serious, comprehensive and near-continuous, if not to the same extent everywhere. In some cases, such as Napoleon's Russian expedition, they were examples of total war, though formally only incursions. These wars had two effects. One was to strengthen state powers in lands where absolutism had been limited, if only to withstand such massive assaults and pay for the mass armies and their artillery. The second was to demonstrate the propaganda effects of even swift forays and incursions, in an era of growing communications and secular ideologies. One has only to consider the remarkable effects of Napoleon's relatively brief campaigns in Italy, and of his forays into Egypt and Syria, not to mention his propaganda addressed to the Illyrians.[70]

The century of total war

If the Napoleonic wars produced so great an ethnic upheaval, one would expect the prolonged and total wars of the twentieth century to harden, and broaden, the lines of ethnicity everywhere. In a sense this is what occurred; but the 'test' of total war also produced some surprises.[71]

The First World War is often treated as a war of nations, but in fact the contenders were still bureaucratic states in which, for the most part, there was a considerable gulf between government and society.[72] Among them, the multinational empires were the first to succumb to the scale and intensity of modern warfare; their adoption of conscription actually 'fostered the disintegration of multinational empires, because universal conscription became an unavoidable condition of military strength and armies raised in this way were of little value unless permeated by patriotism'.[73] Small wonder that they were quickly replaced by ethnically more homogeneous 'successor states'. In this area, then, the 1914–18 War promoted the cause of ethnic nations across Europe, but was not fought by such nations. In the West, the war was fought by nation-states with colonial empires, and it gradually but inexorably extended the powers of the state over civilian life. At first, the war was fought by the state and army machines, until the decimation of the volunteers forced mass conscription even in Britain in 1916, and the creation by the state of the 'home front' as an integral part of the war effort. Only at this critical juncture did Western governments begin to move closer to their peoples.

Within the Western democracies, total war provoked contradictory trends: a movement towards greater national solidarity, in which the war was seen as vital and exciting, and the upper classes were ready for social reforms to reward lower-class participation; and an opposing trend towards the hardening of horizontal class and group solidarities among workers, women and Blacks (in America), accompanied by revulsion against all war and bitter disillusion at the front. After Verdun, France went through a period of grave disaffection: 1917, the year of the 'mutinies', was also a 'year of considerable labour unrest, provoked by the rising cost of living and the steady attrition of the original patriotic enthusiasm'.[74] In Britain, too, 1917 was a year of much labour unrest, mainly due to the Conscription and Munitions Acts, and the bad housing for workers.[75] Hence, says Marwick, 'the increase in social solidarity, for which there is much evidence in 1914 and 1915, was subjected to severe strain in 1917, though partially consolidated again in the hour of victory'.[76]

The experience of the First World War is hard to generalize. But we can infer that protracted and total warfare does generally accentuate national or ethnic self-consciousness (and hence breaks up multinational polities), and it undoubtedly provides a fund of propaganda images and stereotypes, which government agencies can whip up for the war effort.[77] On the other hand, it puts a severe strain on the cohesion of even the more homogeneous societies, and tends to destroy the heterogeneous ones. As Simmel observed:

> A state of conflict, however, pulls the members so tightly together and subjects them to such a uniform impulse that they must either completely get along with, or repel, one another. This is the reason why war with the outside is sometimes the last chance for a state ridden with inner antagonisms to overcome these antagonisms, or else to break up definitely.[78]

The Second World War was more truly a 'war of nations'. Owing to the racial or other ideologies espoused, and the ferocity of the objectives, the war became less a 'test' of institutions and states and their armies than of peoples fighting on two fronts – in the field and, through aerial bombardment, at home. If we include this latter front, the military participation ratio was massive, for the war enveloped all, even if casualties in the West were less than in the First World War.

In the East, casualties and involvement were on a tremendous scale. In Russia, the participation of workers and women was enormous, and sheer necessity reduced the erstwhile distance between Party and country. Thus, '[a]nti-religious propaganda disappeared. Marxist jargon tended to give place to the old patriotic slogans. For all the ruthless discipline, a new unity in national patriotic feeling seemed to be opening between party and country.'[79] Even the non-Russian nationalities, once they saw the brutality of Nazi policies towards them, joined forces with the Russian war effort. Citing Shostakovitch's patriotic symphonies and Pasternak's writings, as well as the tremendous victory celebrations of 9 May 1945, Marwick concludes: 'In general, the effect of the war was to foster national solidarity.'[80] The war also provided a rich store of patriotic imagery, already intimated in Eisenstein's film *Alexander Nevsky*, set to Prokofiev's menacing score. As Marwick observes:

> this was a war in which the Russians as a national grouping were second only to the Jews as a target for systematic brutality on the part of the Germans, and which contained great legendary set-pieces such as the siege of Leningrad and the victory of Stalingrad and countless incidents, sung (literally) and unsung, of individual and group heroism.[81]

Among the Western combatants, too, bombing usually solidified national sentiment. In Germany, there was a high active morale in production and an efficient civil defence, underpinned by Nazi governmental controls. Indeed, arms production was usually resumed only weeks after the most devastating raid, and few questioned the Nazi aim of creating a racially homogeneous empire.[82] In Britain, the response was more complex. On the one hand, few questioned the trend to greatly increased government control of economy and society, which paved the way for the welfare state. The immediate dangers of 1940, too, created a strong national solidarity. On the other hand, once the euphoria of Dunkirk was over, old class divisions reappeared during the prolonged blitz; and despite much general camaraderie, the poor soon complained about the lack of shelters and adequate precautions, especially in London's East End. The middle classes did make cross-class contacts; but after 1942 war-weariness and the increased confidence of workers, and women, who now entered the army and the job market, bred increased labour unrest.[83]

A striking exception to the general rule of increased national unity through total war was provided by France. Swift and sudden defeat had merely confirmed the great divisions of the 1930s, and the distance of the state from society.[84] In the ensuing three-cornered struggle between Pétainists, Communists and Free French, the war bred mutual suspicions and fragmentation; yet, paradoxically, through the Resistance movements, it also fostered the rebirth of national consciousness and a nobler self-image, despite continued dissensions after the war.[85]

The Second World War was also the first global war. In an age of nationalism and fascism, it drew large numbers of colonial peoples into the fray and thereby helped to ignite ethnic consciousness in areas remote from the war's epicentre, with a harvest of anti-colonial 'wars of liberation'.[86] Many of these successor wars, consequent on the geopolitical shifts occasioned by the Second World War, have helped to mould ethnic categories into national communities, such as Algeria, or to bring quarrelling ethnic communities into a single nation, as in Yugoslavia.[87]

Generalizations

From this brief, and admittedly selective, historical review, I should now like to extract some tentative generalizations about the relationships between ethnicity and warfare. The evidence presented seems to lend support to my two main contentions: first, the very general one, that it is more useful to treat warfare, and its types, as the independent variable and one of the chief forces shaping various aspects of ethnicity, and second, the more specific argument that while prolonged or total war generally strengthens ethnic *self-consciousness* and ethnic *imagery*, it may often weaken the *cohesion* of multinational or sharply stratified societies.

Beyond these broad contentions, some further generalizations may be ventured from the mass of often contradictory historical evidence. Some of these generalizations have often been remarked on before, though their ethnic consequences have rarely been noted. I shall divide them into direct and indirect consequences of war, there being three generalizations under each heading.

Direct consequences

1 Mobilisation   A commonly noted effect of prolonged or total warfare is the rapid increase in participants in the war effort, or military participation ratio, to use Andreski's term.[88] The more savage and extended the war, the greater the mobilization and consumption of the population; and hence, the greater the chance of diffusing a sense of ethnic belonging and identity through appropriate imagery. The greater the number of ethnic participants in the conflict, and the more active their participation to meet the common threat, as with the English facing the Armada, or the Dutch Calvinists facing the Spanish threat, the more likelihood there is that a strong ethnic sentiment and community will emerge.[89]

In the modern ideological era, this trend is greatly enhanced, because ethnic sentiment and national cohesion can be strongly influenced by the propaganda of 'populist' ideologies and the impetus they provide for further wars, which in turn require mass mobilization. Indeed, under these conditions, which entrench the idea of the 'nation' as a political norm, war may actually replace other kinds of social change to crystallize the ethnic nation. In Vietnam, for example, revolutionary guerilla warfare mobilized the peasants through 'emergency measures', activating the latent energies of the masses. As Wilson put it, the mobilization process 'uses human energy fully and educates the participants to understand new frames of mind, new beliefs, and new social organisations. A nation is being built.'[90]

Yet not all wars bring mobilization. Small incursions and lightning blitzkriegs may offer no ground, or leave no time, for mass mobilization. 'Partial' wars, that is, those conducted by closed professional armies alone and fought for limited objectives, are designed to avoid any recourse to a high participation ratio, and their effects on ethnic community formation or imagery creation are therefore likely to be gradual and indirect. Besides, as we saw, high mobilization may well strengthen horizontal divisions. The hitherto excluded lower strata become conscious of their bargaining power in the war effort; but in the longer term, if the unit survives, such intracommunal competition may reinforce the ethnic framework and its historic mores.

2 *Propaganda* Propaganda and psychological warfare are the most commonly noted and best-attested effects of protracted warfare.[91] Whether more narrowly treated in terms of simple morale boosting, or more broadly as the 'direct manipulation of social suggestion', the propagandist's aim is the construction of favourable self-images and negative enemy stereotypes. One important resource for this end is the fund of accumulated myths and images common to the community, often drawn from previous wars and encounters. In drawing on this inner resource, war propaganda furthers the community's ethnocentrism, the belief in the centrality and superiority of one's group and its culture.[92] Ethnocentrism inevitably devalues outsiders and their cultures, breeding solipsism or in some cases hostility. There are, however, exceptions to this rule: Meiji Japan and Kemalist Turkey, both triggered into being by invasions, managed to re-create an ethnic imagery with positive self-images, but without (at first) the negative stereotypes of outsiders that conduce to isolation or wars.[93]

Wars also make their own propaganda myths. They furnish epic legends on a grand scale which 'speak' to the people and become subjects for inspiring works of art, like Tolstoy's *War and Peace* or Delacroix's 'Massacre at Chios'; for later generations, the war myths they embody will serve as exemplars of a peculiar ethnic virtue and heroism, as will the heroes they glorify. Indeed, manly virtue lies at the heart of most historicism.[94]

3 *Cohesion* The time-span is crucial in considering the effects of war on ethnic cohesion.

In the short term, wars unless immediately lost, paper over the cracks and create ethnic ardour and solidarity. At Marathon, Borodino, Dunkirk, the invaded forgot their internal differences to ward off the common threat. In the medium term, however, prolonged and/or total wars tend to strain cohesion even in homogeneous communities and bring their horizontal social divisions out more forcibly. As for multinational states, total war generally shatters their unity, as was the case with Tsarist Russia, Ottoman Turkey and Habsburg Austria–Hungary.

But, in the longer term, protracted or intermittent wars, whether direct or fought between third parties, may well reinforce the community's framework, its sense of ethnic individuality and history. In Germany, for example, the First World War destroyed any cohesion it had possessed; yet it also strengthened German ethnic self-consciousness, which was later able to act as a resource for Nazi German imagery and create the impression of a much greater solidarity.[95] From a still longer-term perspective, many of the European states – England, France, Russia, Switzerland, Spain, Poland and Sweden among them – have been beaten into 'national shape' by the hammer of incessant wars, which have also endowed them with a great part of their ethnic cohesion and imagery.[96]

Indirect consequences

4   Centralization   On a number of occasions, we saw that incessant warfare encouraged the growth of state power, and this is one of the most commonly accepted notions. In turn, territorial and bureaucratic centralization help to weld and homogenize quite diverse populations over several generations, turning them into a culturally distinct 'nation'.[97] This is also the emergent pattern today among many 'state-nations' of Africa under military regimes. Fear of 'ethnic balkanization' even prompts African elites to strengthen existing states by invoking the threat of external 'neo-colonialism'.[98]

There is, however, a qualification to this generalization. There have been centralizing and bureaucratic states whose 'étatisme' was actually halted and dissolved by exhausting wars; Andreski cites the cases of Ptolemaic Egypt and twelfth-century Byzantium. He also points out that warlike states like the Arabian Caliphate, the Ottoman Empire and the Sultanate of Delhi were not very centralized and interfered minimally in the lives of their peasants, as the latter were useless in a cavalry-dominated army; and he concludes that only where the whole adult population is involved in the war process do continuous wars produce a high degree of governmental regulation.[99]

All these cases, interestingly, antedate the 'ideological era', which is also an era of growing conscription. Recently, prolonged wars *have* tended to produce *dirigiste* manpower policies and strong drives towards centralization and social intervention. Besides, in an industrial era, only the state can afford the costly military research and technology now needed in total warfare. If the link between a centralizing state and a professional army was forged in an age of bureaucratism and science, today ideological and economic factors have made that link indissoluble; and defence needs, in turn, continually reinforce the sense of national identity in an era of total war and global interdependence.

5   Rationalization   Professionalization of the state and the army is, in large part, a product of the increasing social use of scientific technology, which in turn demands a special training and a utilitarian, secular and rationalistic outlook. Such qualities find their natural home among the intelligentsia who are attracted into government and army posts, thereby outflanking more traditional elites. Today, Westernized diploma-holders increasingly run the modern nation-state, and especially those with a small (or eliminated) bourgeoisie (and landowner class).

Yet the technocratic intelligentsia is also the stratum most susceptible to 'ideological' goals and rationalizing programmes. Nationalism is particularly appealing, and especially to army or guerilla leaders. Hence rationalization and professionalism, by bringing an ideologically minded intelligentsia to power in the state, have indirectly bred a heightened nationalism, even in the most revolutionary and 'Marxist' states.[100] In such circumstances, we should not be surprised by the many 'wars of liberation' and 'people's wars' from China to Angola and Cuba, which only serve to reinforce ethnic solidarity and 'nation-building'.[101]

6 *Colonialism* The advent of colonialism has provided warfare with another channel of influence on ethnicity. When Europe exported her 'balance of power' problems overseas, taking over ailing private commercial ventures, the result was to increase enormously the area in which ethnic sentiments and national cohesion could be revived or crystallized. For it was mainly military-strategic and political reasons that prompted the large-scale territorial annexations, climaxed in the 'scramble for Africa'.[102] In exporting their own conflicts overseas, the European states raised up a hornet's nest of new struggles between colonialism and incipient indigenous nationalisms. For the colonies could be seen as embryonic 'nations', or as territorial strait-jackets imposed across ethnic boundaries. In either case, European inter-state antagonisms fed the Asian and African ethnic renaissance and its wars through the intermediary of the colonial state, itself a deliberate creation of distant treaties and the seed-bed for many new territorial loyalties and ethnic antagonisms among the colonized.

In a brief, exploratory paper like this, only a few of the many links between warfare and ethnic community could be indicated. I hope, however, that enough has been said to demonstrate the importance of the field, and to justify my primary contentions concerning the direct and indirect impacts of war on ethnic and national consciousness and imagery.

Notes

1   Of course, scholars of an older generation like Sorokin, and before him Spencer and Gumplowicz, were very conscious of the primacy of warfare and its impact on society, including ethnic groups. However, for their different reasons, the dominant functionalist and Marxist approaches have

tended to relegate the impact of war, and only since the 1950s have scholars like Andreski, Marwick, Finer and Howard reinstated the status of military factors in social order and change.

2   W. McDougall, *An Introduction to Social Psychology* (London: Methuen, 1915), ch. 11.

3   D. J. Levinson, 'Authoritarian personality and foreign policy', *Journal of Conflict Resolution* 1 (1957), pp. 37–47, reprinted in L. Bramson and G. W. Goethals (eds), *War, Studies from Psychology, Sociology, Anthropology* (New York and London: Basic Books, 1964).

4   K. Popper, *The Open Society and its Enemies*, 4th edn (London: Routledge & Kegan Paul, 1962), vol. 2, ch. 12, pp. 49–51.

5   W. G. Sumner, *War and Other Essays* (New Haven: Yale University Press, 1911). Parsons, too, views solidarity groups like ethnic communities and nations as the main sources and foci of aggression in the modern world. Cf. T. Parsons, 'Certain primary sources and patterns of aggression in the social structure of the Western world' (1947), in T. Parsons, *Essays in Sociological Theory*, rev. edn (Glencoe, IL: Free Press; London: Macmillan, 1964), esp. pp. 314ff.

6   E. Kedourie, *Nationalism* (London: Hutchinson, 1960).

7   L. Wirth, 'Types of nationalism', *American Journal of Sociology* 41 (1936), pp. 723–37; and B. Akzin, *State and Nation* (London: Hutchinson, 1964), ch. 5.

8   Z. Barbu, 'Nationalism as a source of aggression', in *Conflict* (London: Ciba Foundation, 1966).

9   B. Malinowski, 'An anthropological analysis of war', *American Journal of Sociology* 46 (1941), pp. 521–50; and R. E. Park, 'The social function of war', *American Journal of Sociology* 46 (1941), pp. 551–70.

10   On the Czechs, S. Harrison Thompson, *Czechoslovakia in European History* (Princeton: Princeton University Press, 1943).

11   B. Abrahamsson, *Military Professionalization and Political Power* (Beverly Hills CA, and London: Sage Publications, 1972), cites, in support of the view that nationalism is necessarily the ideology of the military, *inter alia*, E. Waldman, *The Goosestep is verboten* (New York: Free Press, 1964), for German military hostility to the Soviets (p. 238).

12   J. P. Nettl and R. Robertson, *International Systems and the Modernization of Societies* (London: Faber & Faber, 1968), pt II.

13   Malinowski, 'Anthropological analysis', on 'Tribe-nation' and 'Tribe-state'.

14   Cf. H. Tint, *The Decline of French Patriotism* (London: Weidenfeld & Nicolson, 1964). On military elites generally, cf. M. Janowitz, 'Military elites and the study of war', *Journal of Conflict Resolution* 1 (1957), pp. 9–18, reprinted in Bramson and Goethals (eds), *War*.

15   B. C. Keeney, 'Military service and the development of nationalism in England, 1272–1327', *Speculum* 22 (1947), pp. 534–49, reprinted in C. L. Tipton (ed.), *Nationalism in the Middle Ages* (New York: Holt, Rinehart & Winston, 1972); and H. Seton-Watson, *Nations and States* (London: Methuen, 1977), ch. 2.

16   E. Renan, *Qu'est-ce qu'une Nation?* (Paris: Calmann-Levy, 1882).

17   G. Simmel, *Conflict, and the Web of Group-Affiliations* (Glencoe, IL: Free Press; London: Macmillan, 1964), p. 88.

18   Ibid., p. 100.

19   Ibid., p. 101.

20   Ibid., p. 92.

21   M. Weber, 'Ethnic groups', in *Economy and Society*, ed. G. Roth and C. Wittich (New York: Bedminster Press, 1968, vol. 1, ch. 5; thus: 'It is primarily the political community, no matter how artificially organized, that inspires the belief in common ethnicity.' On this, cf. also C. Enloe, *Ethnic Soldiers* (Harmondsworth: Penguin, 1980), ch. 1.

22   For the role of cultural 'markers' cf. E. Gellner, 'Scale and nation', *Philosophy of the Social Sciences* 3 (1973), pp. 1–17; and the general discussion of ethnic cleavages today in D. Bell, 'Ethnicity and social change', in N. Glazer and D. P. Moynihan (eds), *Ethnicity, Theory and Experience* (Cambridge, MA, and London: Harvard University Press, 1975), pp. 141–74.

23   Seton-Watson, *Nations and States*, ch. 4.

24   For fuller discussions of ethnic community and nation, cf. A. D. Smith, *Theories of Nationalism* (London: Duckworth, 1971), ch. 7; and *idem*, 'Nationalism: a trend report and bibliography', *Current Sociology* 21/3 (The Hague and Paris: Mouton, 1973).

25   R. Coulborn, *The Origin of Civilized Societies* (Princeton: Princeton University Press, 1959); and R. Braidwood and G. Willey (eds), *Courses towards Urban Life* (New York: Aldine Publishing Company, 1962).

26   S. N. Kramer, *The Sumerians* (Chicago: University of Chicago Press, 1963); C. H. Gordon, *The Ancient Near East*, 3rd edn (New York: W. W. Norton, 1965), ch. 3.

27   On the Hittites, Hurrians and Kassites and the Semitic revival, cf. S. Moscati, *The Face of the Ancient Orient* (New York: Doubleday Anchor, 1962), chs 3, 5.

28   Ibid., p. 110, citing J. B. Pritchard (ed.), *Ancient Near Eastern Texts Relating to the Old Testament*, 2nd edn (Princeton: Princeton University Press, 1955), p. 232.

29   Moscati, *Face of the Ancient Orient*, pp. 110–14; and H. Frankfort, *Kingship and the Gods* (Chicago: Chicago University Press, 1948).

30   G. Roux, *Ancient Iraq* (Harmondsworth: Penguin, 1964), ch. 19.

31   Moscati, *Face of the Ancient Orient*, ch. 3; and the inscriptions in J. B. Pritchard, *The Ancient Near East* (Princeton: Princeton University Press, 1958), section VII.

32   M. Noth, *The History of Israel*, 2nd edn (London: A. & C. Black, 1960), pt I.

33   Ibid., pt III; cf. T. Parsons, *Societies, Evolutionary and Comparative Perspectives* (Englewood Cliffs, NJ: Prentice-Hall, 1966).

34   As in Miriam's song by the Red Sea, Exodus 15; cf. Psalm 24.

35   H. Kohn, *Nationalism and Liberty: The Swiss Example* (London: Macmillan, 1957).

36   P. Berger, 'Charisma, religious innovation and Israelite prophecy', *American Sociological Review* 28 (1963); *idem, The Social Reality of Religion* (London: Faber & Faber, 1969).

37   M. Weber, *Ancient Judaism* (New York: Free Press, 1952), p. 268.

38   Y. Kaufmann, *The Religion of Israel* (London: George Allen & Unwin, 1961), pt III.

39   e.g. Ezekiel 37; Isaiah 42, 53; cf. Kaufmann, *Religion of Israel*.

40   V. Tcherikover, *Hellenistic Civilization and the Jews* (New York: Atheneum, 1970), pt I.

41   M. Pearlman, *The Maccabees* (London: Weidenfeld & Nicolson, 1973); cf. also W. R. Farmer, *Maccabees, Zealots and Josephus* (New York: Columbia University Press, 1956).

42   M. Grant, *The Jews in the Roman World* (London: Weidenfeld & Nicolson, 1973), ch. 6.

43   S. G. F. Brandon, *Jesus and the Zealots* (Manchester: Manchester University Press, 1967).

44   H. Maccoby, *Revolution in Judaea* (London: Ocean Books, 1974), ch. 6; and J. Carmichael, *The Death of Jesus* (Harmondsworth: Penguin, 1966), pp. 125–30.

45   Brandon, *Jesus and the Zealots*, pp. 128–45; Josephus, *The Jewish War* (Harmondsworth: Penguin, 1959).

46   A. Andrewes, 'The growth of the city-state', in H. Lloyd-Jones (ed.), *The Greek World* (Harmondsworth: Penguin, 1965), pp. 26–65; and R. Schlaifer, 'Greek theories of slavery from Homer to Aristotle', in M. I. Finley (ed.), *Slavery in Classical Antiquity* (Cambridge: Heffer & Sons, 1960).

47   On the 'racial factor', cf. A. Andrewes, *The Greek Tyrants* (London: Hutchinson, 1956), ch. 5.

48   Cf. W. G. Forrest, *The Emergence of Greek Democracy* (London: Weidenfeld & Nicolson, 1966); and Andrewes, *Greek Tyrants*, ch. 3.

49   M. Levi, *Political Power in the Ancient World* (London: Weidenfeld & Nicolson, 1965).

50   H. Schwabl, 'Das Bild der fremden Welt bei den frühen Griechen', and Hans Ditter, 'Die Hellenen-Barbaren-Antithese im Zeitalter der Perserkriege', both in Fondation Hardt, *Grecs et Barbares*, Entretiens sur l'antiquité classique 8 (Geneva, 1962).

51   H. Bacon, *Barbarians in Greek Tragedy* (New Haven: Yale University Press, 1962); Schlaifer, 'Greek Theories'.

52   On the 'old continuous nations', cf. Seton-Watson, *Nations and States*, ch. 2; and J. Strayer, 'The historical experience of nation-building in Europe', in K. Deutsch and W. Foltz (eds), *Nation-Building* (New York: Atherton, 1963), pp. 17–26.

53   Cf. H. Kohn, *The Idea of Nationalism* 2nd edn (New York: Macmillan, 1967), ch. 3; but cf. the contrary view of J. Huizinga, 'Nationalism in the Middle Ages', in idem, *Men and Ideas* (New York: Free Press, 1959), reprinted in Tipton (ed.), *Nationalism in the Middle Ages*, pp. 14–24.

54   A. Kemilainen, *Nationalism: Problems Concerning the Word, Concept and Classification* (Yvaskyla: Kustantajat Publishers, 1964).

55   Cf. Smith, *Theories of Nationalism*, ch. 7, and *idem*, 'Nationalism: a trend report and bibliography', section 2. Also E. Kamenka (ed.), *Nationalism: The Nature and Evolution of an Idea* (London: Edward Arnold, 1976), esp, essays by Kamenka and J. Plamenatz.

56   J. Godechot, *France and the Atlantic Revolution of the Eighteenth Century, 1770–1799* (London: Collier–Macmillan, 1971); H. Trevor-Roper, *Jewish and Other Nationalisms* (London: Weidenfeld & Nicolson, 1961).

57   e.g. by Kedourie, *Nationalism*.

58   H. Kohn, 'The origin of English nationalism', *Journal of the History of Ideas* 1 (1940), pp. 69–94.

59   D. Irwin, *English Neo-Classical Art* (London: Faber & Faber, 1966), chs 4, 6; Kohn, *Idea of Nationalism*, ch. 5, pp. 212–14; S. Baron, *Modern Nationalism and Religion* (New York: Meridian Books, 1960), ch. 2.

60   B. C. Shafer, 'Bourgeois nationalism in the pamphlets on the eve of the French Revolution', *Journal of Modern History* 10 (1938), pp. 31–50.

61   S. Andreski, *Military Organization and Society* (London: Routledge & Kegan Paul, 1954), p. 30.

62   M. Howard, *War in European History* (London: Oxford University Press, 1976), p. 55. And he adds: 'In noting this interaction one cannot ignore the development of professional armed forces, itself made possible by the increasing control acquired by the state over the resources of the community, which enabled the state to acquire yet greater control over those resources by serving as an instrument, not only of external defence but of internal compulsion' (ibid.).

63   J. Loquin, *La Peinture d'histoire en France de 1747 à 1785* (Paris: Henri Laurens, 1912); R. Palmer, 'The national idea in France before the Revolution', *Journal of the History of Ideas* 1 (1940), pp. 94–111.

64   J. A. Leith, *The Idea of Art as Propaganda in France, 1750–1799* (Toronto: University of Toronto Press, 1965); and A. Cobban, *Rousseau and the Modern State* 2nd edn (London: Allen & Unwin, 1964).

65   H. Honour, *Neo-Classicism* (Harmondsworth: Penguin, 1968); and F. Cummings, 'Painting under Louis XVI, 1774–1789', in *French Painting 1774–1830: The Age of Revolution* (Detroit: Wayne State University Press, 1975).

66   R. Herbert, *David, Voltaire, Brutus and the French Revolution* (London: Allen Lane, 1972); and N. Hampson, 'The French Revolution and the nationalisation of honour', in M. R. D. Foot (ed.), *War and Society* (London: Paul Elek, 1973).

67   H. Kohn, *Prelude to Nation-States: The French and German Experience, 1789–1815* (Princeton: Van Nostrand, 1967).

68   W. M. Simon, 'Variations in nationalism during the great reform period in Prussia', *American Historical Review* 59 (1954), pp. 305–21; and M. S. Anderson, *The Ascendancy of Europe, 1815–1914* (London: Longman, 1972), chs 2–3.

69 R. A. Kann, *The Multi-National Empire* (New York: Columbia University Press, 1950); H. Seton-Watson, *The Russian Empire 1801–1917* (London: Oxford University Press, 1967); J. Droz, *Europe between Revolutions 1815–1848* (London: Collins, 1967), chs 6–7.

70 F. Markham, *Napoleon and the Awakening of Europe* (Harmondsworth: Penguin, 1975), chs 7–8, 11; and G. Rudé, *Revolutionary Europe* (London: Collins, 1964).

71 The idea that war furnishes a 'test' of social structures comes from the important analysis of total war by A. Marwick, *War and Social Change in the Twentieth Century* (London: Methuen, 1974).

72 M. Howard, 'Total war in the twentieth century: participation and consensus in the Second World War', in B. Bond and I. Roy (eds), *War and Society* (London: Croom Helm, 1975).

73 Andreski, *Military Organization and Society*, p. 83. Conscription was introduced after Sadowa and the Crimean War.

74 Marwick, *War and Social Change*, p. 55. There were 98 strikes in 1915, and 696 strikes in 1917.

75 A. Marwick, *The Deluge: British Society and the First World War* (London: Macmillan, 1965), ch. 6.

76 Marwick, *War and Social Change*, p. 56.

77 Marwick, *The Deluge*, pp. 210–17.

78 Simmel, *Conflict*, pp. 92–3.

79 Marwick, *War and Social Change*, p. 132.

80 Ibid., p. 33.

81 Ibid., p. 123.

82 Ibid., pp. 114ff, 142.

83 Ibid., pp. 153ff.

84 Howard, 'Total war in the twentieth century'.

85 Marwick, *War and Social Change*, citing S. Hoffman, 'The effects of World War II on French Society and politics', *French Historical Studies* 1 (1961).

86 Cf. P. Worsley, *The Third World* (London: Weidenfeld & Nicolson, 1964).

87 On Yugoslavia, cf. R. Burks, *The Dynamics of Communism in Eastern Europe* (Princeton: Princeton University Press, 1961), ch. 6.

88 Andreski, *Military Organisation and Society*, ch. 2, pp. 33ff, the key concept of M.P.R. being defined as 'the proportion of militarily utilized individuals in the total population'. Cf. also S. Andreski, *Elements of Comparative Sociology* (London: Weidenfeld & Nicolson, 1964), chs 7–8.

89 P. Geyl, *The Revolt of the Netherlands* (London: Benn, 1932); and P. Geyl, 'Language and nationality in the Low Countries: a correction', *History* 31 (1946), pp. 137–9; Kohn, 'Origin of English nationalism'.

90 D. A. Wilson, 'Nation-building and revolutionary war', in Deutsch and Foltz (eds), *Nation-Building*, pp. 84–94.

91 M. Grodzins, *The Loyal and the Disloyal: Social Boundaries of Patriotism and Treason* (Cleveland and New York: Meridian Books, 1956); and B. L. Smith, H. D. Lasswell, and R. D. Casey, *Propaganda, Communication and Public Opinion* (Princeton: Princeton University Press, 1946).

92   On this, cf. Weber, 'Ethnic groups', and A. D. Smith, 'Ethnocentrism, nationalism and social change', *International Journal of Comparative Sociology* 13 (1972), pp. 1–20.

93   Cf. M. Kosaka, 'The Meiji era: the forces of rebirth', *Journal of World History* 5 (1959), pp. 621–33; B. Lewis, *The Emergence of Modern Turkey*, 2nd edn (London: Oxford University Press, 1968); R. Bellah, 'Religious aspects of modernization in Turkey and Japan', *American Journal of Sociology* 64 (1958), pp. 1–5.

94   R. Rosenblum, *Transformations in Late Eighteenth-Century Art* (Princeton: Princeton University Press, 1967), ch. 2.

95   D. K. Bracher, *The German Dictatorship* (Harmondsworth: Penguin, 1973), chs 1–3.

96   As is made clear in the account of Seton-Watson, *Nations and States*, ch. 2, and essays in Tipton (ed.), *Nationalism in the Middle Ages*.

97   On the link between the mercenary professional army and growing state power, cf. H. Jacoby, *The Bureaucratization of the World*, trans. E. Kanes (Berkeley and Los Angeles: University of California Press, 1973), pt I, chs 1–2, esp. p. 27, which cites the words of J. Schumpeter, *History of Economic Analysis* (New York: Oxford University Press, 1954), p. 147: 'All this . . . meant management of everything, which in turn meant the rise of modern bureaucracy, a fact that is no less important than is the rise of the business class. The resulting economy was a planned Economy; and it was planned, primarily with a view to war.' Cf. also A. D. Smith, *Nationalism in the Twentieth Century* (Oxford: Martin Robertson, 1979), ch. 7.

98   B. Neuberger. 'The African concept of Balkanization', *Journal of Modern African Studies* 13 (1976), pp. 523–9.

99   Andreski, *Military Organization and Society*, ch. 5, esp. pp. 111–15.

100 On this, cf. Smith, *Nationalism in the Twentieth Century*, ch. 5.

101 Cf. R. A. Scalapino (ed.), *The Communist Revolution in Asia* (Englewood Cliffs, NJ: Prentice-Hall, 1969).

102 D. K. Fieldhouse (ed.), *The Theory of Capitalist Imperialism* (London: Longman, 1967).

7

The Origins of Nations

Anyone exploring the shape and origins of the modern world must soon stumble on the power and ubiquity of nations. In a sense, nothing so clearly marks out the modern era and defines our attitudes and sentiments as national consciousness and nationalist ideology. Not only in everyday political and social life, but also in our underlying assumptions, the nation and its nationalism provide a stable framework for good or ill and define the goals and values of most collective activity. The modern world has become inconceivable and unintelligible without nations and nationalism; international relations, in particular, though they deal in the first place with the relations between states, are built around the premisses of nationalism.

It follows that a fundamental way to grasp the nature and shape of the modern world is through an exploration of the nature and origins of nations. This is, of course, a vast subject, whose investigation could fill several volumes. Here I can only look at the broad outlines of such an investigation. In particular, I shall be concerned with the 'prehistory' of nations, the way in which collective identities in pre-modern eras helped to shape modern nations. Only in this way, through an historical and sociological exploration of how pre-modern communities shaped our world of nations, can we really begin to grasp the power and significance of today's nations and nationalism.

'The Origin of Nations', *Ethnic and Racial Studies*, *12/3* (1989): 340–67. Reproduced with the permission of the editors. (<http://www.tandf.co.uk/journals/routledge/01419870.html>)

The 'National' and 'Nationalism'

We can begin by narrowing down our enquiry to three questions. The first concerns the relationship between abstractions and realities. The 'nation' is often seen by modernists as an abstraction, something that nationalists, and elites in general, have 'constructed' to serve their partisan ends. On this reading, nations lack tangibility or any 'primordial' character. They constitute mere ideals, or mere legitimations and political arguments (Breuilly 1982: 1–41; Hobsbawm and Ranger 1983; Sathyamurthy 1983).

Against this fashionable view, the so-called primordialists argued for the 'reality' of nations, and the almost 'natural' quality of ethnic belonging. National sentiment is no construct; it has a real, tangible, mass base. At its root is a feeling of kinship, of the extended family, that distinguishes national from every other kind of group sentiment (Connor 1978; Fishman 1980; A. D. Smith 1981a: 63–86; Horowitz 1985: 55–92; Stack 1986: 1–11).

Clearly, our investigation of the origins of national sentiment cannot proceed far until this fundamental question of whether the nation be viewed as construct or real historical process is resolved.

The second question is linked to the first. I have emphasized the importance, indeed the indispensability, of nations in the modern era and the modern world. The question arises whether it is fundamental in other eras and pre-modern worlds. Was there 'nationalism' in antiquity? Can we find 'nations' in medieval Europe or Asia? In part, of course, as we saw in Chapter 5, the answer will hinge on our definition of the nation; but equally, it will reflect our reading of the global historical process. If the 'modernists' are right, if the nation is a fundamental feature only of the modern world, this will support, *prima facie*, the idea that nations are primarily abstractions and élite constructs. However, if the 'perennialists' turn out to be nearer the mark, and we find nations and nationalism prior to the rise of the modern world from the sixteenth century (or the French Revolution) onwards, we may well have to change our view of the whole historical process. Nations might still be constructs, but ancient élites, or medieval ones, might be as adept at inventing them as their modern counterparts. This would inevitably devalue the importance attributed to specifically 'modern' developments, like bureaucracy and capitalism, in the rise of nations, which 'modernists' tend to emphasize (Nairn 1977: 92–125; Anderson 1983; Gellner 1983).

The last question again concerns the nature of the concept of the nation. Should we view it as a largely political unit, or mainly a social and cultural entity? Can there be a cultural nationalism, which is not also *ipso facto* political? Or should we regard nations as operating on all these levels at once? These are important questions when it comes to looking at the political ramifications of the national. Again, there are those who would downgrade its cultural importance for collective identity (Breuilly 1982); while others emphasize questions of cultural identity and social cohesion (Barnard 1965; Hutchinson 1987).

The answers to these three sets of questions will, I think, furnish important clues to our exploration of the processes by which nations were formed.

Let me start with a working definition of the nation. A nation is a named community of history and culture, possessing a unified territory, economy, mass education system and common legal rights. I take this definition from the ideals and blueprints of generations of nationalists and their followers. It sums up an 'ideal-type' of the nation that is fairly widely accepted today, even if given units of population aspiring to be full nations in this sense, lack one or other of these characteristics in lesser or greater degree. For example, in a unit of population aspiring to constitute a full nation, certain categories of the population may be excluded from the full exercise of the common legal rights. Or they may not enjoy equal access to the common system of education, or equal mobility in the territorial economy. Alternatively, they may enjoy all these attributes and rights, yet be treated by the majority as in some sense cultural aliens, standing outside the sense of history and much of the culture of the majority, as the Jews were felt to be at the time of Dreyfus, both in France and outside, or the Asians in East Africa after decolonization.

What this means is that the nation is not a once-for-all, all-or-nothing, concept; and that historical nations are ongoing processes, sometimes slow in their formation, at other times faster, often jagged and discontinuous, as some features emerge or are created, while others lag. In Europe, nations have been forming, I would argue, from the medieval period; in several other parts of the world, this process, or processes, have been more recent. It also means that both objective factors outside human control, and human will and action, go into the creation of nations. Geographical environment, and the political accidents of warfare, may provide a setting for a group to form into a nation; but whether it will subsequently do so may depend on how far the group, or its ruling classes, become conscious of their identity, and reinforce it through education, legal codes and administrative centralization (Tilly 1975: 3–163).[1]

If this is accepted, it means in turn that nations can be seen as both constructs or visions of nationalist (or other) élites, but equally as real, historical formations that embody a number of analytically separable processes over long time-spans. It is these processes, as much as any visions, that form the object of our analysis.

Where does this leave 'nationalism'? I should define nationalism as an ideological movement for attaining and maintaining the autonomy, unity and identity of an existing or potential 'nation'. I should also stress its often

minority status as a movement. As a movement, nationalism often ante-
dates, and seeks to create, the nation, even if it often pretends that the
nation already exists (Smith 1973a, 1983a: 153–81).

Of course, nationalists cannot, and do not, create nations *ex nihilo*.
There must be, at least, some elements in the chosen population and its
social environment who favour the aspirations and activities of the nationalist visionaries. To achieve their common goals – autonomy, unity, identity – there need to be some core networks of association and culture,
around which and on which nations can be 'built'. Language-groups are
usually regarded as the basic network of nations; but religious sects, like
the Druse, Sikhs or Maronites, may also form the starting-point for 'reconstructing' the nation. So may a certain kind of historic territory, for
example, the mountain fastnesses of Switzerland or Kurdistan, or island
homelands like Iceland or Japan.

Besides, not all nations are the product of nationalist political endeavour. The English or Castilian nations, for example, owed more to state centralization, warfare and cultural homogeneity than to any nationalist
movement. Vital for any nation is the growth and spread of a 'national
sentiment' outwards from the centre and usually downwards through the
strata of the population. It is in and through the myths and symbols of the
common past that such a national sentiment finds its expression; and these
too may develop over long periods.[2]

The 'Ethnic Core'

So much for initial definitions. Let us turn to the processes of nation formation themselves.

At the turn of the century, it was quite common to argue that nations
were immemorial. People talked of the ancient Greek, Persian and
Egyptian nations, and even equated them with the present-day nations of
those names. They certainly saw modern Bulgarian or French nations as
the lineal descendants of their medieval counterparts. The familiar view
was that nations were natural and perennial; people had a nationality much
as they had speech or sight. Clearly, such a view of the nation is untenable. Nations are not perennial; they can be formed, and human will and
effort play an important part in the process. People can also change their
nationality, or at least their descendants can, over a period of time.
Moreover, it is extremely doubtful, at the least, whether modern Greeks,
Persians and Egyptians are lineal descendants of ancient Greeks, Persians
and Egyptians. Are we not guilty here of a 'retrospective nationalism' to
epochs that lacked all sense of nationality (Levi 1965; Breuilly 1982)?

For these reasons, recent scholars have tended to emphasize the modernity of nations. The modernists argue that the nation is a modern construct of nationalists and other élites, and the product of peculiarly modern conditions like industrialism. They point out that ancient Egypt, and even ancient Greece, could boast no standardized, public, mass education system, and that common legal rights, in so far as they existed, were restricted to particular classes. Because of its territorial unity, ancient Egypt did indeed enjoy more of a common economy than other ancient kingdoms, but it was unusual. In Assyria, Greece, Persia and China, local economies of different regions reflected a lack of territorial compactness of a kind unknown in the contemporary world.[3]

Clearly, in antiquity and much of the medieval era, nations in the sense that we have defined them, viz. named communities of history and culture, possessed of unified territories, economies, education systems and common legal rights, are rarely, if ever, to be found. Yet does this mean that there were no durable cultural communities in antiquity or the Middle Ages? Are we being retrospective nationalists in attributing some common history and culture to ancient Greeks and Persians or medieval Serbs and Irish? I think not. Despite the many changes that these cultures had undergone, they remained recognizably distinct to their own populations and to outsiders; and cultural differentiation was as vital a factor in social life then as now. The only difference then was that the scope and role of cultural diversity operated more at the social than the political level, but even this varied between peoples and eras.

Moreover, cultural differences, then as now, were not just a matter of outside observation. The people who possessed specific cultural attributes often formed a social network or series of networks, which over the generations became what we today designate 'ethnic communities'. These communities of history and culture generally display a syndrome of characteristics, by which they are usually recognized. These include:

1   a common name for the unit of population included;
2   a set of myths of common origins and descent for that population;
3   some common historical memories of things experienced together;
4   a common 'historic territory' or 'homeland', or an association with one;
5   one or more elements of common culture – language, customs, or religion;
6   a sense of solidarity among most members of the community.

I shall call the communities that manifest these characteristics (to a lesser or greater degree) *ethnies* (the French equivalent of the ancient Greek *ethnos*), as there is no single English-language equivalent. By no means all the cultural differences that scholars have distinguished in pre-modern or modern eras are mirrored in such *ethnies*. Many remain as 'ethnic categories'; certainly, in the past, the speakers of, say, Slovakian or Ukrainian dialects, were hardly conscious of their membership in any community. It had to wait for the rise of a romantic nationalism to build communities out of these and other differences (Brock 1976; Szporluk 1979).[4]

However, that still leaves a multitude of *ethnies* in the ancient and medieval worlds, which at first sight resemble, but are not, nations. For example, in Sassanid Persia between the third and seventh century AD, we find a population group with a common name; a sense of a common home-land of 'Iran' that the members opposed to another fabled land of enemies, 'Turan'; some common historical memories and myths of descent related to Zoroaster and the Achaemenid kings; and a sense of solidarity, ever renewed by the protracted struggle with Byzantium (Frye 1966: 235–62; *Cambridge History of Iran* 1983: 359–477).

Although it was divided, both into *poleis* and into sub-ethnic commu-nities, ancient Greece could also be described as an *ethnie* in this sense. We find there, too, a common name, Hellas; a set of common-origin myths about the Greeks and their main divisions; common historical memories centred around the Homeric canon; common Greek dialects and a common Greek pantheon of Olympic deities; an attachment to the Greek 'home-land' around the Aegean; and, above all, a shared sense of being 'Greek' and not 'barbarian'. This did not mean that many Greeks did not inter-marry, that Greek *poleis* did not fight each other most of the time, that they did not form alliances with the Persians against each other, and so on. Yet all Greeks recognized their common Greek heritage and a common Greek cultural community (Fondation Hardt 1962; Andrewes 1965; Alty 1982; Finley 1986).

Perhaps the best-known of ancient and medieval *ethnies*, the Jews, managed to retain their distinctive identity even when most of their members were scattered in diaspora communities. A common name, common myths of origin and descent, sedulously fostered, a whole canon of historical memories centred on charismatic heroes, a common liturgi-cal language and script, an attachment to Eretz-Israel wherever they might find themselves and especially to Jerusalem, all fed a strong bond of ethnic solidarity, which outside hostility renewed with almost monotonous regu-larity. Again, these bonds did not prevent apostasy, intermarriage or inter-nal class and cultural divisions, particularly between Jews of the Ashkenazi and Sephardi rite (Hirschberg 1969; Barnett 1971; Raphael 1985).

One last example, this time from medieval Western Europe, must suffice to illustrate the range of *ethnies*. Apart from their fame as builders of massive castles and cathedrals in the Romanesque style, the Norman evinced a common myth of origins and descent from Duke Rollo, a common name and historical memories of warfare and colonization, common customs and adopted language, along with an attachment to the duchy in northern France that they had conquered and settled. Above all, they maintained for nearly three centuries their *esprit de corps* as a warrior community, even when they conquered Ireland and Sicily (Jones 1973: 204–40; Davis 1976).

'Vertical' and 'Lateral' *Ethnies*

What all these examples have in common is an underlying sense of historical and cultural community. This sense of community pervades and regulates their social life and culture, spilling over at times into the political and military realms. On the other hand, it rarely determines their economic conditions of existence. Generally speaking, economic localism and a subsistence economy fragment the community into a series of interlocking networks. What unites these networks, in so far as it does so, is the common fund of myths, symbols, memories and values that make up the distinctive traditions passed down the generations. Through common customs and rituals, languages, arts and liturgies, this complex of myths, symbols, values and memories ensures the survival of the sense of common ethnicity, of the sense of common descent and belonging, which characterizes a 'community of fate'.

Yet, the example of the Norman conquerors introduces a vital distinction. As with the Sassanid Persians, but even more so, it was really only the upper strata, especially around the Court and priesthoods, that constituted the Norman *ethnie*. The myths of descent and the memories of battle clustered around the ruling house; it was their genealogies and their exploits that Dudo of St Quentin and Orderic Vitalis were called on to record and extol. At the same time, the ruling house represented a whole upper stratum of warrior-aristocrats who had founded a *regnum* in Normandy, based on common customs and myths of descent. Other classes were simply subsumed under those customs and myths; and quite often, the latter were amalgams of the heritage of the conquerors and the conquered (Reynolds 1983).

Compared, however, to the community of Greeks or Jews, that of the Norman or Sassanid Persian ruling classes was rather limited. In one sense, it was wider. The sense of common ethnicity went wherever Normans sailed, and Persian arms conquered. In another sense, it was shallower. It never really reached far down the social scale. For all Kartir's attempts to institute Zoroastrian fire worship as a state religion, many of the Persian peasants were untouched. Although Chosroes I (AD 531–79) attempted to revive ancient Persian culture, he was unable to stabilize the Persian state by extending a sense of common Persian ethnicity. As McNeill puts it:

> As with other urban civilisations that lacked real roots in the countryside, the results were grand and artificial, in theology as in architecture; and Moslem conquest cut off the entire tradition in the seventh century, just as Alexander's victories had earlier disrupted the high culture of the Achaemenids. (McNeill 1963: 400)

This is, perhaps, going too far. A sense of specifically Persian ethnicity remained beneath Islamization, after the Sassanid armies were defeated by the Arabs at Nihavand (AD 642). Islam even stimulated a Persian renaissance in poetry and the arts in the tenth and eleventh centuries, a renaissance that looked back for its inspiration to Chosroes and the Sassanids (*Cambridge History of Iran* 1975: 595–632).

Yet the basic point remains. The Persian Sassanid *ethnie*, like the Norman, the Hittite or the Philistine, was socially limited. It was an aristocratic and 'lateral' *ethnie*, as territorially wide as it was lacking in social depth. In contrast to this type, with its ragged boundaries and aristocratic culture, we find communities with much more compact boundaries, a more socially diffused culture and a greater degree of popular mobilization and fervour. This type of *ethnie* we may call 'vertical' and 'demotic'. The Armenians, Greeks and Jews are classic examples, despite their territorial dispersion, because they lived in often segregated enclaves once they had left their clearly defined homelands. Other examples of 'demotic' or 'vertical' *ethnies* include the Irish, Basques, Welsh, Bretons, Czechs and Serbs, as well as the Druse, Sikhs and Maronites. Such *ethnies* are as stratified as any other, but the strata all share in a common heritage and culture, and in the common defence. Hence the ethnic bond is more exclusive and intensive, and the boundaries are more marked and more strongly upheld. Thus, in contrast to the looser ties that characterized the Philistine aristocratic pentapolis, the Israelite tribal confederation was from the outset marked by a greater ethnocentric zeal and communal mobilization for war, as well as greater ritual involvement of all strata (Kitchen 1973; Seltzer 1980: 7–43).[5]

The distinction between 'lateral' and 'vertical' types of *ethnie* is important for a number of reasons. First, because it highlights a source of conflict between pre-modern ethnic communities, as aristocratic lateral *ethnie* attempted to incorporate and subdue different demotic vertical communities. It also suggests why many *ethnies*, especially of the more demotic variety, persisted over long periods, even when they experienced 'character change'. The Greek *ethnie*, for example, within the Eastern Roman Empire was transformed in many ways by the influx of Slav immigrants. Yet they did not basically change the cultural and religious framework of Greek ethnicity, even though they grafted their customs and mores on to an existing Hellenic culture, especially in the countryside (Campbell and Sherrard 1968: 19–49; Armstrong 1982: 168–200). Similarly, a tenuous sense of Egyptian identity persisted even after the Arab conquest in the seventh century AD, especially among Copts, despite the fact that any attempts to trace 'descent' back to the inhabitants of ancient Egypt were bound to run into the sands. The point is that cultural forms and frameworks may outlive their physical bearers, and even the 'character change' of cultural content that new immigrants and new religious movements bring with them (Atiya 1968: 79–98).

One result of ethnic survival and coexistence over the long term is a patchwork or mosaic of *ethnies* in varying relationships of status and power. Quite often we find a dominant lateral *ethnie* of land-owning aristocrats like the Magyar knights or Polish *szlachta* exploiting a peasantry of a different culture, Croat or Ukrainian, and so helping to preserve these cultural differences as 'ethno-classes'. Wherever we find lateral *ethnies* attempting to expand into territories populated by demotic, vertical communities of culture, the opportunities for a 'frozen' ethnic stratification to develop are greatly increased. This has occurred, not only in Eastern Europe, but in the Middle East, South-East Asia and parts of Africa. The overall result is to preserve ethnic difference and identity right up to the onset of the age of nationalism, and afford ready-made bases for political movements of autonomy (Seton-Watson 1977: 15–142; Orridge 1982).

Already certain implications of the foregoing analysis can be clarified. Only in this modern era could we expect to find unified divisions of labour, mass public education systems and equal legal rights, all of which have come to be part and parcel of a common understanding of what we mean by the concept of the nation. Moreover, the 'modernists' are right when they speak of nations being 'reconstructed' (but not 'invented') out of pre-existing social networks and cultural elements, often by intellectuals.

The modernist definition of the nation omits important components. Even today, a nation *qua* nation must possess a common history and culture, that is to say, common myths of origin and descent, common memories and common symbols of culture. Otherwise, we should be speaking only of territorial states. It is the conjunction, and interpenetration, of these cultural or 'ethnic' elements with the political, territorial, educational and economic ones that we may term 'civic', that produce a modern nation. Today's nations are as much in need of common myths, memories and symbols, as were yesterday's *ethnies*, for it is these former that help to

create and preserve the networks of solidarity that underpin and characterize nations. They also endow nations with their individuality. So that,
while nations can be read as reconstructions of intellectual and other elites,
they are also legitimately viewed as configurations of historical processes,
which can be analysed as real trends.[6]

Because nations embody ethnic as well as civic components, they tend
to form around pre-existing 'ethnic cores'. The fact that pre-modern eras
have been characterized by different types of *ethnie* is therefore vital to
our understanding of the ways in which modern nations emerged. The
number, location and durability of such *ethnies* are crucial for the formation of historical nations. The relations of power and exploitation between
different kinds of *ethnie* also help to determine the bases for historical
nations. It is this latter circumstance that provides an essential key to the
processes of nation formation in modern times.

Bureaucratic 'Incorporation'

The two basic kinds of ethnic core, the lateral and the vertical, also furnish
the two main routes by which nations have been created.

Taking the lateral route first, we find that aristocratic *ethnies* have the
potential for self-perpetuation, provided they can incorporate other strata
of the population. A good many of these lateral *ethnies* cannot do so.
Hittites, Philistines, Mycenaeans, even Assyrians, failed to do so, and they
and their cultures disappeared with the demise of their states (Burney and
Lang 1971: 86–126; Kitchen 1973; Saggs 1984: 117–21). Other lateral
ethnies survived by 'changing their character', as we saw with Persians,
Egyptians and Ottoman Turks, while preserving a sense of common
descent and some dim collective memories.

Still others grafted new ethnic and cultural elements on to their common
fund of myths, symbols and memories, and spread them out from the core
area and down through the social scale. They did so, of course, in varying
degrees. The efforts of the Amhara kings, for example, were rather limited
in scope; yet they managed to retain their Monophysite Abyssinian identity in their heartlands (Atiya 1968; Ullendorff 1973: 54–92). That of the
Castilians was more successful. They managed to form the core of a
Spanish state (and empire) that expelled the Muslim rulers and almost
united the Iberian peninsula. Yet, even their success pales before that of
their Frankish and Norman counterparts.

In fact, the latter three efforts at 'bureaucratic incorporation' were to
prove of seminal historical importance. In all three cases, lower strata and
outlying regions were gradually incorporated in the state, which was

grounded upon a dominant ethnic core. This was achieved by administrative and fiscal means, and by the mobilization of sections of the populations for inter-state warfare, as in the Anglo–French wars (Keeney 1972). An upper-class *ethnie*, in other words, managed to evolve a relatively strong and stable administrative apparatus, which could be used to provide cultural regulation and thereby define a new and wider cultural identity (Corrigan and Sayer 1985). In practice, this meant varying degrees of accommodation between the upper-class culture and those prevalent among the lower strata and peripheral regions; yet it was the upper-class culture that set its stamp on the state and on the evolving national identity.

Perhaps the most clear-cut example is afforded by British developments. As there had been an Anglo-Saxon kingdom based originally on Wessex before the Norman Conquest, the conquered populations could not be treated simply as a servile peasantry. As a result, we find considerable intermarriage, linguistic borrowing, élite mobility and finally a fusion of linguistic culture, within a common religio-political framework.

In other words, bureaucratic incorporation of subject *ethnies* entailed a considerable measure of cultural fusion and social intermingling between Anglo-Saxon, Danish and Norman elements, especially from the thirteenth century on. By the time of Edward III and the Anglo–French and Scottish wars, linguistic fusion had stabilized into Chaucerian English, and a 'British' myth served to weld the disparate ethnic communities together (Seton-Watson 1977: 22–31; L. Smith 1985).

I am not arguing that an English nation was fully formed by the late fourteenth century. There was little economic unity as yet, despite growing fiscal and judicial intervention by the royal state. The boundaries of the kingdom, too, both with Scotland and in France, were often in dispute. In no sense can one speak of a public, mass education system, even for the middle classes. As for legal rights, despite the assumptions behind Magna Carta, they were common to all only in the most minimal senses. For the full development of these civic elements of nationhood, one would have to wait for the Industrial Revolution and its effects (Reynolds 1984: 250–331).

The ethnic elements of the nation, on the other hand, were well developed. By the fourteenth century or slightly later, a common name and myth of descent, promulgated originally by Geoffrey of Monmouth, were widely current, as were a variety of historical memories (MacDougall 1982: 7–17). These were fed by the fortunes of wars in Scotland and France. Similarly, a sense of common culture based on language and ecclesiastical organization had emerged. So had a common strong attachment to the homeland of the island kingdom, which in turn bred a sense of solidarity, despite internal class cleavages. The bases of both the unitary state and a compact nation had been laid, and laid by a lateral Norman-origin *ethnie* that was able to develop its regnal administration to incorporate the Anglo-Saxon population. Yet the full ideology of Englishness had to wait for late-sixteenth- and seventeenth-century developments, when the old British myth gave way to a more potent middle-class 'Saxon' mythology of ancient liberties (MacDougall 1982: chs 2–4).

A similar process of bureaucratic incorporation by an upper-class lateral *ethnie* can be discerned in France. Some fusion of upper-stratum Frankish with subject Romano-Gallic culture occurred under the Christianized Merovingians, but a regnal solidarity is really only apparent in northern France at the end of the twelfth century. It was in this era that earlier myths of Trojan descent, applied to the Franks, were resuscitated for all the people of northern France. At the same time, the *pays d'oc*, with its different language, customs and myths of descent, remained for some time outside the orbit of northern bureaucratic incorporation (Reynolds 1984: 276–89; Bloch 1961: ii. 431–7).

Of course, Capetian bureaucratic incorporation from Philip II onwards was able to draw on the glory and myths of the old Frankish kingdom and Charlemagne's heritage. This was partly because the kingdom of the Eastern Franks came to be known as the *regnum Teutonicorum*, with a separate identity. However, it was also due to the special link between French dynasties and the Church, notably the archbishopric of Rheims. The backing of the French clergy, and the ceremony of anointing at coronations, were probably more crucial to the prestige and survival of a French monarchy in northern France before the battle of Bouvines (1214) than the fame of the schools of Paris or even the military tenacity of the early Capetians. There was a sacred quality inhering in the dynastic *mythomoteur* of the Capetians and their territory that went back to the Papal coronation of Charlemagne and Papal legitimation of Pepin's usurpation in AD 754, which the Pope called a 'new kingdom of David'. The religious language is echoed centuries later, when at the end of the thirteenth century Pope Boniface declared: 'like the people of Israel . . . the kingdom of France [is] a peculiar people chosen by the Lord to carry out the orders of Heaven' (Davis 1958: 298–313; Lewis 1974: 57–70; Armstrong 1982: 152–9).

Though there is much debate as to the 'feudal' nature of the Capetian monarchy, the undoubted fact is that an originally Frankish ruling class *ethnie* managed, after many vicissitudes, to establish a relatively efficient and centralized royal administration over north and central France (later southern France). So it became able to furnish those 'civic' elements of compact territory, unified economy, and linguistic and legal standardization that from the seventeenth century onwards spurred the formation of a

French nation as we know it. The process, however, was not completed until the end of the nineteenth century. Many regions retained their local character, even after the French Revolution. It required the application of Jacobin nationalism to mass education and conscription under the Third Republic to turn, in Eugene Weber's well-known phrase, 'peasants into Frenchmen' (Kohn 1967; Weber 1979).[7]

An even more radical 'change of character' occasioned by attempted bureaucratic incorporation by a 'lateral' ethnic state is provided by Spain. Here it was the Castilian kingdom that formed the fulcrum of Christian resistance to Muslim power. Later, united with the kingdom of Aragon, it utilized religious community as an instrument of homogenization, expelling those who, like the Jews and Moriscos, could not be made to conform. Here, too, notions of *limpieza de sangre* bolstered the unity of the Spanish crown, which was beset by demands on several sides from those claiming ancient rights and manifesting ancient cultures. Quite apart from the Portuguese secession and the failed Catalan revolt, Basques, Galicians and Andalusians retained their separate identities into the modern era. The result is a less unified national community, and more poly-ethnic state, than either Britain or France. With the spread of ideological nationalism in the early nineteenth century, these ethnic communities felt justified in embarking on varying degrees of autonomous development, whose reverberations are still felt today. Yet, most members of these communities shared an overarching Spanish political sentiment and culture, over and beyond their often intense commitment to Basque, Catalan or Galician identity and culture (Atkinson 1960; Payne 1971; Greenwood 1977).

Historically, the formation of modern nations owes a profound legacy to the development of England, France and Spain. This is usually attributed to their possession of military and economic power at the relevant period, the period of burgeoning nationalism and nations. As the great powers of the period, they inevitably became models of the nation, the apparently successful format of population unit, for everyone else. Yet in the case of England and France, and to a lesser extent Spain, this was not accidental. It was the result of the early development of a particular kind of 'rational' bureaucratic administration, aided by the development of merchant capital, wealthy urban centres, and professional military forces and technology. The 'state' formed the matrix of the new population unit's format, the 'nation'. It aided the type of compact, unified, standardized and culturally homogenized unit and format that the nation exemplifies.

Some would say that the state actually 'created' the nation, that royal administration, taxation and mobilization endowed the subjects within its jurisdiction with a sense of corporate loyalty and identity. Even in the West, this overstates the case. The state was certainly a necessary condition for the formation of the national loyalties we recognize today. However, its operations in turn owed much to earlier assumptions about kingdoms and peoples, and to the presence of core ethnic communities around which these states were built up. The process of ethnic fusion, particularly apparent in England and France, which their lateral *ethnies* encouraged through the channels of bureaucratic incorporation, was only possible because of a relatively homogeneous ethnic core. We are not here talking about actual descent, much less about 'race', but about the *sense* of ancestry and identity that people possess. Hence the importance of myths and memories, symbols and values, embodied in customs and traditions and in artistic styles, legal codes and institutions. In *this* sense of 'ethnicity', which is more about cultural perceptions than physical demography, albeit rooted perceptions and assumptions, England from an early date, and France somewhat later, came to form fairly homogeneous *ethnies*. These *ethnies* in turn facilitated the development of homogenizing states, extending the whole idea of an *ethnie* into realms and on to levels hitherto unknown, to form the relatively novel concept of the nation.

The 'Rediscovery' of the 'Ethnic Past'

In contrast to the route of bureaucratic incorporation by lateral *ethnies*, the process by which demotic *ethnies* may become the bases for nations is only indirectly affected by the state and its administration. This was either because they were subject communities – the usual case – or because, as in Byzantium and Russia, the state represented interests partially outside its core *ethnie*. This subdivision also produces interesting variants on the constitutive political myth, or *mythomoteur*, of vertical *ethnies*.[8]

In all these communities, the fund of cultural myths, symbols, memories and values was transmitted not only from generation to generation, but also throughout the territory occupied by the community or its enclaves, and down the social scale. The chief mechanism of this persistence and diffusion was an organized religion with a sacred text, liturgy, rites and clergy, and sometimes a specialized secret lore and script. It is the social aspects of salvation religions, in particular, that have ensured the persistence and shaped the contours of demotic *ethnies*. Among Orthodox Greeks and Russians, Monophysite Copts and Ethiopians, Gregorian Armenians, Jews, Catholic Irish and Poles, myths and symbols of descent and election, and the ritual and sacred texts in which they were embodied, helped to perpetuate the traditions and social bonds of the community.

At the same time, the very hold of an ethnic religion posed grave problems for the formation of nations from such communities. It transpired that 'religion-shaped' peoples, whose ethnicity owed so much to the symbols and organization of an ancient faith, were often constrained in their efforts to become 'full' nations. Or rather, their intellectuals may find it harder to break out of the conceptual mould of a religio-ethnic community. So many members of such demotic *ethnies* simply assumed that theirs was already, and indeed always had been, a nation. Indeed, according to some definitions they were. They possessed in full measure, after all, the purely ethnic components of the nation. Arabs and Jews, for example, had common names, myths of descent, memories and religious cultures, as well as attachments to an original homeland and a persisting, if subdivided, sense of ethnic solidarity. Did this not suffice for nationhood? All that seemed to be necessary was to attain independence and a state for the community (Baron 1960: 213–48; Carmichael 1967; Patai 1983).

Yet, as these examples demonstrate, matters were not so simple. Quite apart from adverse geopolitical factors, social and cultural features internal to the Arab and Jewish communities made the transition from *ethnie* to nation difficult and problematic. The Arabs have been faced, of course, by their geographic extent, which flies in the face of the ideal of a 'compact nation' in its clearly demarcated habitat. They have also had to contend with the varied histories of the subdivisions of the 'Arab nation', ranging from the Moroccan kingdoms to those of Egypt or Saudi Arabia. There is also the legacy of a divisive modern colonialism, which has often reinforced historical differences and shaped the modern Arab states with their varied economic patterns. Mass, public education has, in turn, like legal rights, been the product of the colonial and post-colonial states and their élites. Above all, however, the involvement of most Arabs and most Arab states with Islam, whose *umma* both underpins and challenges the circle and significance of an 'Arab nation', creates an ambiguous unity and destiny, and overshadows efforts by Arab intelligentsia to rediscover an 'Arab past' (Sharabi 1970; A. D. Smith 1973b).

The Jews were also faced with problems of geographic dispersion, accentuated by their lack of a recognized territory and exile from an ancient homeland. True, in the Pale of Settlement and earlier in Poland, something approaching a public religious education system and common legal rights (albeit restricted) had been encouraged by the *kahal* system and its successors. Yet, though Jews, like Armenians, were compelled to occupy certain niches in the European economy, we can hardly characterize their enclave communities as models of economic unity, let alone a territorial division of labour. Quite apart from these obstacles to national unity, there were also the ambivalent attitudes and self-definitions of

Judaism and its rabbinical authorities. Only later did some rabbis and one wing of Orthodoxy come to support Jewish nationalism and its Zionist project, despite the traditional hopes for messianic restoration to Zion of generations of the Orthodox. The concept of Jewish self-help had become alien to the medieval interpretation of Judaism; and the general notion that the Jews were a 'nation in exile' actually strengthened this passivity (Hertzberg 1960; Vital 1975: 3–20).

It was in these circumstances of popular resignation amid communal decline, set against Western national expansion, that a new stratum of secular intelligentsia emerged. Their fundamental role, as they came to see it, was to transform the relationship of a religious tradition to its primary bearers, the demotic *ethnies*. We must, of course, place this development in the larger context of a series of revolutions – socio-economic, political and cultural – which began in the early modern period in the West. As we saw, the primary motor of these transformations was the formation of a new type of professionalized, bureaucratic state on the basis of a relatively homogeneous core *ethnie*. Attempts by older political formations to take over some of the dimensions of the Western 'rational state', and so stream-line their administrations and armies, upset the old accommodations of these empires to their constituent *ethnies*. In the Habsburg, Ottoman and Romanov empires, increasing state intervention, coupled with incipient urbanization and commerce, placed many demotic *ethnies* under renewed pressures. The spread of nationalist ideas from the late eighteenth century on carried with it new ideals of compact population units, popular repre-sentation and cultural diversity, which affected the ruling classes of these empires and even more the educated stratum of their subject communities (see the essays in Sugar and Lederer 1969; more generally, A. D. Smith 1986a: 129–52).

For the subject vertical *ethnies*, a secularizing intelligentsia led by educator-intellectuals supplied the motor of transformation, as well as the cultural framework, which among lateral *ethnies* had been largely provided by the incorporating bureaucratic state. It was this intelligentsia that furnished the new communal self-definitions and goals. These redefinitions were not simple 'inventions', or wholesale applications of Western models. Rather, they were derived from a process of 'rediscovery' of the ethnic past. The process tended to reverse the religious self-view: instead of 'the people' acting as a passive but chosen vessel of salvation, subordinate to the divine message, that message and its salvation ethic became the supreme expression and creation of the people's genius as it developed in history (Haim 1962; A. D. Smith 1983a: 230–56).[9]

At the centre of the self-appointed task of the intelligentsia stood the rediscovery and realization of the community. This entailed a moral and political revolution. In the place of a passive and subordinate minority living precariously on the margins of the dominant ethnic society and its state, a new compact and politically active nation had to be created ('re-created' in nationalist terminology). From now on, the centre stage was to be occupied by the people, henceforth identified with 'the masses', who would replace the aristocratic heroes of old. This was all part of the process of creating a unified, and preferably autarchic, community of legally equal members or 'citizens', who would become the fount of legitimacy and state power. However, for this to occur, the people had to be purified of the dross of centuries – their lethargy, divisions, alien elements, ignorance and so on – and emancipate themselves. That was the primary task of the educator-intellectuals.

The transition, then, from demotic *ethnie* to civic nation carries with it several related processes and movements. These include:

1 a movement from subordinate accommodation and passivity of a peripheral minority to an active, assertive and politicized community with a unified policy;
2 a movement towards a universally recognized 'homeland' for the community, a compact, clearly demarcated territory;
3 economic unification of all members of the territorially demarcated community, with control over its own resources, and movement towards economic autarchy in a competitive world of nations;
4 turning ethnic members into legal citizens by mobilizing them for political ends and conferring on each common civil, social and political rights and obligations;
5 placing the people at the centre of moral and political concern and celebrating the new role of the masses, by re-educating them in national values, myths and memories.

That traditional elites, especially the guardians of sacred texts which had so long defined the demotic *ethnie*, might resist these changes, was to be expected. This meant that the intellectuals had to undercut earlier definitions of the community by re-presenting their novel conceptions through ancient symbols and formats. These were in no sense mere manipulations (though there undoubtedly was individual manipulation, such as Tilak's use of the Kali cult in Bengal); there is no need to unmask what are so patently selective readings of an ethnic past. Yet selection can take place only within strict limits, limits set by the pre-existing myths, symbols, customs and memories of vertical *ethnies*. That still leaves considerable scope for choice of symbol or myth and understanding of history. Can we discern a pattern in the selective readings of educator-intellectuals?[10]

There were, I think, two main patterns by which educator-intellectuals could engage the community for their moral and political goals. Both had to be couched in the language and symbolism of the people, in the sense that any novelties must find an echo in popular historical traditions. The first pattern was the use of landscape, or what we may call 'poetic spaces'. A nation, after all, needs before all else a national territory or homeland, and not just anywhere. The geographic terrain must be simultaneously a historic home. How do you create this sense of 'homeland' for people who are either divided into small localities or scattered outside the chosen area? The answer is to endow the chosen home with poetic and historical connotations, or rather with a historical poetry. The aim is to integrate the homeland into a romantic drama of the progress of the nation. One way to do this is to historicize natural features of the chosen area. This was, of course, a feature of older *ethnies*, with their myths of descent from gods who dwelt on great mountains like Ida, Olympus or Meru. A modern romantic historiography of the homeland turns lakes and mountains, rivers and valleys, into the 'authentic' repository of popular virtues and collective history. So the Jungfrau became a symbol of Swiss virtues of purity and naturalness, and the *Vierwaldstättersee* the national theatre of the historical drama of the foundation of the *Eidgenossenschaft* in 1291. In this poetic history, fact and legend become fused to produce a stirring symbol of purity and rectitude, and a dramatic myth of resistance to tyranny. Again, the English or Russian paeans to their respective landscapes, with rolling meadows or wide open spaces and birch trees, immortalized by painters and musicians like Constable and Elgar, or Levitan and Borodin, celebrate the community's involvement in its homeland habitat, turning bare nature into poetic history (Kohn 1957; Gray 1971: 9–64; Crump 1986).

Another way to integrate the nation with its homeland is to naturalize historical features. Tells, temples, castles and stone circles are treated as natural components of an ethnic landscape, with a historical poetry of their own. The uses of Stonehenge are instructive in this respect. Interpreted in many ways, Stonehenge in the eighteenth- and nineteenth-century 'historical revival' became so much a symbol of the antiquity of Britain and British ancestry, that it was difficult to erase so 'natural' a part of the British scene from the ethnic consciousness of the nation (Chippindale 1983: 96–125). Similarly, the mysterious stone buildings of Great Zimbabwe, which seem to have grown out of their natural surroundings, despite the skill with which the Elliptical Temple was obviously constructed, suggest the rootedness of the modern nation of Zimbabwe in its natural habitat. By implying this close link between history and nature, the modern educator-intellectual is able to define the community in space and tell us 'where we are' (Chamberlin 1979: 27–35).

The other main pattern of involvement of the community in the national revolution was even more potent. If the uses of landscape define the communal homeland, the uses of history, or what I may call the cult of 'golden ages', direct the communal destiny by telling us who we are, whence we came, and why we are unique. The answers lie in those 'myths of ethnic origins and descent' that form the groundwork of every nationalist mythology. Since the aims of nationalist educator-intellectuals are not academic, but social – i.e. the moral purification and political mobilization of the people – communal history must be taught as a series of foundation and liberation myths and as a cult of heroes. Together, these make up the vision of the golden age that must inspire present regeneration (A. D. Smith 1984a).

Typical of such uses of history is the Gaelic revival's vision of a Celtic, pre-Christian Irish golden age set in a half-mythical, half-historical time before the fifth-century conversion to Christianity by St Patrick. When O'Grady and Lady Gregory rediscovered the Ulster Cycle with its legends of Cuchulain, they found a golden age of High Kings, *fianna* bands and *filid* guilds in a rural and free Celtic society that seemed the spiritual model for a modern Irish nation. The rediscovery of an early Celtic art and literature seemed to confirm the image of a once-great community, whose progress had been cut off by Norman, and later Protestant, English invasions. The cult of Celtic heroes in a free Gaelic Ireland suggested what was authentically 'ours' and therefore what 'we' must do to be 'ourselves' once again (Chadwick 1970: 134–5, 268–71; Lyons 1979: 57–83; Hutchinson 1987).

A similar process of ethnic reconstruction took place in Finland during the last century. In this case, a subordinate vertical *ethnie,* differentiated from the Swedish élite and its Russian masters, formed a potential popular base for the reconstructions of nationalist educator-intellectuals like Lönnrot, Runeberg and Snellman from the 1830s on. Of course, the 'Finns' and the 'Finland' of their imaginations bore only a very partial resemblance to earlier Finnish society, particularly its pagan era in the later first millennium AD. This appears to have been the epoch (to judge from its material remains) to which the later *Kalevala* songs and poems collected by Lönnrot in Karelia refer back. Nevertheless, the historicism of Lönnrot and his fellow-intellectuals, with their cults of a golden age of heroes like Väinämöinen and Lemminkainen, answered to a very real need to recover what was thought of as being an ancient but 'lost' period of Finnish history and culture. Popularized by the paintings of Gallen-Kallela and the tone-poems and *Kullervo* symphony of Sibelius, this archaic golden age set in Finland's lakes and forests provided an ideal self-definition and exemplar for the reconstruction of Finnish society and culture as a nation in its struggle against Swedish cultural and Russian political domination (Boulton Smith 1985; Branch 1985: pp. xi–xxxiv; Honko 1985).

The same patterns operated in other reconstructions for a demotic ethnic base. Historicist revivals of ancient Greek culture and heroes, of ancient Israelite archaeology and heroic examplars, of ancient Turkish steppe heroes, and of a Nordic pantheon of gods and heroes in a barbarian golden age among Germans, are some examples of nationalist attempts to re-create ethnic pasts that would define and guide modern nations (Eisenstein-Barzilay 1959; Kohn 1965; Campbell and Sherrard 1968: 19–49; Kushner 1976).

What they all had in common was their provision of 'maps' of ethnic relations and history, and 'moralities' of national endeavour. On the one hand, the educator-intellectuals furnished maps of the nature, descent and role of the community in the modern world; on the other hand, exemplary guides to collective action and models of 'true' and authentic national behaviour. This is the purificatory and activist moral revolution which a 'returning intelligentsia' in search of *its* roots performs and which, for demotic *ethnies*, is a prerequisite for constructing a civic nation.

Intellectuals and professionals, of course, also play a role in the trans-formation of lateral *ethnies*. Yet here their task is secondary. The bureau-cratic state and its incorporating activities provide the framework and the motor of change. Among subordinate, demotic *ethnies*, the state is a target and a culturally alien one. It falls, therefore, to a returning intel-ligentsia to turn elements of an existing culture into a national grid and moral exemplar, if the civic nation is to be formed and its members mobilized for 'nation building'. In the creation of a 'community of history and destiny', the historicism of the educator-intellectuals provides the nation-to-be with its genealogy and purpose (Gella 1976; A. D. Smith 1986a: 174–208).

I have concentrated on the role of historicist intelligentsia in creating nations from, and around, demotic *ethnies*. Such nations form a majority of all nations and aspirant nations today. Modern circumstances have encouraged vertical *ethnies* to proliferate, and their intelligentsia to put forward claims to national status, while at the same time eliminating 'lateral' aristocratic *ethnies*, unless they could transform themselves through an incorporating bureaucratic state into a civic nation. This in turn means that intellectuals and professionals have assumed a disproportion-ate role in contemporary politics outside the West, often with fervently nationalistic outlooks and policies. This is true even where intelligentsias attempt to stem the tide of ethno-national claims and separatism, by attempting to use a Western-style bureaucratic state to incorporate com-peting *ethnies*, as in many sub-Saharan African states. They, too, must try to rediscover an ethnic past, but this time for a series of *ethnies* forcibly brought together by the colonial state. African practice suggests a combination of the two routes to nationhood, with one starting out from a lateral *ethnie* (especially if there is a dominant *ethnie* in the state) and operating through bureaucratic incorporation, the other from a vertical *ethnie* (often a core one) and reconstructing an ethno-national culture through the activities of educator-intellectuals like Senghor and Cheikh Anta Diop (Ajayi 1960; Geiss 1974). How successful such a combination is likely to prove remains to be seen (A. D. Smith 1983b: 122–35).

'Cultural wars'

In delineating the two main bases and routes of nation formation, I have said nothing about the factors that determine which of the rival population units are likely to achieve nationhood – except that they are most likely to stem from a pre-existing ethnic core. Yet, quite evidently, not all units that possess ethnic cores become nations in the sense of that term used here. There have been plenty of examples of ethnic cores that failed to move towards nationhood, like the Copts and Shan, the Sorbs and Frisians. This is not simply a matter of gaining independence or sovereign states of their own, though it may indicate a failure in the face of *force majeure*. More important is the inability to develop the cultural framework that can unite the chosen population unit, and hence the political will and activism to resist encroachment and absorption by more powerful neighbours. This is where the relationship between conflict and cultural resources is crucial (A. D. Smith 1981b (ch. 6 above); Brass 1985).

Just as warfare acts as the agent of state maintenance or state extinction, so cultural conflict – for *ethnies* that lack states of their own – selects out potential nations from those destined to remain in various degrees of accommodation at the margins of other national societies. Clearly, in this competition the 'strength' or 'weakness' of the ethnic base itself is all-important. The 'fuller', and more richly documented, the historical culture which a population unit can claim, the better its chances of achieving political recognition and moving towards the status of a civic nation. Equally important, however, is the emergence of a relatively secularized intelligentsia, secular enough to promote auto-emancipation and political activism as a communal option. This in turn requires a cultural war with rival cultures, of the kind waged by German nationalists against French culture or Indian nationalists against British culture. However, it also entails an internal conflict of 'sons against fathers', of the secular intelligentsia against the guardians of tradition, in the interests of moving a demotic *ethnie* along the road to nationhood. That may mean a judicious borrowing from external cultures, preferably distant ones, such as the Japanese under the Meiji Restoration utilized and assimilated to indigenous norms. Yet over-borrowing may undermine the strength of native traditions and attenuate an ethnic heritage. So a balance must be struck between archaism and syncretism, which is a function of culture conflict and cultural resources. Such balances and conflicts also place a premium on the control of the means of communication and socialization. The Meiji regime could sanction large-scale borrowings, not only because the foundations of a unique historical Japanese culture were so secure, but also because they controlled the means of communication and socialization (Kosaka 1959; Dore 1964; Mazrui 1985).

The ability to wage 'cultural wars' by rejection or selective assimilation is, of course, a function of indigenous cultural resources and their availability for political ends in the hands of the intelligentsia. That is why the main battle of the nationalists is so often fought out within its chosen *ethnie* against the older self-definitions. However, we can only understand the significance of such internal struggles if we take the culture and history of the ethnic core seriously.[11] This leads us back to our initial theses.

Conclusions

Whatever the factors that make one bid for nationhood successful and another less so (and chance, too, plays a part here), the fundamental pre-conditions remain as before.

(1)   The nation, as we have defined it, is a modern phenomenon, and its civic features can only reach full flowering in the modern era, with its specific modes of domination, production and communication. At the same time, modern nations have their roots in pre-modern eras and pre-modern cultures. The origins of such nations must therefore be traced far back, since their ethnic features, though subject to considerable reconstructions, stem from often distant eras and ancient traditions. Modern nations are closely, if often indirectly, related to older, long-lived *ethnies*, which furnish the nation with much of its distinctive mythology, symbolism and culture, including its association with an ancient homeland. It is difficult to see a modern nation maintaining itself as a distinctive identity without such mythology, symbolism and culture. If it does not have them, it must appropriate them, or risk dissolution (A. D. Smith 1986b).

(2)   As we have seen, the nation that emerges in the modern era must be regarded as both construct and real process, and that in a dual sense. For the analyst, a 'nation' represents an ideal-type combining elements in

accentuated form, but equally needs to be broken down into the constituent dimensions of process to which the construct refers. For the nationalist, too, the nation represents an ideal to be striven for and reconstructed, particularly in the case of demotic *ethnies*, where educator-intellectuals' visions assume great importance. Equally, these visions must elicit a definite *praxis* in the context of real transformations that develop in partial independence of human design and nationalist action, transformations like increasing territorialization and economic unification, the rise of mobilized masses and more scientific communication systems. These transformations also force the cultural and political spheres more closely together, so that the emergent nation becomes both a cultural and a political community. Not surprisingly, their coincidence in time and space becomes one of the chief goals of nationalists everywhere (Gellner 1983: 1–7).

(3) The point of departure for any analysis of the modern cultural and political communities we call 'nations' lies in the different kinds of premodern ethnic communities, the aristocratic lateral and the demotic vertical types. These form the main bases and 'ethnic cores' from which the two main routes in the transition to nationhood set out. We can go further. Different types of ethnic base largely determine the forms and mechanisms through which the nation is subsequently formed, in so far as this is achieved. Not only do they influence the role of the state, they also differentiate the social groups – aristocrats, bureaucrats, bourgeoisies, intelligentsia, lower clergy – that are likely to play leading roles in the movement towards nationhood. Even more important, they influence the forms and much of the content of the ensuing national culture, since it is from their myths of descent and the symbols, memories and values of different types of *ethnie*, that the modern mass culture of each nation and its modes of communication and socialization derive their distinctive identity and forms. That is why, in the fields of culture and socialization, there is greater continuity with the past of each *ethnie* than in such rapidly changing domains as science, technology and economics.[12]

(4) In the case of nations formed on the basis of lateral *ethnies*, the influence of the state and its bureaucratic personnel is paramount. It is the culture of an aristocratic *ethnie* that an incorporating bureaucratic state purveys down the social scale and into the countryside and inner-city areas, displacing the hold of eccelesiastical authorities and local nobles (or using them for state ends). This is very much the route followed by those Western societies in which cultural homogenization around an upper-stratum ethnic core proceeded *pari passu* with administrative incorporation.

In the case of nations formed on the basis of vertical *ethnies*, a returning intelligentsia with its ethnic historicism provides the motor force and framework of an absent (because culturally alien) bureaucratic state. In this case, there is a more direct confrontation with the guardians of tradition. Often interwoven with a conflict of generations, the struggle of the intelligentsia is for the cultural resources of the community and their utilization for geo-cultural purposes, i.e. for their territorial and political expansion against rival geo-cultural centres. To these ends, the communal culture must be redefined and reconstituted through a national and civic appropriation of ethnic history, which will mobilize members on the basis of a rediscovered identity (Hobsbawm and Ranger 1983; Lowenthal 1985).

(5) Finally, the continuity that such reconstructions encourage between many nations and their ethnic pasts, despite real transformations, implies a deeper need transcending individuals, generations and classes, a need for collective immortality through posterity, that will relativize and diminish the oblivion and futility of death. Through a community of history and destiny, memories may be kept alive and actions retain their glory. For only in the chain of generations of those who share a historic and quasi-familial bond, can individuals hope to achieve a sense of immortality in eras of purely terrestrial horizons. In this sense, the formation of nations and the rise of ethnic nationalisms appear more like the institutionalization of a 'surrogate religion' than a political ideology, and therefore far more durable and potent than we may care to admit.

For we have to concede that, in the last analysis, there remain 'non-rational' elements of explosive power and tenacity in the structure of nations and the outlook and myth of nationalism. These elements, I would contend, stem from the profound historical roots of the myths, symbols, memories and values that define the ethnic substratum of many modern nations. These are elements that many of us, including many social scientists, would prefer to ignore, but we do so at our peril. The conflicts that embitter the geopolitics of our planet often betray deeper roots than a clash of economic interests and political calculations would suggest, and many of these conflicts, and perhaps the most bitter and protracted, stem from just these underlying non-rational elements. Their persistence, and intensification, in the modern era suggest a long future for ethno-nationalism, and an increasingly violent one, if we fail to address the real issues in the formation of nations and the spread of nationalism.

Notes

1   Further discussions of the subjective and objective features of nations, and of their dynamic and processual character, can be found in Rustow 1967 and Nettl and Robertson 1968.

2   For a general discussion, and an example from ancient Rome, see Tudor 1972.
3   For discussions of ancient empires and their economies, see Larsen 1979, especially the essays by Lattimore, Ekholm and Friedman, and Postgate.
4   The ancient Greek term *ethnos*, like the Latin *natio*, has a connotation of common origin, and so, being alike and acting together; but the emphasis is cultural rather than biological. As always, it is what people believe, rather than objective origins, that is important.
5   In many cases, the evidence from ancient and medieval records does not allow us to infer much about the degree of social penetration of elite culture and the range of ethnic ties, as the other essays in the volume by Wiseman (1973) make clear.
6   Of course, this conclusion owes much to the definition of the nation adopted here. Even so, one would have to distinguish in some way(s) between the types of cultural community in antiquity and the Middle Ages, and the very different kinds prevalent in the modern world. It is therefore better to make the distinctions explicit in the definitions themselves. Though there is a 'before-and-after' model inherent in this conception, the argument advanced here suggests that the earlier components are *not* simply replaced by the later, modern ones; ethnic components do (and must) persist, if a nation is to be formed.
7   Again, the continuity is cultural, and indirect. It remained significant into the nineteenth century to claim descent from 'Franks' and even 'Gauls' for political purposes; the recovery of medieval French art and history also spurred this sense of ethnic identification. By the later Middle Ages, the claim to Frankish descent could hardly be substantiated; but again, it is claims within a cultural framework that count.
8   These are discussed by A. D. Smith 1986a: 47–68; and see Armstrong 1982.
9   It is necessary to distinguish the educator-intellectuals proper from the wider stratum of the professional intelligentsia, on which see Gouldner 1979 and A. D. Smith 1981a: 87–107.
10 For different readings of 'manipulation' and 'mass ethnic response' in Muslim India, see the essays by Brass and Robinson in Taylor and Yapp 1979.
11 That is why some recent devaluations of the role of 'culture' in ethnic identification, particularly among anthropologists, seem beside the point. Of course, cultures change, and at the individual level change contextually, making ethnicity often 'situational'; but at the collective level, and over the long term, cultural *forms* are relatively durable. Provided they are encoded in myths, symbols, traditions, artefacts and the like, they provide a delineated framework and repertoire for future generations, which influence in often subtle ways the perceptions and attitudes of the majority of members of an *ethnie*; cf. the discussion of Armstrong and Gellner in Smith 1984b.
12 This vitally affects the issue of industrial 'convergence' between societies of very different culture. It is in the ethnic heritage of different societies, above all, that divergences persist and spill over into the ideological and political spheres (cf. Goldthorpe 1964 for an early statement).

References

Ajayi, Jacob F. A. 1960: The place of African history and culture in the process of nation-building in Africa south of the Sahara. *Journal of Negro Education* 30 (3), 206–13.

Alty, J. H. M. 1982: Dorians and Ionians. *Journal of Hellenic Studies* 102 (1), 1–14.

Anderson, Benedict 1983: *Imagined Communities: Reflections on the Origin and Spread of Nationalism*. London: Verso.

Andrewes, Antony 1965: The growth of the city-state. In Hugh Lloyd-Jones (ed.), *The Greek World*, Harmondsworth: Penguin, 26–65.

Armstrong, John 1982: *Nations before Nationalism*. Chapel Hill: University of North Carolina Press.

Atiya, Aziz S. 1968: *A History of Eastern Christianity*. London: Methuen.

Atkinson, William C. 1960: *A History of Spain and Portugal*. Harmondsworth: Penguin.

Barnard, Frederik Mechner 1965: *Herder's Social and Political Thought*. Oxford: Clarendon Press.

Barnett, Richard D. (ed.) 1971: *The Sephardi Heritage: Essays on the History and Cultural Contribution of the Jews of Spain and Portugal*, vol. 1: *The Jews in Spain and Portugal Before and After the Expulsion of 1492*. London: Valentine, Mitchell & Co.

Baron, Salo W. 1960: *Modern Nationalism and Religion*. New York: Meridian Books.

Bloch, Marc 1961: *Feudal Society*, 2 vols. London: Routledge & Kegan Paul.

Boulton Smith, John 1985: The *Kalevala* in Finnish art. *Books from Finland* 19 (1), 48–55.

Branch, Michael (ed.) 1985: *Kalevala: The Land of Heroes*, trans. William F. Kirby. London: Athlone Press.

Brass, Paul (ed.) 1985: *Ethnic Groups and the State*. London: Croom Helm.

Breuilly, John 1982: *Nationalism and the State*. Manchester: Manchester University Press.

Brock, Peter 1976: *The Slovak National Awakening*. Toronto: University of Toronto Press.

Burney, Charles and Lang, David M. 1971: *The Peoples of the Hills: Ancient Ararat and Caucasus*. London: Weidenfeld & Nicolson.

Cambridge History of Iran 1983: vol. 3: *The Seleucid, Parthian and Sassanian Periods*, ed. Ehson Yarshater; 1975: vol. 4: *The Period from the Arab Invasion to the Saljuqs*, ed. Richard N. Frye. Cambridge: Cambridge University Press.

Campbell, John and Sherrard, Philip 1968: *Modern Greece*. London: Benn.

Carmichael, Joel 1967: *The Shaping of the Arabs*. New York: Macmillan Company.

Chadwick, Nora 1970: *The Celts*. Harmondsworth: Penguin.

Chamberlin, Eric R. 1979: *Preserving the Past*. London: J. M. Dent & Sons.

Chippindale, Christopher 1983: *Stonehenge Complete*. London: Thames & Hudson.

Connor, Walker 1978: A nation is a nation, is a state, is an ethnic group, is a. . . . *Ethnic and Racial Studies* 1 (4), 377–400.

Corrigan, Philip and Sayer, Derek 1985: *The Great Arch: English State Formation as Cultural Revolution*. Oxford: Blackwell.

Crump, Jeremy 1986: The identity of English music: the reception of Elgar, 1898–1935. In Robert Colls and Philip Dodd (eds), *Englishness, Politics and Culture, 1880–1920*, London: Croom Helm, 164–90.

Davis, R. H. C. 1958: *A History of Medieval Europe*. London: Longmans, Green and Co.

Davis, R. H. C. 1976: *The Normans and their Myth*. London: Thames & Hudson.

Dore, Ronald P. 1964: Latin America and Japan compared. In John J. Johnson (ed.), *Continuity and Change in Latin America*, Stanford, CA: Stanford University Press.

Eisenstein-Barzilay, Isaac 1959: National and anti-national trends in the Berlin Haskalah. *Jewish Social Studies* 21 (3), 165–92.

Finley, M. I. 1986: The Ancient Greeks and their nation. In *idem, The Use and Abuse of History*, London: Hogarth Press, 120–33.

Fishman, Joshua 1980: Social theory and ethnography: neglected perspectives on language and ethnicity in eastern Europe. In Peter Sugar (ed.), *Ethnic Diversity and Conflict in Eastern Europe*, Santa Barbara, CA: ABC-Clio, 69–99.

Fondation Hardt 1962: *Grecs et Barbares*, Entretiens sur l'antiquité classique, 8, Geneva.

Frye, Richard N. 1966: *The Heritage of Persia*. New York: Mentor.

Geiss, Immanuel 1974: *The PanAfrican Movement*. London: Methuen.

Gella, Aleksander (ed.) 1976: *The Intelligentsia and the Intellectuals: Theory, Method and Case Study*, Sage Studies in International Sociology no. 5. Beverly Hills, CA: Sage Publications.

Gellner, Ernest 1983: *Nations and Nationalism*. Oxford: Blackwell.

Goldthorpe, John 1964: Social stratification in industrial society. In Paul Halmos (ed.), *The Development of Industrial Societies*, Sociological Review Monograph no. 8, 97–122.

Gouldner, Alvin 1979: *The Rise of the Intellectuals and the Future of the New Class*. London: Macmillan.

Gray, Camilla 1971: *The Russian Experiment in Art, 1863–1922*. London: Thames & Hudson.

Greenwood, Davydd 1977: Continuity in change: Spanish Basque ethnicity as a historical process. In Milton Esman (ed.), *Ethnic Conflict in the Western World*, Ithaca, NY: Cornell University Press, 81–102.

Haim, Sylvia (ed.) 1962: *Arab Nationalism: An Anthology*. Berkeley: University of California Press.

Hertzberg, Arthur (ed.) 1960: *The Zionist Idea: A Reader*. New York: Meridian Books.

Hirschberg, Hayyim Ze'ev (Joachim W.) 1969: The Oriental Jewish communities. In Arthur J. Arberry (ed.), *Religion in the Middle East: Three Religions in Concord and Conflict*, vol. 1: *Judaism and Christianity*, Cambridge: Cambridge University Press, pp. 119–225.

Hobsbawm, Eric and Ranger, Terence (eds) 1983: *The Invention of Tradition*. Cambridge: Cambridge University Press.

Honko, Lauri 1985: The *Kalevala* process. *Books from Finland*, 19 (1), 16–23.

Horowitz, Donald L. 1985: *Ethnic Groups in Conflict*. Berkeley: University of California Press.

Hutchinson, John 1987: *The Dynamics of Cultural Nationalism: The Gaelic Revival and the Creation of the Irish Nation State*. London: Allen & Unwin.

Jones, Gwyn 1973: *A History of the Vikings*. London: Oxford University Press.

Keeney, Barnaby C. 1972: Military service and the development of nationalism in England, 1272–1327. In Leon Tipton (ed.), *Nationalism in the Middle Ages*, New York: Holt, Rinehart & Winston, 87–97.

Kitchen, K. A. 1973: The Philistines. In D. J. Wiseman (ed.), *Peoples of the Old Testament*, Oxford: Oxford University Press, 53–78.

Kohn, Hans 1957: *Nationalism and Liberty: The Swiss Example*. New York: Macmillan.

Kohn, Hans 1965: *The Mind of Germany*. London: Macmillan.

Kohn, Hans 1967: *Prelude to Nation-States: The French and German Experience, 1789–1815*. New York: Van Nostrand.

Kosaka, Masaaki 1959: The Meiji era: the forces of rebirth. *Journal of World History* 5 (3), 621–33.

Kushner, David 1976: *The Rise of Turkish Nationalism*. London: Frank Cass.

Larsen, Mogens T. (ed.) 1979: *Power and Propaganda: A Symposium on Ancient Empires*. Copenhagen: Akademisk Forlag.

Levi, Mario Attilio 1965: *Political Power in the Ancient World*, trans. J. Costello. London: Weidenfeld & Nicolson.

Lewis, Archibald 1974: *Knights and Samurai: Feudalism in Northern France and Japan*. London: Temple Smith.

Lowenthal, David 1985: *The Past Is a Foreign Country*. Cambridge: Cambridge University Press.

Lyons, Francis S. 1979: *Culture and Anarchy in Ireland, 1890–1930*. London: Oxford University Press.

MacDougall, Hugh 1982: *Racial Myth in English History: Trojans, Teutons and Anglo-Saxons*. Montreal: Harvest House.

Mazrui, Ali 1985: African archives and oral tradition. *The Courier*, February (Paris: UNESCO), 13–15.

McNeill, William H. 1963: *The Rise of the West: A History of the Human Community*. Chicago: University of Chicago Press.

Nairn, Tom 1977: *The Break-up of Britain: Crisis and Neo-nationalism*. London: New Left Books.

Nettl, J. P. and Robertson, Roland 1968: *International Systems and the Modernization of Societies*. London: Faber.

Orridge, Andrew 1982: Separatist and autonomist nationalisms: the structure of regional loyalties in the modern state. In Colin H. Williams (ed.), *National Separatism*, Cardiff: University of Wales Press, 43–74.

Patai, Raphael 1983: *The Arab Mind*, rev. edn. New York: Charles Scribner's Sons.

Payne, Stanley 1971: Catalan and Basque nationalism. *Journal of Contemporary History* 6 (1), 15–51.

Raphael, Chaim 1985: *The Road from Babylon*. London: Weidenfeld & Nicolson.

Reynolds, Susan 1983: Medieval *origines gentium* and the community of the realm. *History* 68, 375–90.

Reynolds, Susan 1984: *Kingdoms and Communities in Western Europe, 900–1300*. Oxford: Clarendon Press.

Rustow, Dankwart 1967: *A World of Nations*. Washington, DC: Brookings Institution.

Saggs, Henry W. F. 1984: *The Might That Was Assyria*. London: Sidgwick & Jackson.

Sathyamurthy, T. V. 1983: *Nationalism in the Contemporary World: Political and Sociological Perspectives*. London: Frances Pinter.

Seltzer, Robert M. 1980: *Jewish People, Jewish Thought: The Jewish Experience in History*. New York: Macmillan.

Seton-Watson, Hugh 1977: *Nations and States: An Enquiry into the Origins of Nations and the Politics of Nationalism*. London: Methuen.

Sharabi, Hisham 1970: *Arab Intellectuals and the West: The Formative Years, 1875–1914*. Baltimore: Johns Hopkins University Press.

Smith, Anthony D. 1973a: Nationalism: a trend report and annotated bibliography. *Current Sociology* 21 (3) (The Hague: Mouton).

Smith, Anthony D. 1973b: Nationalism and religion: the role of religious reform in the genesis of Arab and Jewish nationalism. *Archives de Sociologie des Religions* 35, 23–43.

Smith, Anthony D. 1981a: *The Ethnic Revival in the Modern World*. Cambridge: Cambridge University Press.

Smith, Anthony D. 1981b: War and ethnicity: the role of warfare in the formation, self-images and cohesion of ethnic communities. *Ethnic and Racial Studies* 4 (4), 375–97; ch. 6 this volume.

Smith, Anthony D. 1983a: *Theories of Nationalism*, 2nd edn. London: Duckworth; New York: Holmes & Meier.

Smith, Anthony D. 1983b: *State and Nation in the Third World*. Brighton: Harvester.

Smith, Anthony D. 1984a: National identity and myths of ethnic descent. *Research in Social Movements, Conflict and Change* 7, 95–130.

Smith, Anthony D. 1984b: Ethnic persistence and national transformation. *British Journal of Sociology* 35 (3), 452–61.

Smith, Anthony D. 1986a: *The Ethnic Origins of Nations*. Oxford: Blackwell.

Smith, Anthony D. 1986b: State-making and nation-building. In John A. Hall (ed.), *States in History*, Oxford: Blackwell, 228–63.

Smith, Leslie (ed.) 1985: *The Making of Britain: The Middle Ages*. London: Macmillan.

Stack, John F. (ed.) 1986: *The Primordial Challenge: Ethnicity in the Contemporary World*. New York: Greenwood Press.

Sugar, Peter and Lederer, Ivo (eds) 1969: *Nationalism in Eastern Europe*. Seattle: University of Washington Press.

Szporluk, Roman 1979: *Ukraine: A Brief History*. Detroit: Ukrainian Festival Committee.

Taylor, David and Yapp, Malcolm (eds) 1979: *Political Identity in South Asia*, Collected Papers on South Asia no. 2, Centre of South Asian Studies, School of Oriental and African Studies, University of London. London: Curzon Press.

Tilly, Charles (ed.) 1975: *The Formation of National States in Western Europe*. Princeton: Princeton University Press.

Tudor, Henry 1972: *Political Myth*. London: Pall Mall Press.

Ullendorff, Edward 1973: *The Ethiopians: An Introduction to Country and People*, 3rd edn. Oxford: Oxford University Press.

Vital, David 1975: *The Origins of Zionism*. Oxford: Clarendon Press.

Weber, Eugene 1979: *Peasants into Frenchmen: The Modernization of Rural France, 1870–1914*. London: Chatto & Windus.

Wiseman, D. J. (ed.) 1973: *Peoples of the Old Testament*. Oxford: Oxford University Press.

8

The 'Golden Age' and National Renewal

People often remark on the Janus nature of the nation, at once visionary and nostalgic, backward-looking, yet oriented to the future. Some have seen this as the key to nationalism's success. But they view this duality in essentially instrumental terms: the return to the communal past is necessary if the masses are to be mobilized. For Kedourie,[1] the appeal to the past is part and parcel of the leaders' demagoguery, playing on the atavistic emotions of the masses. For Tom Nairn,[2] élites in the periphery, realizing their help-lessness in the face of the onslaught of uneven capitalism, have to appeal to the sentiments and cultures of the masses. For Hobsbawm,[3] the élites must fabricate a sense of community for the newly enfranchised and mobilized masses; while for Benedict Anderson[4] they must create an imagined poli-tical community among people who will never see each other through the representations and narratives of the printed word.

In each case the élites are pictured as seeking to control the masses through a project of social engineering. This they do by creating a cultural artefact, the nation, in order to prevent social breakdown and channel social change and political mobilization. The concept of a nation, however, cannot be sustained without a suitable past and a believable future, and this requires a community's history and destiny to be formed out of whole cloth. In order to create a convincing representation of the 'nation', a

'The "Golden Age" and National Renewal', in Geoffrey Hosking and George Schöpflin (eds), *Myths and Nationhood* (London: Hurst and Co., 1997). Repro-duced with the permission of the editors.

worthy and distinctive past must be rediscovered and appropriated. Only then can the nation aspire to a glorious destiny for which its citizens may be expected to make some sacrifices.

A 'Usable Past'?

From the standpoint of 'modernists' and instrumentalists, whose theoretical assumptions were scrutinized in Part I, the communal past forms a repository or quarry from which materials may be selected in the construction and invention of nations. The assumption here is that nations need *usable pasts*, their uses being largely determined by the needs and preoccupations of present-day élites. Curiously, this is an assumption shared by many nationalists in their drive to create nations.[5]

There are a number of dimensions of a usable past. The first is that history serves the interests of élites who use selected aspects of the past to manipulate mass emotions. To generate but also control mass mobilization, élites invent traditions and tailor national myths and symbols for mass consumption. As Saddam Hussein pictures himself as a latter-day Assyrian monarch, the former Shah holds court at Persepolis on the 2,500th anniversary of the Achaemenid kings, while Tilak invokes the cult of Kali to stir up the Bengali masses against partition.[6]

Second, the communal past can be treated as the legitimizer of unpalatable social change. When the nationalist regimes of new states need to force through unpopular measures and radical policies, it is often necessary to appeal to precedent and the traditions of 'our forefathers' in order to smooth their passage. Again, the example of Tilak and his use of the *Bhagavad Gita* is a case in point: Krishna's advice to the hero, Arjuna, on the need for courage in battle was used to inspire collective resistance to the British.[7]

Third, the communal past can provide a series of *exempla virtutis* to inspire public emulation, indeed a public morality. This was the aim of the French *patriots* in the Revolution, when they appealed to the civic virtue and heroism of Brutus, Scipio and Cincinnatus; or the American patriots who saw Washington as a latter-day example of classical virtue.[8]

Fourth, where territory is contested, the communal past may be used to provide prior title for one or other ethnic community or nation. Here, different but parallel communal pasts are usually invoked, as has been the case with Tamils and Sinhalese, and with Israelis and Palestinians, each national community selecting different periods and aspects which undergird its claim.[9]

Finally, the communal past is malleable. It represents, in the instrumentalist view, a construct of present generations, to serve their needs and interests, with each generation tending to change 'its' past in line with its perspective, providing new selections of, and interpretations for, what it considers significant. Thus different generations have reinterpreted the Swiss foundation myth, the Oath of the Rütli (1291),[10] for their own ends; successive generations of Afrikaners have reinterpreted the message of the battle of Blood River (1838);[11] and a modern generation of Israelis have found in the siege of Masada (AD 73)[12] a new significance unknown to older generations.

The past may have many uses, but it also has drawbacks in the formation of nations. It is often an ethnic past, when what is required is a more unifying civic nationalism which will draw in other *ethnies* who have no connection with the communal past of the dominant *ethnie*. It is therefore likely to prove divisive. Moreover, the malleability of the past, while helpful for such ethnic incorporation, may engender successive revisions and contestations, which have an unsettling effect on 'national identity'. Alternatively, a particular official version of the communal past can become a fixation and evoke nostalgia for the 'good old days' at a time of rapid change; and it may be simply irrelevant to the needs of the present, a utopian diversion from the real tasks ahead.[13]

All this may well be true in particular cases, but none of these considerations go to the heart of the matter. The question we have to consider is why so many people so often turn back to the collective past and seek in it something that appears to be missing in the present and which they think will assist them in shaping the future. We have to ask why it is that cultural collectivities so often define themselves in terms of a distinctive past and seek in that past a guide to their destiny. And we need to understand why a heroic past proves so often to be a 'usable past' and vice versa, and why it helps to shape the future even as it is shaped by the present. This applies with special force to the concept of the nation. If we succeed in answering these questions, we may go a long way to explaining the enormous appeal and durability of nations and nationalism.

The hypothesis that I want to consider is that the collective appropriation of antiquity, and especially of shared memories of the 'golden age', contributes significantly to the formation of nations. The greater, the more glorious, that antiquity appears, the easier it becomes to mobilize people around a common culture, to unify the various groups of which they are composed, and to identify a shared national identity.

The Appropriation of 'Antiquity'

The concept of 'antiquity' in which the ideal of the golden age is embedded and which forms the object of nationalist rediscovery and reappropriation, is multifaceted and subject to continual reinterpretation.

Its primary referent for early modern European intellectuals was classical antiquity, the civilization of Greece seen at first mainly through the lens of philosophy and imperial Rome, and from the eighteenth century, more directly, from a study of Homer and Athenian art and literature. In this context, the battle of the ancients and moderns and, later, Winckelmann's essays on Greek art set the tone for later interpretations, not just of Greek civilization, but of the whole notion of a golden age and its links with the possibility of, and need for, a 'classical revival'. The golden age of Periclean Athens had, by the beginning of the nineteenth century, become the standard and model for subsequent ideals of the golden age in other periods and civilizations.[14]

With the burgeoning of Romanticism, a second, broader concept of antiquity emerged. Now it embraced not just classical Greece and Rome, but the whole ancient world: ancient Egypt and Mesopotamia, Persia and Anatolia. This new concept went hand in hand with the amazing archaeological discoveries of the nineteenth century in Assyria and Sumeria, Achaemenid Iran and Hittite Anatolia, and fed the Romantic quest for an idealized distant past of humanity and a growing interest in archaeological verisimilitude of the 'first civilizations'. It also reflected an increasing differentiation of antiquity as a separate epoch from more recent, medieval histories.[15]

By the early twentieth century, the net of 'antiquity' had been extended to all pre-medieval civilizations: Shang China, the Indus Valley civilization of Harappa and Mohenjo-daro, Minoan Crete and, later, Han China, the kingdom of Axum, even the Maya of Yucatan. Each of these civilizations could then be fitted into the familiar tripartite periodization of evolutionary social theory (ancient/medieval/modern) and thereby reflect the upward march of humanity towards the apex of civilization, the modern West.[16]

By the mid-twentieth century, the evolutionist account was seriously undermined, and with it the tripartite historical progression. This allowed a much wider and more flexible range of pre-modern civilizations to be included under the rubric of 'antiquity': the Incas and Aztecs, Oyo and Benin, Ghana and Songhai, the Caliphates, Muscovy, Sung China, the Shogunates of Japan, as well as Western feudal states. Once again, this selection reflected a Western bias, but this time with only two stages – 'before and after (European colonialism)'.[17]

Now, at each stage, the number and types of golden ages increased, and with them the range and meanings of the concept. From being at the outset an epoch of moral virtue and literary and artistic creativity, as in Periclean Athens or Republican Rome, that idea of the golden age was extended to cover every kind of collective achievement from religious zeal to military expansion and economic success. From an age of virtue it became a moment of 'glory'. At the same time, it retained its original ideas of purity, authenticity and normative distinctiveness. In Herderian fashion, it defined the 'true character' of a people, or even humanity, what it would and should be if only the people had been 'true to themselves' and had been left alone.[18]

Of course, the ideal of a golden age is not a creation of the nationalists and the Romantics. It can be found among several peoples in the ancient world. The Sumerians of the late third millennium under the Third Dynasty of Ur harked back to an idealized Sumer of the pre-Akkadian Early Dynastic era.[19] The Egyptians of the Saite and Ptolemaic periods looked back to earlier periods and dynasties. Hesiod wrote of a golden age of the human race, while ancient Greeks of the classical era idealized the heroes of their Homeric epics,[20] and the Romans looked back to the moral virtues of a Cincinnatus and Scaevola,[21] or located a mythical golden age among the Hyperboreans at the northernmost rim of the world.[22]

We find a similar nostalgia for golden ages of heroism and chivalry among the Welsh and Anglo-Normans for the age of Arthur,[23] among later Frenchmen for the era of Charlemagne, among Arabs of the later Sultanates for the Age of the Companions or the Caliphates, and among Persians of the Samanid and Seljuk eras for the age of the Sassanids and their legendary battles with the land of Tur'an.[24] Above all, there is the attempt to link present dynasties and peoples with illustrious ancient pedigrees stretching back to Aeneas or Noah.[25]

As modernization invaded different parts of the globe, the number and range of rediscovered golden ages multiplied. This was partly the result of the sheer spread of social change, which disrupted so much of traditional routines and mores, and partly the result of the scientific discoveries and reconstructions of past epochs through disciplines like history, archaeology, philology and anthropology. But perhaps the most important spur to the proliferation of golden ages was the nationalist intellectuals' drive to rediscover the past of every ethnic community for which they wished to secure political recognition. For nationalists, 'antiquity' became almost synonymous with ethnic liberation and efflorescence. Even civic nationalists had to hold up to their countrymen and women a shining exemplar of communal life in the distant past, preferably in the same area, but certainly linked by cultural affinity if not direct ethnic descent. Soon, however, it was not enough to look back to ancient Sparta and Republican Rome, in the manner of the French *patriots* of the Revolution; the true golden age had to be located in the pasts of the ethnic community or nation, and it had to be a heroic age which could dignify the nation-to-be.[26]

Types of Golden Age

Typically, we find more than one type of golden age being reappropriated by the nationalist intellectuals of particular communities. These ages may be economic, an era of flourishing cities and great wealth and fertility – the Indus Valley civilization of Harappa and Mohenjo-daro, the city-states of Sumer, the Minoan palace-cities of ancient Crete, or the civilization of Teotihuacan in Mexico – a kind of Rousseauan dream of natural efflorescence before the corruptions introduced by modern civilization. Alternatively, they may be political, ages of rapid military expansion and imperial grandeur, such as we find under the late Assyrian monarchs from Tiglath-Pileser III to Asshurbanipal, or the Persian empire of the Achaemenids ruling from Susa and Persepolis, or the great age of Augustus and imperial Rome. More often still, the golden age is religious. It is an age of holiness and purity, manifest in the excavations and monuments associated with ancient texts and rites and temples, whether among the Maya of Yucatan, or the early Christian Irish monasteries, the age of Solomon and the Temple in Jerusalem, the Indian temples at Benares and other holy sites, or the Armenian or Russian churches and monasteries of the early medieval era – each of them associated with sacred texts. Finally, there is the golden age of intellect and beauty, in which philosophical, literary and artistic creativity was particularly concentrated: the Periclean age in ancient Athens, the Arab Caliphates from Baghdad to Cordoba, post-Vedic India's city-states, the China of Confucius and the late Chou dynasty. Though these kinds of golden age frequently overlap with each other, they present a standard of heroism, glory and creativity which subsequent ages failed to match, but which can spur modern generations to emulation.

Both the range and interpretations of golden ages, as seen through the lens of modern nationalisms, are illustrated by examples from communities as far apart as Mexico, Ireland and India. In the Irish case, two such golden ages achieved widespread popular support in the nineteenth century. One was Christian and Catholic, and centred on the activities of St Patrick and the subsequent age of monastic Christianity, exemplified in the characteristic round towers and crosses of the Irish countryside, studied by the archaeologist George Petrie. This was an age that combined saintly conduct and holiness with scholastic learning, as Irish missionaries and monks travelled throughout the Western world to instruct and convert the heathen, and hold up a beacon of learning in the era of barbarian kingdoms.[27]

The other golden age was pagan, the earlier centuries of the High Kings of Tara and the heroes of the Ulster cycle of epics, an era of warrior bands and companies of bards, which had been rediscovered by O'Grady and Lady Gregory and popularized by Yeats. The heroes of this era – Cuchulain, Fin MacCool and Oisin – championed an aristocratic warrior order which appealed to intellectuals in search of strength and nobility in an era of oppression and rural strife in the aftermath of the Great Potato Famine. Both of these golden ages served to remind Irishmen and women of a great, if distant, past before their island fell under British domination, and thereby instilled a measure of pride at a time of renewed nationalist activity in the 1880s and 1890s.[28]

Mexico presented a different, but equally complex, cultural ground. There had been an early 'Aztecist' rediscovery by some Creole intellectuals, notably Clavijero, in the late eighteenth century, but it was not until the late nineteenth and early twentieth century that a more systematic rediscovery and appropriation of the pre-Colombian pasts of Meso-America began. Again, a number of possible golden ages presented themselves. One was the wealth and scale of the central plateau city of Teotihuacan from the third to seventh centuries AD, with its huge temples and buildings, excavated and popularized by Manuel Gamio, who thereby demonstrated the vibrant life and strength of pre-Colombian 'Indian' civilization. From this point, a panorama of Meso-American civilizations was opened up, stretching from the Olmecs of the pre-Christian era to the Toltecs and Aztecs of the tenth to fifteenth centuries AD.[29]

Yet it was the Aztec city-state civilization of the central Mexican plateau, rather than the more distant Maya civilization of Yucatan, that was favoured by the Revolutionary governments after 1917. The reason was largely political. A new political order required a myth of the golden age that would help to weld an ethnically disparate nation together, by suggesting it was reviving its age of native independence and past political grandeur. Under President Obregon and his Minister of Education, Vasconcelos, the artistic movement of muralism was encouraged by public commissions to portray an idealized version of the glorious Aztec past and its tragic fate. The murals of Orozco, Diego Rivera and Siqueiros portrayed a heroic vision of the Aztec political golden age that underpinned the official cultural nationalism of the post-Revolutionary Mexican state with its use of Aztec symbolism and its ideal of racial mixing or *mestizaje* in mass civic education. But, despite the undoubted artistic flowering, the official cultural project and its muralist expression had only limited success. The modern Mexican state had inherited from the former Spanish provincial territory too many indigenous *ethnies* with their own languages and myths of origin for the Nahuatl Aztec–Spanish political mythology to take root outside the central plateau – quite apart from the modern distaste for aspects of the Aztec past.[30]

In modern Egypt, too, a similar duality of golden ages emerged in the late nineteenth century. With the rediscovery by Western archaeologists of the Pharaonic past, an Egyptian Pharaonic identity could be counterposed to the more traditional Arab–Islamic identity. By the turn of the century, there was an attempt to reform and liberalize the traditional Islamic iden- tification under the auspices of Muhammad Abduh, which opened the way for a more secular liberal politics under Lufti al-Sayyid. At the same time, there was also an influential movement of retraditionalization through a return to a purer Islam (*salafiyya*), preached by Rashid Rida, which sought to re-link Egypt and the Egyptians to a wider Arab world.[31]

The problem of such Islamic Arabism, in the eyes of its critics, was that it tended to ignore the special needs of Egypt and the Egyptians. This was a theme stressed by Mustafa Kamil in his attacks on British hegemony, and later by Muhammad Heikal in his attempts to locate Egyptian identity in a special land with a millennial Pharaonic history. There was the additional problem of the Christian Copts, who claimed to be the true Egyptians through lineal descent. Moreover, Islamic Arabism tended to assume a radical *discontinuity* not only between pre-Islamic and Islamic Egypt, but between the inhabitants of Egypt during each epoch. This seemed implausible in a population inhabiting a compact territory with its own very distinctive habitat and civilization. Pharaonism, *per contra*, rep- resented a movement that stressed the clear links between modern Egypt and its ancient past, so visible to its present-day inhabitants through its extant monuments, and it therefore sought to explain the distinctive character and needs of Egypt and Egyptians by reference to its unique and formative early civilization. This in turn helped to elevate Egypt and its inhabitants in both psychological and political terms at a time of foreign occupation. Unlike the Islamic golden age of the Mamluks, the Pharaonic golden age was decisively indigenous and political in character. It was an age of native imperial grandeur, and thus seemed more appropriate for an ideology of national liberation from an alien imperial power – until a new enemy, Zionism, reactivated the religious identity of Egypt and its Arab golden ages.[32]

A similar contrast between a more secular, political and a strongly reli- gious identity and antiquity surfaced in Iran in the later twentieth century under the Pahlavis. The late Shah favoured a return to the golden age of the Persian Achaemenids with its imperial grandeur, as it fitted well with his own imperial dreams of an efficient, highly modernized and Western- ized Iran. In this spirit, he convened in 1975 an imperial spectacle at the palace of Darius and Xerxes in Persepolis to mark the 2,500th anniversary of the Achaemenids, celebrating a pagan, pre-Islamic and secular era of imperial power and monumental art, brought to light by Western archaeology and scholarship. But the Shah's programme and his historical model failed to command any following among the ordinary people, let alone the bazaar merchants and clergy. They looked with more favour on the golden age of early Islam, and especially to the martyrdom of Hussein, the son of Ali, at Karbala in AD 680 and to his successors, the Imams. The Shiite version of Islam which became dominant in Iran since the Safavids in the sixteenth century, and which was further strengthened by Khomeini's return and the clergy's hegemony, has at present ousted the secularizing Achaemenid mythology and replaced it with a revolutionary Islamic myth with its own sacred memories of an age of religious fervour and martyrdom.[33]

Even greater possibilities were afforded to Russian nationalists by the vicissitudes of Russian ethno-history. What they tended to share, notably the Slavophiles, was an idealization of 'Old Russia' before the Westernization introduced by the Petrine reforms. That 'Old Russia' could stand for the early Romanov period in the seventeenth century, or for the apogee of Muscovite glory under Tsars Ivan the Great and Ivan the Terrible, or for the earlier resistance to the Tartar yoke and Teutonic Knights from Alexander Nevsky to Ivan III, or even for Kievan Rus' from the tenth to twelfth centuries. Alternatively, there were the golden ages of pure religion, notably the monastic epoch of the fourteenth century. In each case, 'holy Mother Russia' was opposed in power and value to its enemies, from the Cumans and Tartars to the modern West of capitalism and Nazism – even Stalin invoked the Church and Russian national symbolism in the dark days of the Great Patriotic War, and supported Eisenstein's epic films about Alexander Nevsky and Ivan the Terrible.[34]

For Russian nationalists, pre-Petrine Muscovy especially held up a model of purity, devotion and popular faith, for which they pined as the antidote to the class conflict and individualism of the West. From Dostoevsky and Mussorgsky's *Boris Godunov* and *Khovanshchina* to the historical painters Vrubel' and Vasnetsov and Stravinsky's *Rite of Spring* – based on Roerich's archaeology of ancient Russian tribal rites – a critique of Western values was mounted in the name of an idealized Russian past which, by cutting itself off and standing apart from the world, based state power on indigenous Christian faith, or even subordinated power to the pagan religion of the people and hailed backwardness as evidence of purity and superior faith.[35]

The same subordination of power to faith can be found among some Indian nationalists, for whom the post-Vedic era of classical city-states marked the apogee of Hindu Indian civilization even more than the later Gupta empire, exactly because it saw the creation of so many Hindu religious texts like the Upanishads and epics like the *Mahabharata*, along with the formation of new Indian religions like Buddhism and Jainism. This was the era that fired the imaginations of men like Pal, Banerjea and Aurobindo, a predominantly intellectual and religious golden age that could be counterposed both to Christianity and to the secular values of the West. The claim that 'India' had as great a civilization, and a philosophical and religious one at that, as any European 'nation', was an essential component of an increasingly Hindu Indian nationalism. The fact that this was essentially a North Indian golden age, and excluded Muslims and Sikhs and their golden ages, only served to strengthen the exclusive and hegemonic tendencies in Indian nationalism.[36]

If religious creativity was the criterion of Hindu Indian nationalist appropriation of the past, politics and statehood became the standard for Zionist ideals of Jewish history and destiny. From the early days of the Berlin and Galician *Haskalah*, the Davidic and Maccabean kingdoms became the guiding star of political Zionism. In terms of territorial extent, military prowess and political power, the united monarchy and the Hasmonean kingdom suggested former eras of unifying sovereignty and secular splendour that were designed to console a politically powerless and scattered people – a choice that was soon reinforced by the growing conflict with the Palestinians and the surrounding Arab states, and by the terrible experience of the Holocaust. The spectacular discoveries of Solomonic constructions at Hatsor, Megiddo and Gezer, as well as Yadin's excavations at Masada and Nachal Hever, attested to the apparent desire of the Israelites at the time of Solomon to maintain a strong state, and of the Jews in the period from the Zealots to Bar-Kochba to strive again for their independence from Rome.[37]

It was only to be expected of a people whose religion had played so important a role in its formation and development that this exclusively secular political model would not go unchallenged. For religious Jews, including religious Zionists, other periods of Israelite and Jewish history, especially the Mosaic era and the age of the Second Temple and the Sanhedrin, the age of the rabbis which saw the creation of the Mishnah and Talmud, possessed far greater significance. In a sense, they adhered to the traditional conception of Jewry in the diaspora, except that they too located the golden age, not in Mesopotamia or Spain or Poland, but in ancient Palestine. But this choice also brought the deep tensions in Jewish ethnohistory to the fore. These were not simply the opposition between the religious and the secular, of kings versus sages, so familiar in modern Israeli politics. The deeper tension that Zionism exposed was over the value to be placed on the Palestinian as opposed to the diaspora periods of Jewish history – a tension that the growing Israeli reappraisal of the Holocaust and the millennial history of Jewish persecution heightened, bringing in its wake a new appreciation of the high points of diaspora existence – economic, intellectual and religious.[38]

Similar combinations of themes – virtue, holiness, heroism, power, wealth and creativity – can be found among other peoples in all parts of the world. They have played an important role in cementing ethnic communities in the past and continue to do so in current debates about national identity, providing touchstones and inspiration even for more sceptical modern generations in moments of crisis and rapid change.

Functions of the Golden Age

These examples suggest not only the range of models and historical periods selected for idealization, but also the ways in which politics and religion are frequently fused to generate powerful concepts of an ethnic past that can fire the imaginations of the members of a community.

These concepts serve a number of functions for both individuals and communities in a nationalist epoch. The first is to satisfy the quest for *authenticity*. For nationalists themselves, this has become a *leitmotif* of their struggle. They seek to 'realize themselves' in and through the nation-to-be, believing that the nation has always been there, concealed under the debris of the ages, waiting to be 'reborn' through the rediscovery of the 'authentic self'. The interesting thing is that many people, who are not part of the nationalist élite or movement, have engaged in their own quests for 'authentic identity' and have come to embrace the need for authenticity in their own lives and as part of a wider community that needs to be purified of external accretions.[39]

In this context, an 'authentic identity' can have two meanings. The first is that of origin: 'who we are' is determined by 'whence we came', a myth of origins and descent – from Philip of Macedon, Oguz Khan, Hengist and Horsa. The second is that of difference: 'who we are' is determined by our relations with the 'outsider', the other who is marked off from 'us' by not sharing in our distinctive character, our individuality. Memories of one or more golden ages play an important part here, for they hold up the values and heroes that we admire and revere – which others cannot and do not, because they have different values and heroes.

In this sense, the model of a golden age is used to establish and delineate the nature of the 'true self', the authentic being, of the collectivity. This is essential to an evolutionary perspective that sees nations as developing from small, original and pure beginnings in some distant time to a first pristine flowering in the golden age, followed by decline and ossification – until it experiences a second birth at the hands of the nationalists.

The very distance of that pristine epoch lends to the community and its history an aura of mystery and an immemorial quality; conversely, the immemorial existence of the nation is a guarantee of its authentic nature, its original, unmixed and uncontaminated personality.[40]

The return in time is accompanied by a return in space, back to the 'homeland'. This is the second function of memories of the golden age: to locate and *re-root* the community in its own historic and fertile space. Like the community itself, the golden age (or ages) possesses a definite historical location and clear geographical dimensions in the land of the ancestors. The land is an arena or stage for the enactment of the heroic deeds and the contemplation of eternal verities which are among the main achievements of the heroes and sages of the golden age. It is also a landscape and soil that influences the character of that age, not only by giving birth to its heroes and sages, but also by forming and moulding the community of which they are members. Hence the need, in the eyes of nationalists, to re-root the community in its own terrain and liberate the land of the fathers and mothers, so that it may once again give birth to heroes and sages and create the conditions for a new collective efflorescence. Only by re-rooting itself in a free homeland can a people rediscover its 'true self', its ethno-historical character, in habitual contact with its sacred places and poetic landscapes.[41]

Another important function of memories of the golden age is to establish a sense of *continuity* between the generations. The return to a golden age suggests that, despite the ravages of time and the vicissitudes of social change, we are descendants of the heroes and sages of that great age. This is achieved through the periodization of ethno-history. The flux of ceaseless change is thereby rendered manageable through an intellectual framework which gives the people's history coherence and design, by relating earlier to later stages of their past. In this way, the nation is depicted as an outgrowth of earlier periods of the community's history, establishing itself as its lineal descendant through linkages of name, place, language and symbol, and in the stratification or layering of collective experiences, with lower 'layers' setting limits to higher ones, despite some breaks in experience. On this view, we can only grasp the 'meaning' of later periods of a particular community's history by studying the earlier, heroic periods. By establishing genealogical descent as well as cultural affinity with the heroic age(s), later generations realize their own genuine heroic individuality. Hence the task of nationalists is essentially one of political archaeology: to rediscover and reconstruct the life of each period of the community's history, to establish the linkages and layerings between each period, and hence to demonstrate the continuity of 'the nation', which is assumed to persist as a discrete, slowly changing identity of collective values, myths, symbols and memories, as, for example, many English people tacitly assume continuity through descent from their 'true ancestors', the Anglo-Saxons.[42]

A fourth function of memories of a golden age is to remind the members of a community of their past greatness and hence their inner worth. The quest for collective *dignity* has become a key element in national struggles everywhere, and the memory of a golden age affords a standard of comparison and evaluation in relation to both the past of the community and the histories of its neighbours. An appeal to the golden age elevates the inner, or 'true', essence of the community *vis-à-vis* both outsiders and the present degradations of the community. This is the point at which memories of the golden age are linked to myths of ethnic election: the chosen are worthy, their inner dignity contrasts sharply with their outward shame and humiliation.[43]

Memories of a golden age also proclaim an imminent status reversal: though at present 'we' are oppressed, shortly we shall be restored to our former glory. Thus contemporary Mongols, in their new-found freedom, can worship openly once again the figure of Genghis Khan in their aspiration to reclaim the power and glory that once was theirs, but has been lost for so many centuries to others. Memories of the golden age proclaim the hope of restoration of the community to its former high estate and true mission, thereby revealing the community's true worth and its ancient and noble pedigree. In their several ways, the discoveries at Great Zimbabwe, Teotihuacan, Masada and Vergina revealed to each community and to the world what nobility they once possessed and what they were capable of becoming if only they were free to follow their inner rhythms. Similarly, the compilation of Karelian ballads by Elias Lönnrot and his edition of the *Kalevala* restored to a small, neglected and politically submerged people a dignity and nobility that made the Finns, in their own eyes, the possessors of a history and an epic comparable to the Iliad, Ossian, the Nibelunglied and the Bible.[44]

Finally, the memories of a golden age mirror and point towards a glorious *destiny*, stemming from the true nature revealed in and by that golden past. In nationalist metaphor, its noble past prepares a community for its ordained destiny, and provides it with a hidden direction and goal beneath the obscuring present. In more concrete terms, each generation's understanding of the communal past and particularly of its golden age(s) helps to shape the future of that community. The selected elements of the heroic era in each generation's understanding will guide the community towards its goal and be re-created in its visionary future. So 'we shall be renewed as in the days of old', and 'be as we once were', in spirit.

In returning to the golden age of the Ramayana, Hindu Indian nationalists do not seek to resurrect it, but to recover the qualities of its heroes so as to re-create in modern terms the glory of the Indian past. Arab invocations of the Age of the Companions imply no return to the seventh century, rather the quest for inspiration and guidance from a pure and holy past for the creation of a united Arab nation. The ideal of St Joan which enthralled so many nineteenth-century French nationalists did not entail a return to a golden age of royal faith of the fifteenth century, but a desire to liberate modern France from its corruptions, divisions and defeatism by ridding it of its external and internal enemies and providing inspiration and an emblem for a people that had lost its way. So the vision of the desired future transmutes the meaning of memories of the golden age in each generation, adapting them to present conditions (though within strict limits), and thereby enabling them to galvanize the community for collective action to achieve a better future. Equally, the memories of a golden age hold the key to unlocking the secrets of a community's destiny, providing a rough-and-ready compass for the journey, as well as a 'map' and a 'morality' for the road, one which will enable the members to return to their core ethnic values and realize their 'inner being'. In this way, they may be able to secure the only immortality which now has any meaning, the favourable judgement of their posterity.[45]

Nations without a Golden Age?

If the possession and recovery of one or more golden ages contributes so much to the formation of nations, what of communities that appear to lack a glorious past, or indeed any past to speak of? Our hypothesis about the functions of the golden ages may hold for communities endowed with a rich and well-documented ethno-history, but it seems irrelevant to peoples with 'impoverished' or poorly documented ethno-histories, or for that matter to more recent immigrant states which are in the process of creating nations. We are back, it seems, with another version of Hegel's theory of 'historyless peoples'.

Let me start with the 'historically impoverished peoples'. Such 'impoverishment' is, of course, a relative matter and one that new historical, philological and archaeological discoveries can easily alter. I am thinking, for example, of the late eighteenth-century Romanian Uniate intellectuals' rediscovery of their 'Dacian' past[46] or the nineteenth-century rediscovery of Benin and Oyo,[47] as well as the Finnish case mentioned above. There are also, however, peoples whose ethno-histories have been submerged in those of more powerful or better-known neighbours. The Slovaks provide an example of a people whose intellectuals had actively to rediscover ancient heroes and a former Moravian kingdom in the ninth century, one that was separate from the better-known Bohemian kingdom and heroes

of the neighbouring Czechs.[48] Another example is afforded by the Ukrainians, whose distant illustrious past was incorporated in that of their Great
Russian neighbours, who also claimed ethnic and cultural descent from
Kievan Rus' from the tenth to twelfth centuries.[49] In these cases, scholarship and nationalist fervour did succeed in supplying both peoples with an
ethno-history of their own, including a golden age.

There are other cases, however, where records are more meagre and
where history has been largely oral. Ghana provides an example of a state
composed of several *ethnies*, including some with well-known ethno-
histories like the Ashante, but which as a 'nation-to-be' could not boast a
past that included most of the population. Its leaders, especially Nkrumah,
had therefore to annex an ancient African history, that of the empire of
Ghana, some 300 miles away, and regard it as its own, so as to confer on
the population of the newly independent state a sense of dignity and enable
its leaders to mobilize the people on the basis of a vision of former greatness.[50] Similarly, the ruins of Great Zimbabwe have been seen by some
African nationalists as evidence of the former greatness of the indigenous
people of the area, even though little is known about these mysterious
ruins. Likewise, in Australia, sites like Ayers Rock have become increasingly national symbols of an 'Aborigine nation' that clearly did not exist
prior to the coming of the Whites and probably not till well into this
century.

So pressing, however, is the need for an ethnic golden age in the construction of nations that states and populations that lack their own epochs
of former glory may well annex the golden ages of other related communities or of lands with which they have historic connections. This has
occurred among Blacks in the United States, who have looked to 'Ethiopia'
as the great independent kingdom of Africa able to boast several ages of
virtue and glory.[51] Alternatively, small communities have identified with
the golden ages of a wider cultural-ancestral community, as occurred
among some Turkic-speaking *ethnies* who identified with their forbears in
Central Asia.[52] This may explain the attraction of 'Pan' nationalisms for
those ethnic communities which lack their own well-documented and distinctive ethno-histories.[53] The heroic ages of large groups of peoples –
Slavs, Turks, Arabs – can be appropriated, as were the empires of Ghana
and Songhai by African nationalisms.

What of that other category of nations apparently without history, the
new immigrant national state? In Australia and New Zealand, Canada, the
West Indies, the United States and Argentina, the indigenous populations
were either penned in or decimated or exterminated. Among those where
some members survived the massacres and diseases brought by the Euro-
peans, we are witnessing now the birth or revival of a pan-indigenous

sentiment and network, together with claims to lands appropriated and cultures denigrated by the colonialists. Among Mohawks, Cree, American Indians, Aborigines and others, there are incipient movements for land rights and a return to the inspiration of a hidden and despised past, which may yet serve to unite and mobilize the often fragmented ethnic communities into a political nation.[54]

In fact, they may also be competing with the white colonists who may possess their own golden ages, be it those of the Pilgrim and later Founding Fathers of the White Americans, or the War of Independence fought by the Creoles of Argentina in 1810, the memories of the first settlements in Australia in 1788 and of the ANZAC expedition and sacrifice in 1916, or of the battle of Quebec in 1759 and the 1867 Act of Confederation in British Canada (contested, of course, by the Quebecois with their own golden age). In these cases, the golden age is not only recent; as Benjamin West remarked of Wolfe's sacrifice on the Heights of Quebec, the classical *exemplum virtutis* was enacted in 'modern dress', and so was 'movable' and relative to the needs and preoccupations of the present generation. At the same time, even relatively recent immigrant national states appear to require some kind of memory of a golden age and heroic past if they are to weld together into a single cohesive nation so many immigrant part-*ethnies*. In fact, golden ages are not necessarily distant and venerable. They are constantly being created out of the crises and achievements of successive generations of a community, but once they are recognized by later generations as heroic, they become an object of reverence and a standard for emulation.[55]

The attempt to use memories of a relatively recent golden age to create nationwide loyalties in immigrant national states is not without problems. For one thing, important groups of new immigrants may not accept these memories, or be indifferent or hostile to them – as is often the case with indigenous peoples in these states. They are, after all, the memories of the dominant *ethnie*. Thus Hispanics in the United States may reject the Founding, let alone the Pilgrim Fathers; Aborigines will be indifferent to ANZAC Day; and Indians in Trinidad will have their own memories of a golden past. In the more liberal democracies, this may prompt a move to celebrate ethnic diversity through policies of 'multiculturalism'. But this may in turn provoke a backlash from the radical Right of the dominant *ethnie*. Moreover, unless it is verifiably remarkable, a recent golden age rarely carries the resonance and potency of a well-documented and well-rehearsed antiquity. It may confer a measure of dignity, but doubts about its authenticity are liable to creep in. This in turn may erode any sense of continuity and hence its usefulness as a guide to communal destiny.[56]

Authenticity, Inspiration and Reinterpretation

These considerations raise some more general issues about the uses of the ethnic past, and suggest that some pasts are more 'usable' than others – not in the crude rationalistic sense of manipulation of mass emotions by élites for their own ends, or of social engineering of myths, symbols and memories to create new traditions, but in helping to form nations through such processes as *vernacular mobilization* and *cultural politicization.*[57]

Can we spell out in more detail the elements that go into the making of a past that can help to form nations? There are, I think, three elements that are essential for this purpose: authenticity, inspiration and the capacity for reinterpretation.

The phrase 'an authentic past' has several meanings. It can refer to the reappropriation of a communal possession, to the representativeness of shared cultural elements, to their indigenous and original qualities, and to their correspondence with 'objective' truth. An ethnic past can, and should, be authentic in all these ways if it is to serve the formation of nations. A 'usable past' and a model golden age is not a form of invented tradition; nor is it made up of 'shreds and patches'; nor again is it merely an imagined community. It refers to definite historical periods with their own dimensions and properties. At the same time, such a past is not any past, however well documented. It must be demonstrably 'our' past, or at least 'ours' by extension, and so capable of being connected and made relevant to the present of the people concerned. An ethnic past must also express the distinctive spirit of a period and community; and it must be created from within, not imported and imposed from without. Finally, the better documented and more securely dated and attested the golden age, the more it can bear the weight of emotion placed upon it, and withstand processes of demythologization.[58]

The second element in a nationally 'usable' ethnic past is its potential for inspiration. Again, there are several aspects. Not only must it be able to boast a golden age for this purpose, one which is well attested; the heroic epoch must be able to kindle the imagination, not just of a few romantic intellectuals, but of large numbers of the population. It must have 'mythic' quality: that is, it must contain a widely believed tale or tales of a heroic or sacred past that can serve present needs and purposes, as the Homeric poems so clearly served the needs and purposes of an early aristocratic era in the Greek city-states, or as the heroic tales of Aeneas and Romulus served the needs of the senatorial oligarchy and imperial family in late republican and early imperial Rome.[59]

In the era of modern nations, the tales of a heroic past must have a much wider resonance. They must be applicable to all the citizens of the nation and must strike a chord in the hearts of the common people as well as the élites. To play its part in the formation of the nation, the golden age must be able to act as a model and guide to its destiny, demonstrating the capacity of the nation in the past to create a culture worthy of emulation, and highlighting the qualities – personal, political, intellectual and social – that can inspire national renewal and spur public emulation. This is undoubtedly what occurred at the onset of romantic neo-classicism in late eighteenth-century Europe and America, when the Greek and Roman past and its heroes were held up for public admiration and emulation in the French and American revolutions and thereafter in many lands. Soon the heroes and golden ages of peoples and cultures far removed from Europe were being extolled as guides and models in the creation of the new nations of Latin America, Asia and sub-Saharan Africa. In Africa, the quest for authentic pasts that could inspire the common people would evoke those qualities and dimensions that had in the past helped to create heroic cultures and great civilizations, as the researches of Edward Blyden and Cheikh Anta Diop sought to demonstrate.[60]

And third, the ethnic past and its golden ages must be capable of re-interpretation. These are, after all, periods of the community's history that have been selected and reassessed in the light of (a) present social and political needs – here the present shapes the past; (b) the special qualities of that past, by tradition and common consent, and preferably also by modern scholarship – here the past shapes the future; (c) its transmission in records and/or through oral memories.

Thus the golden age of Periclean Athens was disinterred by Greek intellectuals and professionals in the eighteenth century, and became influential among state élites after the Greeks won their independence. Clearly, the present needs and preoccupations of Greek élites led them to select and reinterpret this ancient epoch as a model for the future. But equally, the quite distinctive qualities of the past, according to older traditions as well as modern scholarship, helped to shape the future course of the Greek state – in mass education, in law, in language, even in the economy, to the detriment perhaps of Greek modernization, yet to the advantage and power of Greek national pride and cohesion. At the same time, the hold of this seminal epoch on the modern Greek consciousness was increased by its transmission in records that are also sometimes masterpieces of art.[61]

Conversely, the return to the Davidic and Hasmonean kingdoms by modern Jews was partly shaped by the powerlessness of Jewish communities in the diaspora, a condition that was deepened by the experience of the Holocaust. But the choice of these models of ancient valour and power also helped to shape the destiny of an embattled modern Israel. The archaeological excavations at Megiddo, Hatzor, Nachal Hever and Masada simply reinforced the popular sense of authentic heroism and military exploits.[62]

The attempt by post-revolutionary regimes in Mexico to reassess the role of the pre-Colombian past and to establish the 'Aztec model' as canonical for *mexicanidad* is a further example of this two-way process. On the one hand, the needs of revolutionaries reacting to the Iberian positivism of the Diaz regime led to a revaluation of the heroic Aztec past. On the other hand, that past helped to shape the policies of post-revolutionary governments in mass education and culture in favour of the 'fusion of races'. Again, the Aztec past was chosen partly because, of all the pre-Colombian cultures, the Aztec was the best known and attested, as well as being the most central. The fact that state cultural nationalism has so far failed to inspire the indigenous groups does not mean that for the *mestizo* majority, it has not served its purpose.[63]

These examples reveal that the selected golden age sets up the parameters which help to delineate present action and future goals. This is because it answers to the quests for authenticity, rootedness, continuity, dignity and destiny that I enumerated earlier. These quests determine which golden age is likely to be selected in any one generation. This is not just a question of competition for power between élites with different visions; rather, the relationship of these élites to 'the people' whom nationalism vests with power and authority, determines which of several golden ages will be chosen as a guide to national destiny. And where 'the people' are divided into rival *ethnies*, it is likely that the golden ages of the dominant community will triumph. As the majority of the population emerge into the political arena, the type of golden age selected, or the type of re-interpretation accorded to it, will gradually change – often from dynastic to more communal golden ages. Hence the growing cult of St Joan in France, interpreted as a popular heroine of French religious nationalism; and the failure of the Achaemenid dynastic golden age sponsored by the Shah to strike a chord in the hearts of the Iranian masses. Lacking roots among 'the people', the age of Darius and Xerxes appeared to be inauthentic and remote, unable to inspire the people.[64]

Conclusion

The return to a golden age is an important, and probably an essential, component of nationalism. Its role is to re-establish roots and continuity, as well as authenticity and dignity, among a population that is being formed into a nation, and thereby to act as a guide and model for national destiny.

An ethnic past is usable if it can be claimed as 'authentic' on several levels, if it can inspire the mass of the population, and if it is relatively well attested. Equally important for a usable ethnic past is that it live in popular memory, that it can be recovered through artefacts, records and oral transmission, and that it can then be transmitted through a system of popular, public education as well as in the mass media.

Also important is the verifiability of the selected golden age. Nationalist fabrications may succeed for a moment, but their inevitable exposure is likely to divert energy and induce cyncism and apathy for the national cause. To inspire wonder and emulation, the golden age must be well attested and historically verifiable. Pure 'invention of tradition' is ineffective.

The memory of a golden age plays a vital part, then, in mobilizing, unifying and directing the energies of 'the people' to meet the challenges of nation formation through a myth of national history and destiny. By serving as a model and guide to that destiny, ethnic antiquity, and especially the golden age, becomes a source of continual inspiration, establishing the authenticity and continuity of the community's culture and conferring dignity on nations-to-be and well-established nations alike.

Notes

1 Elie Kedourie, *Nationalism* (London: Hutchinson, 1960), Introduction.
2 Tom Nairn, *The Break-up of Modern Britain: Crisis and Neo-nationalism* (London: New Left Books, 1977), ch. 2.
3 Eric Hobsbawm and Terence Ranger (eds), *The Invention of Tradition* (Cambridge: Cambridge University Press, 1983), ch. 7.
4 Benedict Anderson, *Imagined Communities: Reflections on the Origins and Spread of Nationalism* (London: Verso, 1983), chs 2–3.
5 Nkrumah annexed the ancient empire of Ghana some 300 miles away for this purpose, and Ataturk proposed the Sun Language theory to explain the origins of the Turks. On this general issue, see Elisabeth Tonkin, Maryon McDonald and Malcolm Chapman (eds), *History and Ethnicity*, ASA Monographs 27 (London and Boston: Routledge, 1989), Introduction.
6 Hobsbawm and Ranger (eds), *Invention of Tradition*, ch. 1; but see also Paul Brass, *Ethnicity and Nationalism* (London: Sage, 1991), chs 1–2.
7 See Mary Matossian, 'Ideologies of "delayed industrialization": some tensions and ambiguities', in J. H. Kautsky (ed.), *Political Change in Underdeveloped Countries* (New York: Wiley, 1962); M. Adenwalla, 'Hindu concepts and the *Gita* in early Indian thought', in R. A. Sakai (ed.), *Studies on Asia* (Lincoln: University of Nebraska Press, 1961), pp. 16–23.
8 Robert Rosenblum, *Transformations in Late Eighteenth-Century Art* (Princeton: Princeton University Press, 1967), ch. 2.

9   See K. M. de Silva, *A History of Sri Lanka* (London, Berkeley and Los Angeles: University of California Press and C. Hurst & Co., 1981); Sylvia Haim (ed.), *Arab Nationalism: An Anthology* (Berkeley and Los Angeles: University of California Press, 1962).

10 Georg Kreis, *Der Mythos von 1291: zur Enstehung des schweizerischen Nationalfeiertags* (Basel: Friedrich Reinhardt Verlag, 1991).

11 Leonard Thompson, *The Political Mythology of Apartheid* (New Haven and London: Yale University Press, 1985).

12 Barry Schwarz, Y. Zerubavel and B. M. Barnett, 'The recovery of Masada: a study in collective memory', *Sociological Quarterly* 27, 2 (1986), pp. 147–64.

13 See Yael Zerubavel, 'The multivocality of national myth: memory and counter-memories of Masada', *Israel Affairs* 1, 3 (1995), pp. 110–28.

14 On the classical revival in general, see Hugh Honour, *Neo-Classicism* (Harmondsworth: Penguin, 1968). For the acceptance and application to nineteenth-century French and English society of the classical Greek canon, see Athena Leoussi, 'The social significance of visual images of Greeks in English and French art, 1833–80' (unpublished Ph.D. thesis, University of London, 1992).

15 Sabatino Moscati, *The Face of the Ancient Orient* (New York: Anchor Books, 1962); Glyn Daniel, *The First Civilisations* (Harmondsworth: Penguin, 1971).

16 On evolutionism and its models of the development of civilization, see Shmuel Eisenstadt (ed.), *Readings in Social Evolution and Development* (Oxford and London: Pergamon Press, 1970); for a critique, see Robert Nisbet, *Social Change and History* (Oxford, London and New York: Oxford University Press, 1969).

17 See Nisbet, *Social Change*.

18 See Isaiah Berlin, *Vico and Herder* (London: Hogarth Press, 1976).

19 George Roux, *Ancient Iraq* (Harmondsworth: Penguin, 1964), ch. 10.

20 B. G. Trigger, B. J. Kemp, D. O'Connor and A. B. Lloyd, *Ancient Egypt: A Social History* (Cambridge: Cambridge University Press, 1983), p. 3.

21 Pierre Grimal, *Hellenism and the Rise of Rome* (London: Weidenfeld and Nicolson, 1968), pp. 211–41.

22 Stuart Piggott, *The Druids* (London: Thames and Hudson, 1985), ch. 4.

23 J. Alcock, *Arthur's Britain* (Harmondsworth: Penguin, 1973).

24 Richard Frye, *The Heritage of Persia* (New York: Mentor, 1966), ch. 6.

25 John Armstrong, *Nations before Nationalism* (Chapel Hill, NC: University of North Carolina Press, 1982), chs 2–3; Susan Reynolds, 'Medieval *origines Gentium* and the community of the realm', *History* 68 (1983), pp. 375–90.

26 See Robert Herbert, *David, Voltaire, Brutus and the French Revolution* (London: Allen Lane, 1972). This development can be traced in European painting and sculpture from the late eighteenth to the early twentieth centuries, as well as in some Latin American art in the twentieth century. In the early stages, Greco–Roman models and themes predominated; later subjects

and modes of portrayal drawn from medieval and pre-colonial histories and sources prevailed, as the spirit of historical verisimilitude and archaeological drama became widespread. See Rosenblum, *Transformations in Late Eighteenth-Century Art*, ch. 1; *French Painting, 1775–1830: The Age of Revolution*, comp. Detroit Institute of Arts (Detroit: Wayne State University Press, 1975); Dawn Ades (ed.), *Art in Latin America: The Modern Era, 1820–1980* (London: South Bank Centre, Hayward Gallery, 1989); A. D. Smith, 'Art and nationalism in Europe', in J. C. H. Blom et al. (eds), *De onmacht van hetgrote: Cultuur in Europa* (Amsterdam: Amsterdam University Press, 1993), pp. 64–80.

27 See Jean Sheehy, *The Rediscovery of Ireland's Past* (London: Thames and Hudson, 1980); Liam de Paor, 'The Christian connection', in L. Smith (ed.), *The Making of Britain: The Dark Ages* (London: Macmillan, 1984), pp. 77–90.

28 Nora Chadwick, *The Celts* (Harmondsworth: Penguin, 1970), pp. 100–9; F. S. Lyons, *Culture and Anarchy in Ireland, 1890–1930* (London: Oxford University Press, 1979), ch. 3; John Hutchinson, *The Dynamics of Cultural Nationalism: The Gaelic Revival and the Creation of the Irish Nation State* (London: Allen and Unwin, 1987), chs 2–4.

29 James Phelan, 'Neo-Aztecism in the eighteenth century and the genesis of Mexican nationalism', in Stanley Diamond (ed.), *Culture in History: Essays in Honour of Paul Radid* (New York: Columbia University Press, 1960), pp. 760–70; D. A. Brading, *The Origins of Mexican Nationalism* (Cambridge: Centre for Latin American Studies, University of Cambridge, 1985); Enrique Florescano, 'The creation of the *Museo Nacional de Antropologia* of Mexico and its scientific, educational and political purposes', in Elisabeth Boone (ed.), *Collecting the Pre-Colombian Past* (Washington, DC: Dunbarton Oaks Research Library and Collection, 1993), pp. 81–103.

30 Jean Franco, *The Modern Culture of Latin America* (Harmondsworth: Penguin, 1970); Ades (ed.), *Art in Latin America*, ch. 7; Natividad Gutierrez, 'The culture of the nation: the ethnic past and official nationalism in twentieth-century Mexico' (unpublished Ph.D. thesis, University of London, 1995).

31 Nadav Safran, *Egypt in Search of Political Community: An Analysis of the Intellectual and Political Evolution of Egypt, 1804–1952* (Cambridge, MA: Harvard University Press, 1961).

32 James Jankowski, 'Nationalism in twentieth-century Egypt', *Middle East Review* 12 (1979), pp. 37–48; Simon Shamir (ed.), *Self-Views in Historical Perspective in Egypt and Israel* (Tel-Aviv: Tel Aviv University Press, 1981), pp. 39–49; Israel Gershoni and James Jankowski, *Egypt, Islam and the Arabs: The Search for Nationhood, 1900–1930* (New York and Oxford: Oxford University Press, 1987), chs 6–8.

33 See Richard Cottam, *Nationalism in Iran* (Pittsburgh: Pittsburgh University Press, 1979), chs 2–3, 6, 8; Nikki Keddie, *Roots of Revolution: An Interpretive History of Modern Iran* (New Haven and London: Yale University Press, 1981).

34   Baron Meyendorff and Norman Baynes, 'The Byzantine inheritance in Russia', in Norman Baynes and H. St. L. B. Moss (eds), *Byzantium: An Introduction to East Roman Civilization* (Oxford, London and New York: Oxford University Press, 1969); Michael Cherniavsky, 'Russia', in Orest Ranum (ed.), *National Consciousness, History and Political Culture* (Baltimore and London: Johns Hopkins University Press, 1975); Richard Pipes, *Russia under the Old Regime* (Harmondsworth: Penguin, 1977), ch. 9.

35   Edward C. Thaden, *Conservative Nationalism in Nineteenth-Century Russia* (Seattle: University of Washington Press, 1964); Camilla Gray, *The Russian Experiment in Art, 1863–1922* (London: Thames and Hudson, 1971), chs 1–2.

36   B. T. McCulley, *English Education and the Origins of Indian Nationalism* (Gloucester, MA: Smith, 1966); Elie Kedourie (ed.), *Nationalism in Asia and Africa* (London: Weidenfeld and Nicolson, 1971), Introduction; Mark Juergensmeyer, *The New Cold War? Religious Nationalism Confronts the Secular State* (Berkeley: University of California Press, 1993), pt 2.

37   Michael Meyer, *The Origins of the Modern Jew: Jewish Identity and European Culture in Germany, 1749–1824* (Detroit: Wayne State University Press, 1967); Yigael Yadin, *Masada* (London: Weidenfeld and Nicolson, 1966), and *idem, Bar-Kochba* (London: Weidenfeld and Nicolson, 1971); see Doron Mendels, *The Rise and Fall of Jewish Nationalism* (New York: Doubleday, 1992).

38   Dan Segre, *A Crisis of Identity: Israel and Zionism* (London: Oxford University Press, 1980); Yechiam Weitz, 'Political dimensions of Holocaust memory in Israel', *Israel Affairs* 1, 3 (1995), pp. 129–45.

39   The concept of authenticity is often closely linked to metaphors of rebirth and awakening, of the kind discussed by Raymond Pearson ('Fact, fantasy, fraud: perceptions and projections of national revival', *Ethnic Studies*, 10, 1–3 (1993), pp. 43–64). But it is also possible to strip the quest for authenticity of its evolutionary moorings, if the 'true self' following its own inner dictates is seen as having been always 'there' beneath any historical accretions, and hence sometimes clear and visible, at other times concealed and indistinct.

40   A. D. Smith, 'National identity and myths of ethnic descent', *Research in Social Movements, Conflict and Change* 7 (1984), pp. 95–130, and *idem*, 'Gastronomy or geology? The role of nationalism in the reconstruction of nations', *Nations and Nationalism* 1, 1 (1995), pp. 3–23; Pearson, 'Fact, fantasy, fraud'.

41   A. D. Smith, 'States and homelands: the social and geopolitical implications of national territory', *Millennium, Journal of International Studies* 10, 3 (1981), pp. 187–202.

42   Hugh McDougall, *Racial Myth in English History: Trojans, Teutons and Anglo-Saxons* (Montreal: Harvest House, and Hanover, NH: University Press of New England, 1982); Lesley Johnson, 'Imagining communities' (paper for the conference 'Imagining communities: medieval and modern', convened by the Centre for Medieval Studies, University of Leeds, 1992); Smith, 'Gastronomy or geology?'

43 See A. D. Smith, 'Chosen peoples: why ethnic groups survive', *Ethnic and Racial Studies* 15, 3 (1992), pp. 436–56; Donald Akenson, *God's Peoples* (Ithaca, NY: Cornell University Press, 1992).

44 *Kalevala: The Land of Heroes*, trans. W. F. Kirby (London: The Athlone Press, and New Hampshire: Dover, 1985), introduction by Michael Branch; Lauri Honko, 'The *Kalevala* Process', *Books from Finland* 19, 1 (1985), pp. 16–23; E. R. Chamberlin, *Preserving the Past* (London: T. M. Dent and Sons, 1979).

45 See Anderson, *Imagined Communities*, ch. 1; A. D. Smith, *The Ethnic Origins of Nations* (Oxford: Blackwell, 1986), ch. 8.

46 R. R. Florescu, 'The Uniate Church: catalyst of Rumanian nationalism', *Slavonic and East European Review* 45 (1967), pp. 324–42.

47 John Peel, 'The cultural work of Yoruba ethno-genesis', in Tonkin et al., *History and Ethnicity*, pp. 198–215.

48 See Roger Portal, *The Slavs: A Cultural and Historical Survey of the Slavonic Peoples*, trans. Patrick Evans (London: Weidenfeld and Nicolson, 1969); David Paul, 'Slovak nationalism and the Hungarian state, 1870–1910', in Paul Brass (ed.), *Ethnic Groups and the State* (London: Croom Helm, 1985), pp. 115–59; Robert Pynsent, *Questions of Identity: Czech and Slovak Ideas of Nationality and Personality* (London and Budapest: Central European Press, 1994).

49 David Saunders, 'What makes a nation a nation?: Ukrainians since 1600', *Ethnic Studies* 10, 1 (1993), pp. 101–24.

50 See Denis Austin, *Politics in Ghana, 1946–60* (London: Oxford University Press, 1964); Robert Rotberg, *The Rise of Nationalism in Central Africa* (Cambridge, MA: Harvard University Press, 1965); *idem*, 'African nationalism: concept or confusion?', *Journal of Modern African Studies* 4 (1967), pp. 33–46; Chamberlin, *Preserving the Past*; Ali Mazrui, 'African archives and oral tradition', *The Courier*, February 1985, pp. 13–15.

51 Theodore Draper, *The Rediscovery of Black Nationalism* (London: Secker and Warburg, 1970).

52 David Kushner, *The Rise of Turkish Nationalism* (London: Frank Cass, 1976).

53 Hans Kohn, *Pan-Slavism*, 2nd edn (New York: Vintage Books, 1960); Immanuel Geiss, *The Pan-African Movement* (London: Methuen, 1974); Jacob Landau, *Pan-Turkism in Turkey* (London: C. Hurst & Co., 1981).

54 F. Svensson, 'The final crisis of tribalism: comparative ethnic policy on the American and Russian frontiers', *Ethnic and Racial Studies* 1, 1 (1978), pp. 100–23.

55 For West's remark, see *American Art, 1750–1800: Towards Independence*, comp. Victoria and Albert Museum (London, 1976), pp. 82–6. On the mingling of Puritan millennialism and nationalism in the United States, see E. L. Tuveson, *Redeemer Nation: The Idea of America's Millennial Role* (Chicago and London: University of Chicago Press, 1968), and Conor Cruise O'Brien, *God Land: Reflections on Religion and Nationalism* (Cambridge, MA: Harvard University Press, 1988). For Australian nationalism and the ANZAC Day and monument, see Bruce Kapferer, *Legends of Peoples, Myths of States:*

Violence, Intolerance and Political Culture in Sri Lanka and Australia (Washington, DC and London: Smithsonian Institution Press, 1988).

56   The problem with multiculturalism in this context is not just dominant ethnic resentment, but how to ensure cohesion and mobilization and even self-sacrifice among ethnically heterogeneous populations whose separate ethnic components are encouraged to celebrate their diverse origins and their distinct cultures and golden ages. For the Australian example, see Stephen Castles, Bill Cope, Mary Kalantzis and Michael Morissey, *Mistaken Identity: Multiculturalism and the Demise of Nationalism in Australia* (Sydney: Pluto Press, 1988). For a brief discussion of the model of a 'plural' nation, see A. D. Smith, *Nations and Nationalism in a Global Era* (Cambridge: Polity, 1995), ch. 4.

57   See A. D. Smith, *National Identity* (Harmondsworth: Penguin, 1991), ch. 3.

58   Ibid., ch. 8; Smith, *Nations and Nationalism*, ch. 3. The term 'authenticity' is used in several ways. It can mean what the proposer chooses to regard as genuinely his, her or theirs; so, for example, 'authentic music' means 'my' music. Or it can mean that which inheres in the spirit of an age or community and expresses their spirit in pure form. Here 'authentic music' means 'representative of place or period' played on 'authentic instruments'. Authenticity can also refer to original as opposed to derivative, and indigenous as opposed to alien, cultural elements; in this sense 'authentic music' is the true expression of its creator and has no forerunners or models from which to borrow. Finally, it can mean that which is 'true' in the sense of valid; here music is 'authentic' if it is what its composer actually wrote, note for note, without any subsequent addition or embellishment. See Berlin, *Vico and Herder*, for Herder's understanding of 'authentic' culture and experience.

59   Henry Tudor, *Political Myth* (London: Pall Mall Press, 1972); G. S. Kirk, *Myth: Its Meanings and Functions in Ancient and Other Cultures* (Cambridge: Cambridge University Press, 1973); Sebastian Garman, 'Foundation myths and political identity: ancient Rome and Saxon England compared' (unpublished Ph.D. thesis, University of London, 1992).

60   See Robert July, *The Origins of Modern African Thought* (London: Faber & Faber, 1968); H. S. Wilson (ed.), *The Origins of West African Nationalism* (London: Macmillan & Co., 1969).

61   A. Pepelassis, 'The image of the past and economic backwardness', *Human Organisation* 17 (1958), pp. 19–27; John Campbell and Philip Sherrard, *Modern Greece* (London: Ernest Benn, 1968); Paschalis Kitromilides, '"Imagined communities" and the origins of the national question in the Balkans', *European History Quarterly* 19, 2 (1989), pp. 149–92.

62   Amos Elon, *The Israelis: Founders and Sons* (London: Weidenfeld and Nicolson, 1972); Zerubavel, 'Multivocality of National Myth'.

63   See Brading, *Origins of Mexican Nationalism*; Ades (ed.), *Art in Latin America*; Gutierrez, 'Culture of the nation'.

64   See Marina Warner, *Joan of Arc* (Harmondsworth: Penguin, 1983), ch. 13; Cottam, *Nationalism in Iran*, chs 10–13.

9

Romanticism and Nationalism

In this last chapter, I focus on the ideology of nationalism, its nature, content and role, and more especially its relationship with Romanticism. The common view of nationalism in the West is profoundly negative. On the one hand, it is seen as a Romantic doctrine, incoherent, threadbare and irrational; on the other hand, as a subversive and destructive political force. For Michael Freeden, nationalism is a 'thin-centred' ideology which 'arbitrarily severs itself from wider ideational contexts, by the deliberate removal and replacement of concepts'. So it cannot offer 'complex ranges of argument', because 'many chains of ideas . . . are simply absent' (Freeden 1998: 750). The charge of intellectual poverty and incoherence is echoed by Benedict Anderson.[1] For John Dunn, on the other hand, it is the moral depravity of nationalism that is most striking: 'Nationalism is the starkest political shame of the twentieth century, the deepest, most intractable and yet most unanticipated blot on the political history of the world since the year 1900' (Dunn 1979: 55). And not just since 1900, but for at least a century before. For, from the later eighteenth century, the ideal of the nation has become paramount in Western politics, even if, according to Eric Hobsbawn, its most divisive and reactionary 'ethno-linguistic' varieties appeared only after 1870 (Hobsbawm 1990: ch. 4).

Romanticism has had an equally bad press. To the parallel charges of incoherence and irrationality are added an unnatural exaggeration and wildness. Already in the early nineteenth century, Goethe told Friedrich Wilhelm Riemer in 1808: 'There is nothing natural or original in Romanticism – rather it is contrived, affected, intensified, exaggerated, bizarre, even distorted and caricature-like' (cited in Porter and Teich 1988: 110). And in 1829 he told Johann Paul Eckermann: 'Romanticism is disease, classicism is health' (cited in Berlin 1999: 112 and 158n). And in our own time, speaking of Max Stirner's theory of the will and his commitment to unbridled imagination and its self-destructive consequences, an otherwise sympathetic Isaiah Berlin concludes: 'To this extent romanticism, if it is driven to its logical conclusion, must end in some kind of lunacy' (Berlin 1999: 145). For the critics, then, Romanticism and nationalism are perceived as bed-fellows: together they lead their adherents to excess, self-delusion and self-destruction.[2]

In what follows, I shall seek to develop this analysis of Romantic nationalism through a consideration of one of its most influential critiques. I shall then indicate some of the limitations and excesses of this critique, and look at some recent alternative characterizations of nationalism which seek to de-romanticize it. Thereafter, I will argue that there are indeed strong Romantic components in all nationalisms, albeit in varying degrees and in a broader sense than the German Romantic version which is usually singled out by the critics of nationalism. For, as I hope to show, the Romantics were pre-eminent in rediscovering and disseminating the myths, memories, symbols and traditions of diverse ethnic communities, which nationalists then used to create political nations. Thus, an understanding of the Romantic contribution will allow us to obtain a more rounded picture of nationalism, and of its specifically Romantic components – components that retain their cultural and political significance to this day.

The Critique of Romantic Nationalism

The critique of Romantic nationalism is given its most pungent and impassioned expression in the work of Elie Kedourie. For Kedourie, there is really only one version of nationalism, and that is the doctrine formulated by the German Romantics after 1806, the year of Napoleon's humiliating defeat of Prussia at Jena. It was in the following year that Johann Gottlob Fichte gave his seminal *Addresses to the German Nation*, which for Kedourie marks the first statement of the genuine doctrine of nationalism, a doctrine that, in Kedourie's words, 'was invented in Europe at the beginning of the nineteenth century' (Kedourie 1960: 1).

Now, for Fichte and other German Romantics, like Schlegel, Müller, Schleiermacher, Arndt and Jahn, language was the key criterion and the main characteristic of nations. In this, the Romantics followed Johann Gottfried Herder's argument that human beings expressed themselves most intimately and authentically in their vernacular language, and that, though other aspects of culture, notably music and dance, were important communal modes of self-expression, language was the most authentic and most natural. In Herder's words, 'The language in which we make love, pray and dream, that is our most intimate language, our language of worship' (Herder 1911: xxiv. 43, cited in Llobera 1994: 170). Or, even more directly, 'Let us follow our own path . . . let all men speak well or ill of our nation, our literature, our language: they are ours, they are ourselves, and let that be enough' (cited in Berlin 1976: 182).

The German Romantics also shared Herder's organic naturalism. For Herder, the nation was part of nature and was formed originally by natural factors:

> A people can maintain its national character for thousands of years and, if its prince, who has this heritage, has a concern for it, it can be developed through education along the lines most natural to it. For a people is a natural growth like a family, only spread more widely. (Herder 1911: xiii. 384, cited in Llobera 1994: 169)

Not only were nations natural growths for Herder and the German Romantics, they were also historical products of the soil, both physical and spiritual, to which the members belonged. In Isaiah Berlin's rendering of the doctrine:

> A man belongs to where he is, people have roots, they can create only in terms of those symbols in which they were brought up, and they were brought up in terms of some kind of closed society which spoke to them in a uniquely intelligible fashion. (Berlin 1999: 63)

Expressionism, naturalism, historicism and, Berlin adds, cultural populism, the belief that individuals belong to a national group and that all ideals and creativity are products of these quite different cultural groups: all these Romantic ideals originated with Herder, and they fed into nationalism.[3]

Kedourie takes this a step further. Not only did these Romantic ideals feed into nationalism, they formed it. Nationalism is a political version of Romanticism. Yes, concedes Kedourie, there was the example and the legend of the French Revolution. But this was soon understood as collective Will in action, the unbridled assertion of national self-will with all its bloody consequences. It was, above all, in Germany that the spontaneous outburst of the Revolution was taken to heart as an object lesson in applied philosophy for the nefarious ends of political action, subversion and destruction. Hence, according to Kedourie, it is to the German Romantic doctrine that we must turn, if we are to grasp the nature of nationalism (Kedourie 1960: ch. 1).

In the doctrine of unbridled Romantic nationalism, nations are held to be natural. They are like organisms and are therefore subject to natural laws of efflorescence and decay. Equally, nations are distinctive. They have incommensurable cultures and identities, and unique souls or essences. At the same time, nations are deemed to be products of human action, for they express the striving of a collective Will. Nationalism itself is nothing other than the conscious reawakening of nations to renewed life, to rebirth and regeneration on their own soil. Thus nationalism expresses the special mission and glorious destiny of the unique nation. To realize its true nature, every nation must be free and able to express itself in perfect freedom. As for individuals, they are simply the products and specimens of their nation and its unique culture which stamps them indelibly, wherever they happen to be.[4]

This is the doctrine that with variants was espoused by those German Romantics concerned with history and politics – especially Fichte, Müller, Arndt and Jahn. It is also the doctrine that Kedourie castigates as incoherent, unrealistic, irrational and destructive. Specifically, Kedourie charges Romantic nationalism with four sins.

The first is vagueness and incoherence. Nationalists are never sure which characteristics define the nation – language, customs, religion, territory, or simply will. In fact, says Kedourie, citing a passage by the Jewish nationalist Ahad Ha'am, beneath the rhetoric and the various criteria of the nation, the doctrine is remarkably consistent: it is the collective Will that defines what is to constitute the nation, and it is striving and struggle that mould and shape it. This was the legacy of Immanuel Kant, especially of his ethics. For Kant had claimed that freedom was humanity's greatest good, and that the only good will is the free will. But, argues Kedourie (1960: chs 2–3), will is inherently unstable and unpredictable. Renan expressed the matter succinctly when he said that the nation is like a daily plebiscite, and therefore, adds Kedourie, it must fall into querulous anarchy or hypnotic despotism. He might have added that the national Self that is said to strive and will is notoriously hard to pin down, as several historical plebiscites have demonstrated.

Second, nationalism is, for Kedourie, politically subversive and destabilizing. As Lord Acton had warned a century ago, it aimed to make the nation the mould and measure of the state, to make culture and polity congruent. But the fact is that they are so obviously not congruent; to try to make them congruent is bound to cause misery and bloodshed. In a world where states had been formed by all kinds of expedients, from dynastic marriage to warfare, the attempt to overturn the *ancien régime* and redraw the political map to fit linguistic and ethnic populations can only end in terror and massacre, especially in areas of mixed ethnicity like the Balkans.

In fact, the nationalists, Heine's 'well-weaponed Fichteans', by turning conflicts of interest into wars of principle, can only exacerbate tensions and undermine sound practical arrangements for preserving the peace between different ethnic groups, bringing murder and havoc in their wake (Kedourie 1960: ch. 5).

Third, the nationalist vision is inherently unattainable. It is a species of chiliastic doctrine, seeking perfection on earth. This reveals nationalism as the secular heir of antinomian medieval Christian millennialism. Like the latter, nationalism preaches an ethic of brotherly love, the purification of the elect, the destruction of the barriers between the public and the private domains of life, and the abolition of this corrupt world for a new dispensation of absolute love and justice on earth. This bears no resemblance to the real world of politics and society which is inevitably an imperfect patchwork of often unsatisfactory compromises. Nationalism scorns this imperfect world, and strives ceaselessly for perfectibility and the unattainable ideal of popular sympathy and love, much as the Franciscan Spirituals and Anabaptists had done in earlier epochs. Like millennialism, too, Romantic nationalism appeals to the ambitious and talented, but often excluded and marginal men, who feel shut out of society and politics, whether in the Central and Eastern European empires or in the overseas colonies. As a result, nationalism expresses all the discontent and resentment of an excluded intelligentsia, with its messianic yearning for a transfigured world of new, that is, nationally transvalued values, none of which, according to Kedourie, have any place in the real world (Kedourie 1971: introduction).[5]

Finally, nationalism is inherently violent and self-destructive. It is, Kedourie tells us, quite simply a derangement of the senses, to use Rimbaud's phrase. Nationalism is like an opiate that takes away the senses of those to whom it is administered, as well as those who administer it to others. And it proceeds through violence and terror; for, as St Just says, virtue requires terror. Such a doctrine can only end in the violent revolutionary nihilism of a Bakunin or a Nechayev, in which the normal traditional communities of family, neighbourhood and religion are suddenly and violently replaced by a wholly abstract love of the nation. It is quite in keeping that for Michel Aflaq, the founder of the Syrian Ba'ath (or Resurrection) Party, a party responsible for massacre and mass terror, 'Nationalism is love'. Just as people must be forced to be free, so they must be taught to love, if necessary through terror. And Kedourie goes on to list in lurid detail the many violent lessons of nationalistically applied love – from the Mau Mau oaths to Tilak's invocation of the dread Kali, Hindu goddess of dark destruction, with her garland of human heads around her neck (Kedourie 1971: introduction).

This is a bleak picture. Though Kedourie is more respectful of Herder, he clearly regards Romantic or German nationalism as one of the most pernicious doctrines and greatest tragedies to have befallen a hapless humanity. As a witness of some of nationalism's early excesses in the Middle East, his critique is informed by bitter personal insight into the psychology of nationalism and its destructive effects, particularly for religious and ethnic minorities in countries afflicted with this virus. And yet, for all its originality and erudition, Kedourie's analysis is flawed in a number of respects. So, it is exactly for this reason that scrutiny of his critique can provide us with a better understanding of the nature and contribution of Romantic nationalism.

'Civic' or Sanitized Nationalism?

The earliest response to Kedourie's impassioned attack on nationalism came from his colleague, Ernest Gellner. Gellner agreed with Kedourie's basic premiss that nationalism was a logically contingent phenomenon; human beings did not have, or need to have, a nationality as they had to have eyes and ears. But this anti-naturalism did not imply that nationalism was simply a misguided invention of German Romantic intellectuals, or that it was a collective version of a Kantian doctrine of the will. On the contrary, not only was Kant himself guiltless – after all, his good will is predicated of individuals, not groups – but, more important, nations and nationalism had become a sociological necessity in the *modern* epoch. Before the advent of industrial modernity, there was indeed no need or room for nations and nationalism in an agro-literate society; the elites and the mass of food-producers only had economic relations, they did not share, or have to share, a common culture. But in the modern era, the tidal wave of modernization and its industrial machine demanded a mobile, literate work-force and therefore both a general education and specialized skills. Modern work was increasingly semantic, and so messages had to be standardized and context-free. This in turn required the production of educated – that is, numerate and literate – citizens to run the industrial machine. Hence, the mark of modernity was the rise of literate 'high cultures' dependent on compulsory, mass, public education and specialist skills. It was these taught high cultures that attracted the loyalty of the newly urbanized peasants in the anonymous city; and that, according to Gellner, is the core of nationalism. It is, says, Gellner, nationalism that invents nations, not the other way round; and it is modernity that requires nationalism, or identification with high cultures (Gellner 1964: ch. 7; 1983).

And what of Romanticism? Gellner's conclusion that nationalism is a hard-headed, practical programme of pulling oneself up by one's bootstraps for economic development, left little role for intellectual *schwärmerei*. Nationalism likes to dress itself up in peasant garb and extol folk-songs and dances, but that is a nationalist conceit. In reality, it is a determinedly modernizing movement, in which the philosopher-kings, however much they may talk like *narodniks*, are inevitably vigorous Westernizers. Nationalism is the culture and politics of modernity *tout court* (Gellner 1964: ch. 7).[6]

In a similar vein, Tom Nairn also spoke of the way in which nationalism, that most idealist of phenomena, was the product of the most objective and material of conditions: namely, the 'machinery of world political economy'. For Nairn, the romantic intellectuals in the world's periphery, realizing that they could not match the power of capitalist imperialism, appealed to the masses; in his words, they invited the masses into history, and wrote the invitation card in the language and culture of the people. That is why nationalism is always cross-class and populist. Here, Romanticism, with its cult of the common people and the soil, played a useful role in forging a common national culture for elites and masses in their struggle against Western imperialism. (Nairn 1977: chs 2, 9).

This is, of course, a fairly instrumentalist approach to the Romantic elements in nationalism. The intellectuals, on behalf of a nascent native bourgeoisie, exercise the simple function of resistance to the imperialist machinery of world political economy. But at least Nairn, conscious of the role of Walter Scott and others in forging a Scottish national culture, does not entirely dismiss or neutralize Romanticism.[7]

The same cannot be said for that other strategy for sanitizing nationalism: the recently developed ideal of a purely 'civic' nation and nationalism. Of course, the distinction between civic and 'ethnic' nationalism can be traced back to Hans Kohn's (1967a) dichotomy of, on the one hand, a rational, contractual and voluntary 'Western' nationalism and, on the other hand, an organic, mystical and authoritarian 'Eastern' nationalism – east, that is, of the Rhine. The distinction also appears in Kedourie's (1960) contrast between the German Romantic nationalism which he abhors and the more acceptable British or Whig doctrine of nationality advanced by Lord Acton, which values nationality only in so far as it brings good government.[8]

But neither Kohn nor Kedourie had specifically invoked ethnicity as the foil to a rational, liberal Western nationalism. This was the work of a more recent generation, reacting to the resurgence of ethnicity in the West itself – among Bretons, Basques, Catalans and Quebecois – and latterly in the successor states of the former Soviet Union and the Balkan states. For writers like Yael Tamir (1993), Michael Ignatieff (1993), Maurizio Viroli (1995) and David Miller (1995), it is the spectre of an ethnic nationalism that haunts Europe and the globe. This appeal to blood and roots is a retrograde movement, liable to rekindle the fires of xenophobia, racism and anti-Semitism. It rests, says Hobsbawm (1990), on the fear of massive recent changes and especially of the stranger, brought so near by the vast population movements associated with globalization. The only way to exorcise the demon of ethnicity is to strengthen civil society and support or institute a civic nation and nationalism. Only this type of national loyalty will accommodate the polyethnic nature of most states, exactly because it is so pre-eminently rational, inclusive and multicultural, and as such capable of a liberal ethical defence.[9]

Now, however laudable, the civic strategy is fraught with dangers of its own. Leaving aside the objections of ethical universalists to any kind of particularistic nationalism, the civic nationalist project requires a degree of sophistication and mass political tolerance, and a sufficient degree of political solidarity, to hold together the various ethnic or regional segments of society. Neither has been easy to obtain, as the experience of both Western and post-colonial states has shown. Moreover, a purely civic version of nationalism, an elite project so often far removed from popular forms of the ideology, risks the danger of provoking oppositional outbursts and movements under the Romantic banners of ethnicity when, as so often occurs, it fails to fulfil the expectations of the citizens.

There are other problems with the civic approach. For one thing, it fails to grasp the implications of the fact that 'civic' and 'ethnic' elements are closely intertwined in most nations and nationalisms, and that the confidence and tolerance of certain national communities rests as much on the sense of the common origins, history and distinct culture of the dominant ethnic community, or *ethnie*, as of any civic institutions and inclinations. Even then, that tolerance can hardly be taken for granted, and ethnic backlashes may invoke a Romantic conception of the primordial genealogical nation. Second, the belief that civic nationalism is somehow always constructive, and ethnic nationalism destructive, misses the vital point that all nationalisms are able to inspire in their adherents a variety of objectives and sentiments, and that, given the circumstances, these can produce very different policies. Nationalism is not just Janus-headed, it is protean and elusive, appearing in a kaleidoscopic variety of guises, yet remaining always recognizable as the ideology of and for a nation. Finally, civic nationalism cannot in the end help invoking place, time, community and destiny, the four fundamental dimensions of all nationalisms: a homeland or territory, a particular history and unique past, a distinctive community of shared public culture, and a belief in the special future or destiny of the nation. But, as we shall see, these are the very dimensions also singled out by 'Romantic' ethnic nationalists, and they underlie both the most rational and civic of French nationalisms and the most Romantic of German nationalisms.

What this means is that the contrast between 'civic' and 'ethnic' nationalisms is not as clear-cut and exclusive as the liberal theorists of civic nationalism suggest or desire. We have only to recall the French treatment of minorities, notably the Jews from the Enlightenment to Vichy, to see that a civic type of nationalism is often little more inclusive and tolerant than many ethnic forms; and that romantic, indeed Romantic, elements could be found even in the Dreyfusard and socialist versions of French nationalism. In short, all these attempts to sanitize nationalism fail.[10]

The 'Romanticism' of Nationalism

We must therefore retrace our steps and put the Romanticism back into nationalism, but not in the manner of Kedourie. For Kedourie, as we said, the only real nationalism was the German Romantic version. This was his primary error. It led him to mistake the part for the whole, one influential version for the totality of nationalist ideologies. For, just as there have been several versions of Romanticism, so there have been other forms of nationalism which do not share the strongly essentialist, organic and deterministic assumptions of German Romantic nationalism. But, neither are these different kinds of nationalism divorced from Romanticism, as Gellner and the civic model suggest. For nationalist movements, however hard-headed and practical their goals, always incorporate certain of the ideas and assumptions that Romanticism either originated or spread. Their central concepts are steeped in Romantic beliefs, but not necessarily those of the German Romantics – beliefs, I might add, that are still very much part of our popular culture in our supposedly 'post-Romantic' and 'post-modern' epoch.

Of course, as so many scholars have underlined, Romanticism, or perhaps we should say Romanticisms, is a highly complex and multifaceted phenomenon – a revolution that is at once an artistic and literary movement, a moral philosophy, and a psychological sensibility, and thus even more protean and elusive of definition than nationalism. Yet, in most of the products of Romanticism, we find three features continually recurring:

1 the primacy of individual or collective will and action, or will in action;
2 the cult of the particular and of cultural diversity;
3 the yearning for authentic and free self-expression. (See Berlin 1999)

These ideals of active will, cultural diversity and unfettered self-expression informed and gave rise to the characteristic products of Romanticism: its return to, and love of, Nature; its love of innocence and childhood; its elevation of the artist as hero; its cult of the infinite and of genius; its exaltation of love and love's dreams; its glorification of the rebel; its quest for the heart's truth; its yearning for ideal pasts and sublime destinies; and so on; and, as I shall argue, its equally passionate assertion of national identity and national will.[11]

Now, in order to appreciate the profoundly Romantic impulses of all nationalism, we need to recall its central meanings. So, let me start with some working definitions. 'Nationalism' I would define as *an ideological movement for attaining and maintaining autonomy, unity and identity on behalf of a group deemed by some of its members to constitute an actual or potential 'nation'.* The concept of 'nation' in turn may be defined as *a named human population occupying a historic territory and sharing common myths and memories, a distinctive public culture and common laws and customs.*[12]

What of the ideology that animates nationalist movements and whose chief concern is the nation? To repeat, there are many kinds of nationalism: religious and secular, conservative and socialist, liberal and racist. Nevertheless, we can, I believe, discern a 'core doctrine' of nationalism, which I would summarize as follows.

1   The world is divided into nations, each with its own character, history and destiny.
2   The nation is the source of all political power.
3   An individual's primary loyalty must be to her or his nation.
4   To be free, individuals must realize themselves in the nation.
5   All nations must have maximum autonomy and self-expression.
6   A world of peace and justice requires free nations.

These are the recurrent ideas and themes found in all nationalist movements, as they were of nationalism's 'founding fathers' – of Montesquieu, Rousseau and Burke, Herder and Fichte, Zimmerman, Jefferson and, later, Mazzini. And these ideas and themes are, in the broad sense of the term intimated above, Romantic, though not of the specifically German Romantic variety; and, with the exception of the first proposition, they were relatively novel, being largely unimportant, if not unknown, before the eighteenth century. (See Smith 1983: ch. 7.)

Of course, the concept of the nation itself had been around for far longer. Indeed, it is possible to trace it back to the ancient Greeks and the Hebrew Bible. Among ancient Jews and Armenians, a strong sense of ethnic community became increasingly national, and even perhaps nationalist, in content, because of the heavy emphasis placed on the homeland, on a distinct public, religious culture, and on common laws and customs. But such ancient, or indeed later medieval nations, differed from many modern ones both in their extent and, more important, in their social depth. Though we cannot be sure how many members were aware of, and involved in, the wider community, it is safe to say that, for the most part, the mass of the peasantry did not actively participate in the life of the ancient or medieval nation. In contrast, in the modern world, after the French and American revolutions, the majority of the population in the West did become increasingly involved, though as active citizens only in the twentieth century. (See Connor 1994: ch. 8; Smith 2000, ch. 2.)

Now, among the wider political and social processes that mobilized greater numbers of people than ever before, and brought them into the political arena, Romanticism played a pivotal role. It helped to interpret these broader changes, by opening up the pre-existing world of nations in the West and helping to create new nations in Eastern Europe, Asia, Africa and Latin America. And it did so through the key concepts of nationalism which Romantics either originated or disseminated. Though we commonly downplay or dismiss this 'romantic element', as we like to call it, and try to distinguish between 'hopelessly romantic' nationalisms like those of early nineteenth-century Poland or Greece, and practical, business-like nationalisms like those of the present-day Scots or Quebecois, the basic concepts and assumptions of both kinds of nationalism are remarkably similar; and, as I shall argue, Romantic through and through.

Romantic Assumptions of Nationalism

What are these Romantic concepts and assumptions?

Perhaps the most important is that of *identity*. Identity for the Romantic and nationalist is more than 'sameness over time'. It is what makes a phenomenon distinctive, incommensurable, unique. It is the particular stamp of the group, its unique style and voice. We find it already in discussions of 'national character' at the end of the seventeenth century. In the first half of the eighteenth century, writers like Lord Shaftesbury and Montesquieu speak of the 'genius of the nation' and the 'spirit of the nation', which is always felt to be *sui generis*. In the hands of Rousseau, it became a guiding principle: 'The first rule that we must follow is that of national character. Every people has, or must have, a character; if it lacks one, we must begin by endowing it with one' (Rousseau 1915: ii. 319, *Project Corse*).

For Herder, too, collective identity, particularly of the nation, was part of God's plan, and hence part of nature. It had a similar significance for Zimmerman in Switzerland, Burke in England, and Mazzini in Italy. It continues to underlie the efforts and policies of many nationalists and nationalist leaders to this day – in Quebec and Euzkadi, in Croatia and Serbia, Macedonia, Israel and Palestine, among Kurds and Sikhs, Moro and Achinese, but also in France and Britain, Germany and Italy, where discussions of 'who we are' in an increasingly ethnically mixed state have become widespread and passionate.[13]

The quest for a national identity, which began in earnest in the late eighteenth century, was part and parcel of the wider Romantic yearning for *authenticity*, which became a key nationalist aspiration. The idea of 'national identity' or character is predicated on the belief that there is a true self of some kind. This may not be conceived of as an 'essence', but rather as a distinctive or original contribution. Alternatively, the authentic may be simply that which is 'our own' and nobody else's, that which 'we' do not share with others. It was Herder who emphasized and popularized the ideal of authenticity, and hence of cultural purification, which so easily spills over into social exclusion, even though, as an Enlightenment thinker, Herder did not draw such a conclusion. (See Barnard 1965; Berlin 1976.)

But, where is 'authenticity' to be found? Where must we seek our true and original state? There are basically two nationalist replies to this question: in Nature and in History.

As far as *nature* is concerned, the quest for authenticity leads back to the soil of the *homeland*, the land of one's family and ancestors, the land of one's upbringing and occupation. What is authentic about the homeland is its fusion of people and terrain. This is achieved through the creation of an *ethnoscape*: that is, the identification of a land with 'its' people and a people with 'its' land, and the emotions to which this attachment gives rise. In this perspective, we are the children of our soil, and our true character is the product of our interaction with the homeland through the generations. This was very much what Swiss nationalist writers and poets like Gottfried Keller felt about their unique Alpine homeland and its shaping of an authentic Swiss national identity. It was also what animated many Finnish nationalists like Runeberg, Lönnrot and Sibelius in the nineteenth century, especially in their quest for the authentic Finn in Karelia. And we can also find it in the elevation of Constable's vision of a southern English landscape, or in Elgar's passion for the Malverns, both seen by many as 'true expressions' of an 'authentic rural England' to this day (see Kohn 1957; Branch 1985: introduction; Colls and Dodd 1986).[14]

As for *history*, it was not just the German Romantics who delved into a misty past to authenticate a vision of the regenerated and genuine volkisch Germany. Through philology and archaeology, history and folklore studies, the true lineaments of the 'people' of all culture communities could, it was thought, be uncovered to reveal their 'irreplaceable culture values', to use Max Weber's revealing phrase. Above all, the study of history could take us back to our 'golden age' (or ages), when the nation was great and glorious, creative and virtuous. Thus, already in mid-eighteenth-century Britain, the study of early Welsh, Irish and Scots histories and ancient poetry by Romantic nationalist antiquarians and poets like Edward Jones, Charles O'Connor and Thomas Gray paved the way for the Romantic cult of medievalism across Europe. In France, that most civic and republican of nations, the study of golden ages, Gallic or Frankish, of a millennial French past flourished under the impulse of Romantic ideals of national identity, authenticity and historical empathy. In secular and modernizing Kemalist Turkey, reacting against Ottomanism and pan-Turkism, Ataturk himself promulgated his Romantic Sun Language theory of the primordial origins of the Turks in Central Asia and their wanderings to Anatolia. Even in an immigrant society like the United States, a vernacular American ancestralism grew up at the time of the Revolution, opposing itself to the interference and impositions of the 'wicked stepmother', Great Britain; and in subsequent epochs of their relatively short history, Americans have sought the 'authentic American' in the age of Washington and Jefferson, or that of Lincoln, or in the Wild West (Trumpener 1997: introduction; Poliakov 1974: ch. 1; Lewis 1968: ch. 10; Burrows 1982).

What of the Romantic insistence on free will and unfettered action? How does nationalism reflect this ideal? The most obvious expression of such freedom is the doctrine of national self-determination, which, as we saw, Kedourie attributed to Fichte's collective emendation of Kant's belief in the cardinal value of an individual's free will.

But this is only one source. The ideal of national self-determination expresses a wider Romantic belief in *autonomy*: the pursuit of one's inner rhythms or dictates without any external interference. For the Romantics, this inner autonomy was essential for both authenticity and fraternity. Though the concept of *autonomia* could be traced back to the ancient world, it received its philosophical underpinning only in the later eighteenth century, in terms of the universal need for human beings to realize themselves and obey only their inner dictates if they were to be truly free. For nationalists, real freedom was positive: a realization of one's true nature through the exercise of the individual or collective moral will. Clearly, this ideal was heavily influenced by, if not a direct political expression of, the Rousseauan and Romantic assertion of active will (see Cohler 1970).

Similarly, with those other great nationalist ideals of unity and fraternity. On the one hand, *unity* implied territorial unification of all the many regions and cities that made up the homeland, and a commitment to unfettered mobility throughout the national territory. It also entailed a commitment to 'redeem' those territories and the resident populations who were felt to belong to the nation, if necessary by force, as in Alsace and Lorraine at the end of the nineteenth century. On the other hand, unity had a social dimension. It implied the social unification of the national population, and inculcation in them of feelings of *fraternity* (and latterly sorority). Here, too, the Romantic impulse was evident. For, while the absolute monarchs of several European states had already begun to homogenize their populations, it was only the Romantic ideals of will, action and diversity that generated a subjective yearning for broad national unity and deep fraternity, because only through unity and fraternity could the national will be expressed and national action be effective.[15]

On an ideological level, then, the characteristic nationalist ideals of national identity, authenticity, autonomy, unity and fraternity, history and the homeland, were largely collective and political expressions of the broader Romantic drive for cultural diversity, free self-expression and active will. In this sense, all nationalisms, even the most pragmatic, are *au fond* Romantic, even if some forms of Romanticism are non-national.

The Role of Romantic Intellectuals

But there is a further sense in which Romanticism makes its presence felt in every nationalism: in the important role played by, and accorded to, Romantic artists and intellectuals in the genesis and life of the nation. What is it about nations and nationalist ideals that have proved so attractive to them over the last 200 years?

The short answer, of course, lies in the nature of the age of nationalism's genesis in Europe. Though local conditions and power structures have played a major role in the rise of each nationalist movement, the distinctive character of nationalism was shaped by the spirit and concerns of the period in which it emerged in Western and Central Europe. This was an age of revolutions, but also of the neoclassical revival and early Romanticism – a conjunction of processes and ideologies that gave ample opportunities for the new classes of the bourgeoisie and intelligentsia, and created a much larger and more adventurous audience for the varied ideas and artistic representations of the new Romantic sensibility and moral ideals (see Butler 1982).

Among these ideals, that of the nation proved to be especially potent and fertile. Its multifaceted but emotionally charged character chimed well with the two great intellectual, moral and artistic traditions of Europe, the Christian and the classical. It proved relatively easy to locate the new kind of nation in these earlier traditions of republican antiquity and biblical ethnicity. The stage had indeed been well set by three centuries of humanist antiquarianism and biblical 'ethnic theology', which had attuned the minds and hearts of the growing reading publics to the ideas of 'national character', ethnic genealogy and republican patriotism. These ideas were given fresh impetus by the Romantic quest for cultural diversity and free self-expression, and by the neoclassical emphasis on simplicity, will and martial activism. These are themes that can be found already in the 1760s and 1770s in the new passion for the sublime in nature and literature, in the cults of Ossian, Dante and Shakespeare, in the re-creation of medieval tales and histories by the Gothic novelists and by painters like Runciman and Fuseli, in the neoclassical history paintings of Gavin Hamilton and Benjamin West, in Gluck's purification of operatic forms, and of course in Rousseau and the German *Sturm und Drang* movement – the immediate cultural seed-bed for the rise of a secular nationalism in the West (Rosenblum 1967: esp. ch. 2; see also Kidd 1999).

But such reasons are historical and time-limited. There are deeper grounds for the continuing hold of Romantic nationalism over the minds and hearts of intellectuals, artists and, more generally, the educated classes over the last two centuries.

Perhaps the most important reason is the nationalist stress on cultural originality and uniqueness. Obvious enough to later ages, perhaps, but not at all to late eighteenth-century artists and publics for whom tradition, especially classical tradition, had provided the models of both art and public morality. In one sense, nationalism and the nation appeared to accentuate this tradition. But, in another sense, they also undermined a universal classicism by insisting on the particularism, the uniqueness, of nature and history, and hence the parity of all homelands and of all pasts – at least, all authentic pasts. This tied in with the new emphasis upon imagination, myth and memory; and thus, the ability of the artist and writer to conjure and convey times and places far removed from her or his own, and thereby to make popular myths and symbols and ethnic memories and traditions vivid and palpable to large numbers of people through a variety of media (see Anderson 1991).

This, according to Robert Rosenblum, is exactly what late eighteenth- and nineteenth-century artists became increasingly adept at doing. Theirs was a new 'historical mobility' which encouraged artists to move freely between periods and cultures, and evoke the myths, memories and atmosphere of each with increasing archaeological verisimilitude – in terms of specific customs, landscapes and accessories. Thus the American Quaker, Benjamin West, who settled in London and became court painter to George III, was able to paint scenes from Greek history (*Leonidas Banishing Cleombrotus*, 1768), from Roman history (the frieze-like procession of *Agrippina Landing at Brundisium with the Ashes of Germanicus*, 1768), from Israelite history (the supernaturalism of *Saul and the Witch of Endor*, 1777), from early British history, courtesy of Shakespeare, in *King Lear in the Storm* (1788), from medieval French history (*Death of Chevalier Bayard*, 1772), from medieval British history (*The Burghers of Calais*, 1788), from early American history (*William Penn's Treaty with the Indians*, 1772), and from contemporary British history – that celebrated early icon of nationalism, *The Death of General Wolfe*, 1770, a piece of modern reportage that turns death in battle for king and country into a sacrificial rite – not to mention scenes from the New Testament, Saxon and Scots histories, the British in India, Renaissance history and literature, even Persian history (Von Erffa and Staley 1986; Abrams 1986).

Nor was West unusual. Fuseli drew and painted scenes from Dante, Shakespeare, Spenser, Greek and Roman history, the *Nibelunglied* and the Edda, as well as his native Swiss history, notably its foundation document, *The Oath of the Rütli of 1291* (1781) between the three forest cantons on Lake Lucerne: Uri, Schwyz and Unterwalden. The French were equally historically mobile. Girodet painted scenes from Greek mythology and history, the Aeneid, the Old and New Testaments, Ossian (the visionary *Ossian Receiving Napoleonic Officers*, 1802), contemporary French history (*The Revolt of Cairo, 1798*, 1810), as well as poetic subjects like *The Sleep of Endymion* (1791). The same spectrum of historical and literary reference can be found in Ingres: Greek and Roman history, the Bible, Ossian (the hallucinatory *Dream of Ossian*, 1813), Renaissance literature, and modern and medieval French history (especially his tribute to the growing cult of St Joan, *Joan of Arc at the Coronation of Charles VII in Rheims Cathedral*, 1854, with its atmospheric medievalism and emotionally militant piety). (See Rosenblum 1967: ch. 2 and 1985: esp. 160–3; see also Antal 1956.)

This new emphasis on unique cultural memory and historical antiquity which Romantic nationalism did so much to encourage undoubtedly propelled artists, composers and writers to the forefront of the quest for a new sense of national identity. This was pre-eminently their domain and their 'task', since theirs was the power to convey the peculiar contours and

qualities, and the particular symbols, myths and memories, of the enduring nation as it travelled across time from a primeval and heroic past to an
equally glorious destiny. Through the evocation of homeland and history,
of poetic landscapes and golden ages, of chosen peoples and heroic sacrifices, intellectuals and artists could re-present to their compatriots in word
and sound, paint and stone, the continuity of the national community of
their imagination and sentiment, and thereby help to create that community out of the heritage of myths, memories, symbols and traditions of the
wider population (see Smith 1999a).

A second reason for the attraction of the national ideal can be found in
the Romantic quest for freedom of self-expression. Here, too, nationalism,
with its assault on tyranny and corruption, and its support of self-
awareness and self-assertion, encouraged intellectual and artistic freedom
within the bosom of the nation, particularly during the struggle for national
independence, when the movement needed to build a clear collective
identity and self-consciousness. This often provided artists with a role
and a sense of mission on behalf of 'the people'. In this respect, nationalism proved doubly attractive. Not only did it give Romantic intellectuals
and artists a sense of fulfilment; it also offered them a way of reconnect-
ing with 'the people', from whom modern education had often estranged
them. Thus, a composer like Verdi, whose great chorus, *Va pensiero*, in
Nabucco (1842) struck such a powerful chord with so many Italians, could
for some years find himself propelled into the forefront of the Risorgi-
mento's struggle against Austrian rule as 'its' artistic voice – a fate that
also befell Sibelius in late nineteenth-century Finland and the populist
Muralists, Rivera, Orozco and Siqueiros in post-revolutionary Mexico.
These were all in their different ways examples of Romantic nationalist
artists prizing freedom, authenticity, originality and self-assertion, in the
service of the nation (see Layton 1985; Osborne 1997: 47–60; Franco
1970).

Finally, despite the excesses and outrages committed in the name of
nationalism, there is a dynamic ethical dimension to the appeal of the
nation: namely, the ideal of national self-determination. The pre-eminent
artist of the French Revolution, Jacques-Louis David, provides the most
obvious example of this national appeal, for his art embodied the Romantic ideal of will in action. That, surely, is what David's great neoclassical
heroes, from the Horatii to Socrates, Brutus and Leonidas, so vividly
convey. It may be a will in action with disastrous consequences, as the
Horatii found and Brutus knew, but the will of the individual expressed
that of the community through its self-determining character. If, as Kant
tells us, the only good will is a free will, one unhindered by external interference such as family ties, then David's great neoclassical heroes embody

the underlying and genuine goodness of the nation; for theirs is the singular assertion of that freedom and power over the strongest of natural attachments (Herbert 1972).

In this respect, David conveys a specifically Romantic neoclassicism, not just in the nostalgic desire to return to a purer and nobler antiquity, but in the philosophic sense of interpreting the powerful emotions and dynamic actions of the ancient heroes as *exempla virtutis*, of the good will in action triumphing over the natural passions. Now this was the Spartan conclusion that Rousseau and Kant developed out of the classicism of the Enlightenment; and in so doing, they broke with its harmonious system of rational ideas which had sustained that classical vision. For will in action is not ultimately to be reined in and tamed; it is a part of nature, and hence is the law itself. Now, by the same token, the goodness of nations lies in their free will; and the free will of the nation, as the Abbé Siéyès reminded his readers in 1789, exists only in the natural order, and hence its will is always the supreme law. It cannot be gainsaid. But, then, who is to interpret the will of the nation? This question was to become the Achilles' heel of Romantic nationalism and its ideal of the free national will (Siéyès 1789, cited in Cobban 1957: 165; see also Kohn 1967b).

Conclusion

Here, I have only been able to touch on some of the many issues and themes that make up the complex of Romantic nationalism. I have sought to show that all nationalisms are, in the broad sense of the term, Romantic in their core conceptions, sentiments and activities. All nationalisms are committed to the Romantic ideals of cultural diversity, authentic self-expression, and will in action, even where some of them supplement these ideals with other, more 'civic' and liberal notions, or with various racial or religious motifs. But, equally, Romanticism cannot be equated with nationalism as an ideology of culture and politics. The Romantic quest for cultural individuality and self-expression could, and often did, lead in other directions: to an apolitical aestheticism, for example, or to a religious conservatism, or indeed to forms of socialism, though most of the latter had some national, if not nationalist, referent. Conversely, while all nationalisms contain Romantic elements, they differ in the extent of their Romanticism. This is not just a matter of circumstance which may induce a measure of pragmatism. Some nationalisms draw on civic traditions and utilitarian philosophies, which may then modify, though they never dominate, the Romantic elements, as the French and British examples demonstrate.

Beyond this general mapping, I have also argued that we cannot support the traditional picture of Romanticism as standing in radical opposition to classicism, much less to neoclassicism. While it is true that in the field of general ideas and philosophy, as Berlin demonstrated, a radical break can be discerned in the work of Herder, Kant and the later German Romantics, this is not paralleled to anything like the same degree in the arts and literature. Of course, neoclassicism marked a radical change in style, if not iconography, and it became one of the first expressions and languages of nationalism. But in that case, it must be placed under the heading of Romanticism, and we must therefore speak, as does Robert Rosenblum, of a Romantic neo-classic style. Similarly, the break with the Rococo classicism of the Enlightenment initiated by pre-Romanticism is much less marked in the arts. Rather, we should speak of a shift in thought and sensibility over a half century, the very period during which nationalism emerged as a Romantic political doctrine and movement out of earlier beliefs in a territorial 'national character' and a biblical 'ethnic theology' (see Kidd 1999).

This tells us that continuity as much as change marks the transition to Romantic nationalism. This was ensured by the aspirations and activities of the Romantics themselves. The work of popular and vernacular historical 'rediscovery' by Romantic artists, poets, historians and composers ensured the continuities, albeit selective ones, between modern ideals and pre-modern ethnic and religious symbols, myths, memories and traditions. It was not simply a question of salvaging and recycling heroic or popular materials from the classics, the Bible and medieval histories for the sake of period drama and picturesque colour. Such externals became important only in so far as they expressed the inward authenticity and continuity of the nation over *la longue durée*. For the Romantics, an enduring authenticity had taken the place and become the new meaning of 'the sacred' in the earlier religious traditions. For them, the sacred had been transferred from humanity's primordial relationship with God to its rediscovered bond with Nature, with history, and with the nation. In that way, the authenticated nation partook, in the eyes of Romantic nationalists, of the divine; for, as a sacred communion of the dead, the living and the yet unborn, the nation expressed and carried across the generations the intimate sentiments and ideals, and the genuine myths and memories of a people. By rediscovering and politicizing these popular symbols, motifs and traditions, a Romantic nationalism links past, present and future, thereby ensuring that its undoubted radicalism returns on itself and builds a world of cultural nations within the political framework of a world of states (see Smith 2003: ch. 2).

Notes

1 For an early intellectual and moral critique, see Acton 1948; for a more recent critique, see Parekh 1995. For Anderson, nationalism 'never produced its own grand thinkers; no Hobbeses, Tocquevilles, Marxes or Webers' (1991: 5). True, but it had its Montesquieu, Rousseau, Herder and Fichte.
2 On the excesses of Romanticism, see the essays by Engelhardt and Pirie in Porter and Teich 1988; and Berlin 1999: ch. 5.
3 See especially Berlin 1976 and Barnard 1965.
4 For the German Romantics, see Kohn 1965; for the metaphors of Romantic awakeners, see Pearson 1993.
5 Kedourie's ideas on millennialism were shaped by Norman Cohn (1957). For a critique, see Smith 1979: ch. 2.
6 On Gellner's theory, see the critical essays in Hall 1998, and Smith 1998: ch. 2.
7 See also Nairn 1997 for a more political approach.
8 For an incisive critique of Kohn and Kedourie, see Hutchinson 1987: ch. 1.
9 Though not in the eyes of a critic like Brian Barry (1999) for whom not even a multiculturalist nationalism can meet the universalist ethical criteria of liberalism.
10 On the Dreyfus trial, see Kedward 1965. For the illiberalism of 'civic' nationalism in France, see Smith 1995: ch. 4.
11 For a penetrating account of the social and intellectual background of (especially) literary Romanticism, see Butler 1982; see also Trumpener 1997.
12 This definition differs from that given in Smith 1991: ch. 1 in being less specifically modernist.
13 For the concept of national character, see Kemilainen 1964. For current discussions of hybridized national identities, see Bhabha 1990: ch. 16 and Billig 1995.
14 On landscape and national identity, see the essays in Hooson 1994. On ethnoscapes, see Smith 1999b.
15 For cultural unity in France, see Lartichaux 1977 and Kohn 1967b.

References

Abrams, Anne Uhry 1986: *The Valiant Hero: Benjamin West and Grand-Style History Painting*. Washington, DC: Smithsonian Institution Press.
Acton, Lord 1948: 'Nationality'. In *idem, Essays on Freedom and Power*, Glencoe, IL: Free Press.
Anderson, Benedict 1991: *Imagined Communities: Reflections on the Origins and Spread of Nationalism*, 2nd edn. London: Verso.

Antal, Frederick 1956: *Fuseli Studies.* London: Routledge & Kegan Paul.

Barnard, Frederick 1965: *Herder's Social and Political Thought: From Enlightenment to Nationalism.* Oxford: Clarendon Press.

Barry, Brian 1999: 'The limits of cultural politics'. In Desmond Clarke and Charles Jones (eds), *The Rights of Nations*, Cork: Cork University Press, 127–44.

Berlin, Isaiah 1976: *Vico and Herder.* London: Hogarth Press.

Berlin, Isaiah 1999: *The Roots of Romanticism.* London: Chatto & Windus.

Bhabha, Homi (ed.) 1990: *Nation and Narration*, London and New York: Routledge.

Billig, Michael 1995: *Banal Nationalism.* London: Sage.

Branch, Michael (ed.) 1985: *Kalevala: The Land of Heroes*, trans. W. F. Kirby. London: Athlone Press; New Hampshire: Dover.

Burrows, Edwin 1982: Bold forefathers and the cruel stepmother: ideologies of descent in the American Revolution (Paper for Conference on *Legitimation by Descent*, Paris: Maison des Sciences de l'Homme).

Butler, Marilyn 1982: *Romantics, Rebels and Reactionaries.* Oxford and New York: Oxford University Press.

Cobban, Alfred 1957: *A History of Modern France*, vol. 1. Harmondsworth: Penguin.

Cohler, Anne 1970: *Rousseau and Nationalism.* New York: Basic Books.

Cohn, Norman 1957: *The Pursuit of the Millennium*, London: Secker & Warburg.

Colls, Robert and Dodd, Philip (eds) 1986: *Englishness: Politics and Culture, 1880–1920.* London: Croom Helm.

Connor, Walker 1994: *Ethno-Nationalism: The Quest for Understanding.* Princeton: Princeton University Press.

Dunn, John 1979: *Western Political Thought in the Face of the Future.* Cambridge: Cambridge University Press.

Franco, Jean 1970: *The Modern Culture of Latin America.* Harmondsworth: Penguin.

Freeden, Michael 1998: Is nationalism a distinct ideology? *Political Studies* 46, 748–65.

Gellner, Ernest 1964: *Thought and Change.* London: Weidenfeld & Nicolson.

Gellner, Ernest 1983: *Nations and Nationalism.* Oxford: Blackwell.

Hall, John (ed.) 1998: *The State of the Nation: Ernest Gellner and the Theory of Nationalism.* Cambridge: Cambridge University Press.

Herbert, Robert 1972: *David, Voltaire, Brutus and the French Revolution.* London: Allen Lane.

Herder, Johann Gottfried 1911: *Sämmtliche Werke*, 33 vols, ed. Bernard Suphan. Berlin: Weidmann.

Hobsbawm, Eric 1990: *Nations and Nationalism since 1780.* Cambridge: Cambridge University Press.

Hooson, David (ed.) 1994: *Geography and National Identity.* Oxford: Blackwell.

Hutchinson, John 1987: *The Dynamics of Cultural Nationalism: The Gaelic Revival and the Creation of the Irish Nation State.* London: Allen & Unwin.

Ignatieff, Michael 1993: *Blood and Belonging: Journeys in the New Nationalism.* London: Chatto & Windus.

Kedourie, Elie 1960: *Nationalism.* London: Hutchinson.

Kedourie, Elie (ed.) 1971: *Nationalism in Asia and Africa.* London: Weidenfeld & Nicolson.

Kedward, Roderick (ed.) 1965: *The Dreyfus Affair.* London: Longman.

Kemilainen, Aira 1964: *Nationalism: Problems Concerning the Word, the Concept and Classification.* Yvaskyla: Kustantajat Publishers.

Kidd, Colin 1999: *British Identities before Nationalism: Ethnicity and Nationhood in the Atlantic World, 1600–1800.* Cambridge: Cambridge University Press.

Kohn, Hans 1957: *Nationalism and Liberty: The Swiss Example.* London: Macmillan.

Kohn, Hans 1965: *The Mind of Germany.* London: Macmillan.

Kohn, Hans 1967a: *The Idea of Nationalism* (1944), 2nd edn. New York: Collier–Macmillan.

Kohn, Hans 1967b: *Prelude to Nation-States: The French and German Experience, 1789–1815.* New York: Van Nostrand.

Lartichaux, J-Y. 1977: Linguistic politics in the French Revolution. *Diogenes* 97, 65–84.

Layton, Robert 1985: The *Kalevala* and music. *Books from Finland* 19 (1), 56–9.

Lewis, Bernard 1968: *The Emergence of Modern Turkey.* London: Oxford University Press.

Llobera, Josep 1994: *The God of Modernity.* Oxford: Berg.

Miller, David 1995: *On Nationality.* Oxford: Oxford University Press.

Nairn, Tom 1977: *The Break-up of Britain: Crisis and Neo-nationalism.* London: New Left Books.

Nairn, Tom 1997: *Faces of Nationalism: Janus Revisited.* London: Verso.

Osborne, Charles 1997: *The Complete Operas of Verdi: A Critical Guide.* London: Indigo.

Parekh, Bikhu 1995: Ethnocentricity of the nationalist discourse. *Nations and Nationalism* 1 (1), 25–52.

Pearson, Raymond 1993: Fact, fantasy, fraud: perceptions and projections of national revival. *Ethnic Groups* 10 (1–3), 43–64.

Poliakov, Leon 1974: *The Aryan Myth.* New York: Basic Books.

Porter, Roy and Teich, Mikulas (eds) 1988: *Romanticism in National Context.* Cambridge: Cambridge University Press.

Rosenblum, Robert 1967: *Transformations in Late Eighteenth-Century Art.* Princeton: Princeton University Press.

Rosenblum, Robert 1985: *Jean-Auguste-Dominique Ingres.* London: Thames & Hudson.

Rousseau, Jean-Jacques 1915: *The Political Writings of Rousseau,* 2 vols, ed. C. E. Vaughan. Cambridge: Cambridge University Press.

Siéyès, Abbé Emmanuel Joseph 1789: *Qu'est-ce que le Tiers État?* Paris.

Smith, Anthony D. 1979: *Nationalism in the Twentieth Century.* Oxford: Martin Robertson.

Smith, Anthony D. 1983: *Theories of Nationalism,* 2nd edn. London: Duckworth.

Smith, Anthony D. 1991: *National Identity.* Harmondsworth: Penguin.

Smith, Anthony D. 1995: *Nations and Nationalism in a Global Era.* Cambridge: Polity.

Smith, Anthony D. 1998: *Nationalism and Modernism.* London and New York: Routledge.

Smith, Anthony D. 1999a: *Myths and Memories of the Nation.* Oxford: Oxford University Press.

Smith, Anthony D. 1999b: Sacred territories and national conflict. *Israel Affairs* 5 (4), 13–31.

Smith, Anthony D. 2000: *The Nation in History.* Hanover, NH: University Press of New England; Cambridge: Polity.

Smith, Anthony D. 2003: *Chosen Peoples: Sacred Sources of National Identity.* Oxford: Oxford University Press.

Tamir, Yael 1993: *Liberal Nationalism.* Princeton: Princeton University Press.

Trumpener, Katie 1997: *Bardic Nationalism: The Romantic Novel and the British Empire.* Princeton: Princeton University Press.

Viroli, Maurizio 1995: *For Love of Country.* Oxford: Clarendon Press.

Von Erffa, Helmut and Staley, Allen 1986: *The Paintings of Benjamin West.* New Haven and London: Yale University Press.

Index